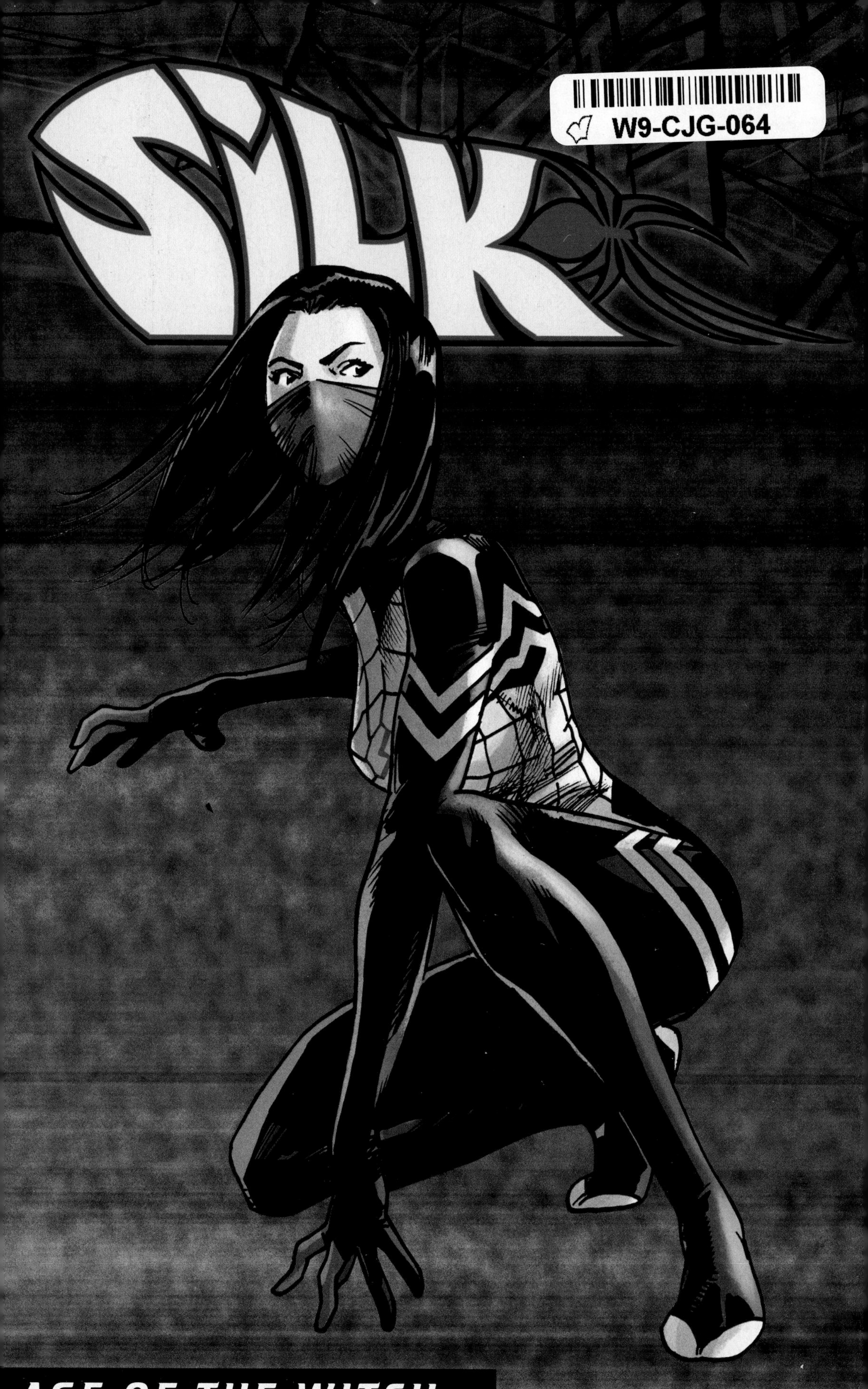
SILK

AGE OF THE WITCH

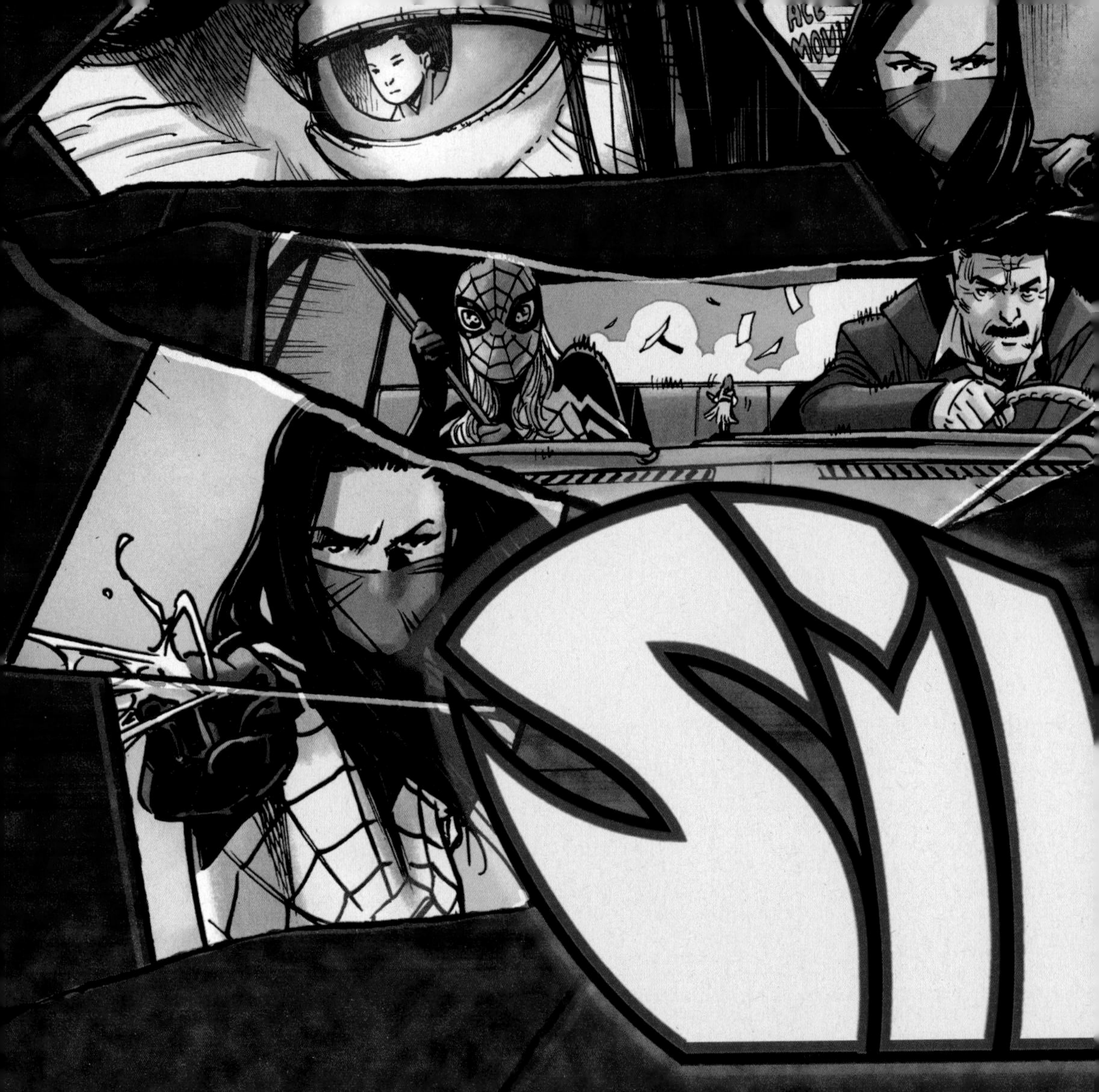

collection editor	**DANIEL KIRCHHOFFER**
assistant managing editor	**MAIA LOY**
associate manager, talent relations	**LISA MONTALBANO**
director, production & special projects	**JENNIFER GRÜNWALD**
vp production & special projects	**JEFF YOUNGQUIST**
book designer	**SARAH SPADACCINI**
senior designer	**JAY BOWEN**
svp print, sales & marketing	**DAVID GABRIEL**
editor in chief	**C.B. CEBULSKI**

SILK VOL. 2: AGE OF THE WITCH. Contains material originally published in magazine form as SILK (2022) #1-5. First printing 2022. ISBN 978-1-302-93279-4. Published by MARVEL WORLDWIDE, INC., a subsidiary of MARVEL ENTERTAINMENT, LLC. OFFICE OF PUBLICATION: 1290 Avenue of the Americas, New York, NY 10104. © 2022 MARVEL No similarity between any of the names, characters, persons, and/or institutions in this book with those of any living or dead person or institution is intended, and any such similarity which may exist is purely coincidental. **Printed in Canada.** KEVIN FEIGE, Chief Creative Officer; DAN BUCKLEY, President, Marvel Entertainment; JOE QUESADA, EVP & Creative Director; DAVID BOGART, Associate Publisher & SVP of Talent Affairs; TOM BREVOORT, VP, Executive Editor; NICK LOWE, Executive Editor, VP of Content, Digital Publishing; DAVID GABRIEL, VP of Print & Digital Publishing; SVEN LARSEN, VP of Licensed Publishing; MARK ANNUNZIATO, VP of Planning & Forecasting; JEFF YOUNGQUIST, VP of Production & Special Projects; ALEX MORALES, Director of Publishing Operations; DAN EDINGTON, Director of Editorial Operations; RICKEY PURDIN, Director of Talent Relations; JENNIFER GRÜNWALD, Director of Production & Special Projects; SUSAN CRESPI, Production Manager; STAN LEE, Chairman Emeritus. For information regarding advertising in Marvel Comics or on Marvel.com, please contact Vit DeBellis, Custom Solutions & Integrated Advertising Manager, at vdebellis@marvel.com. For Marvel subscription inquiries, please call 888-511-5480. **Manufactured**

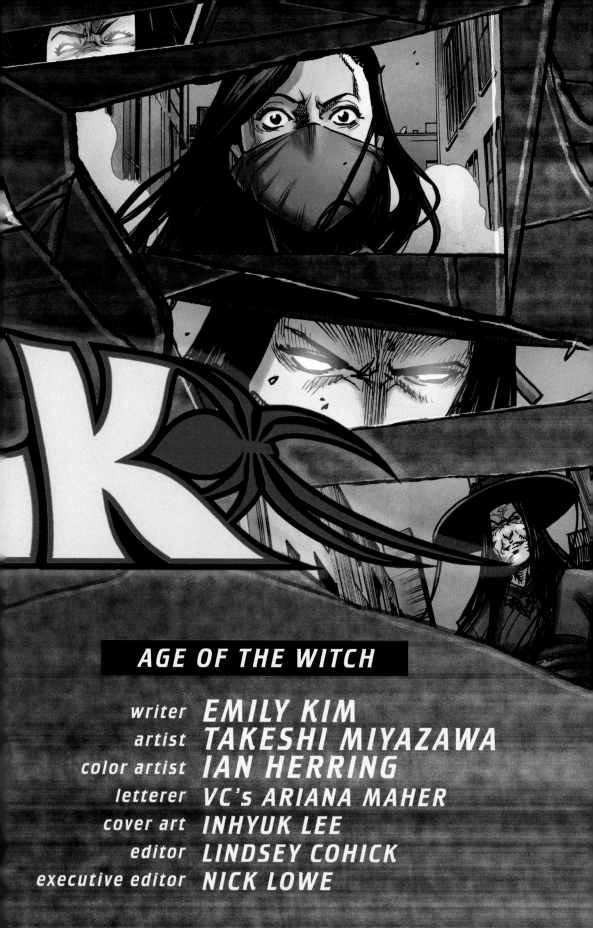

AGE OF THE WITCH

writer **EMILY KIM**
artist **TAKESHI MIYAZAWA**
color artist **IAN HERRING**
letterer **VC's ARIANA MAHER**
cover art **INHYUK LEE**
editor **LINDSEY COHICK**
executive editor **NICK LOWE**

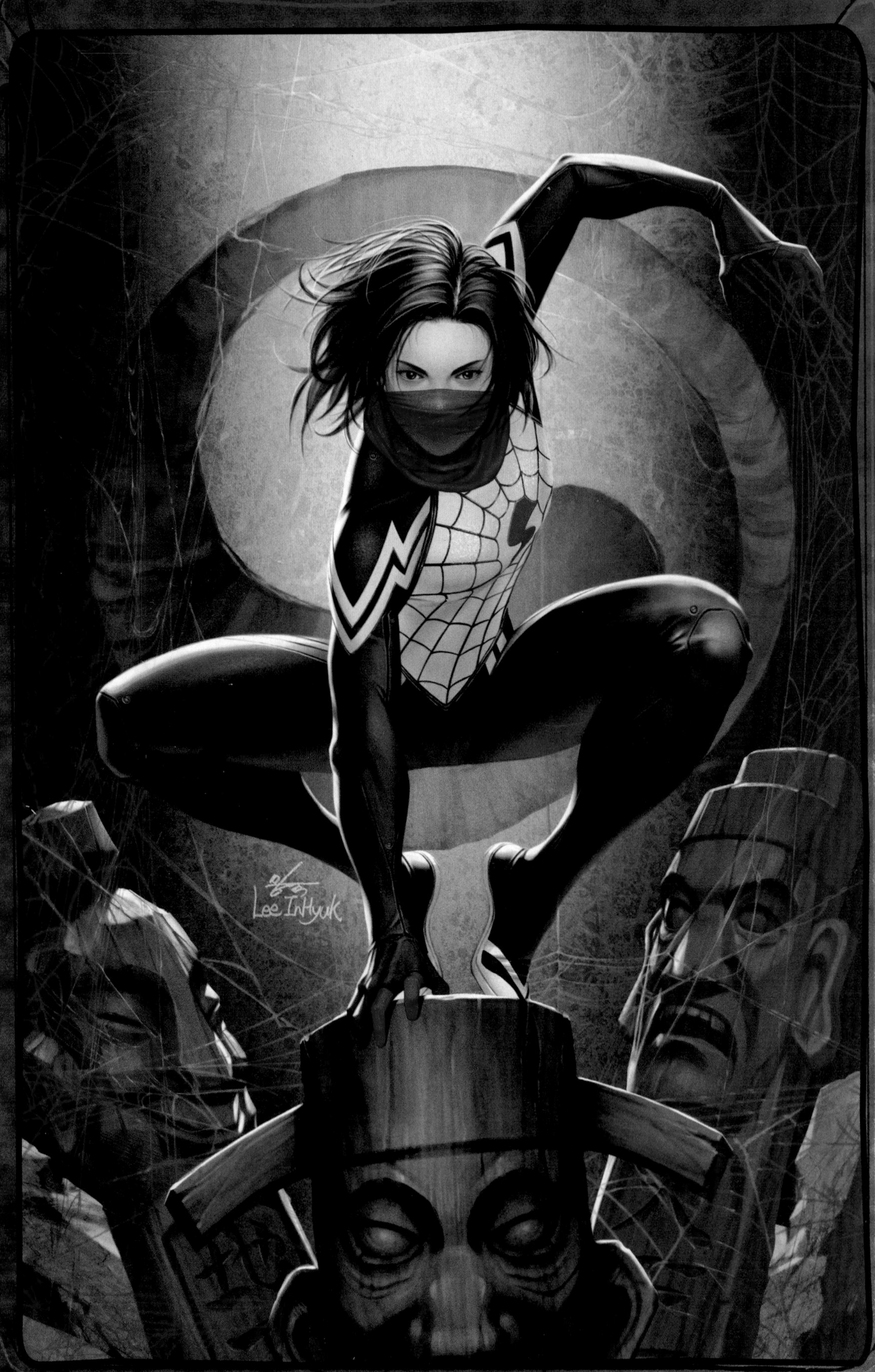
Lee InHyuk

SILK #1

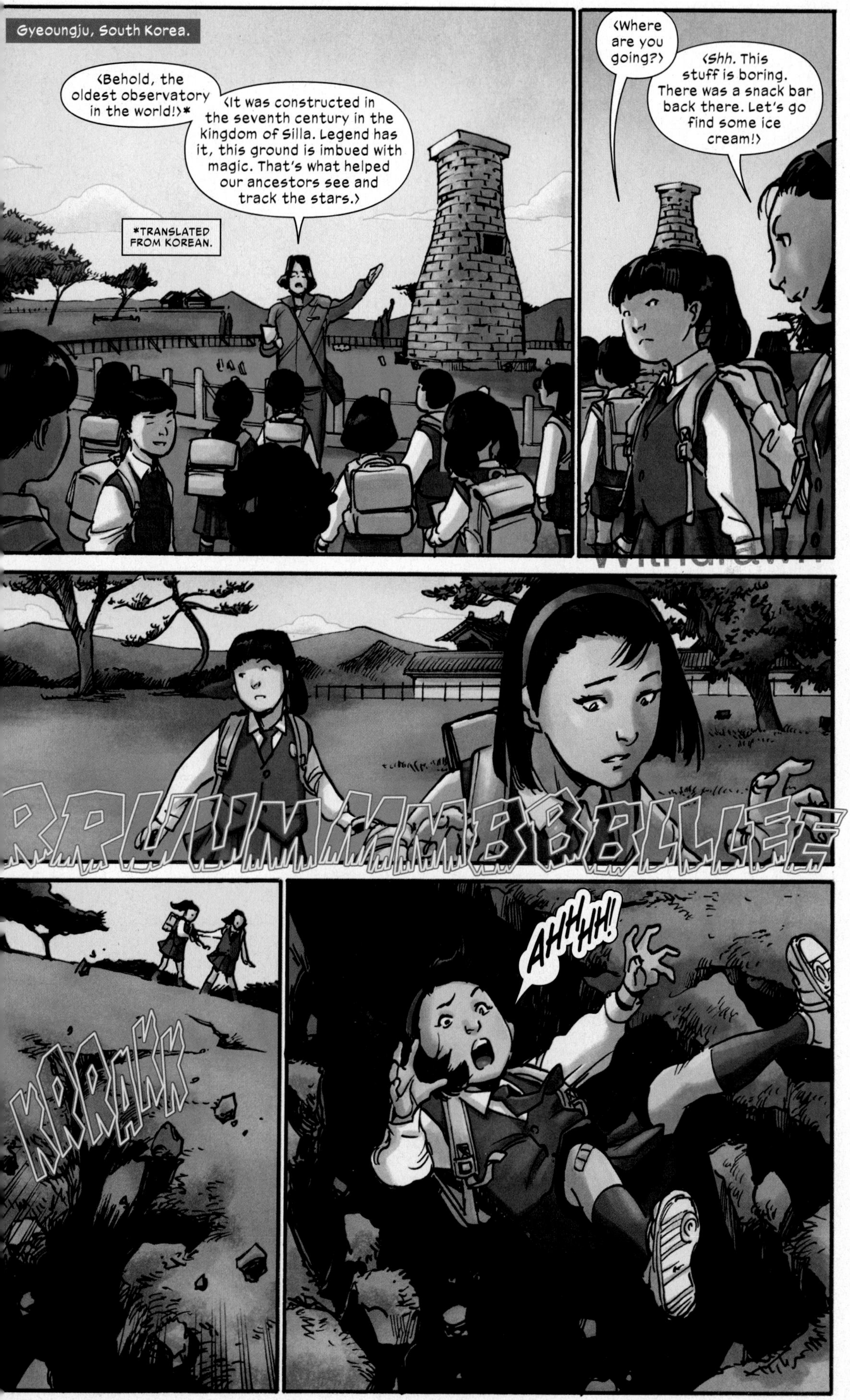

Gyeoungju, South Korea.
‹Behold, the oldest observatory in the world!›*
‹It was constructed in the seventh century in the kingdom of Silla. Legend has it, this ground is imbued with magic. That's what helped our ancestors see and track the stars.›
*TRANSLATED FROM KOREAN.
‹Where are you going?›
‹Shh. This stuff is boring. There was a snack bar back there. Let's go find some ice cream!›
RRUUMMMMBBBLLEE
KRRAKK
AHHHH!

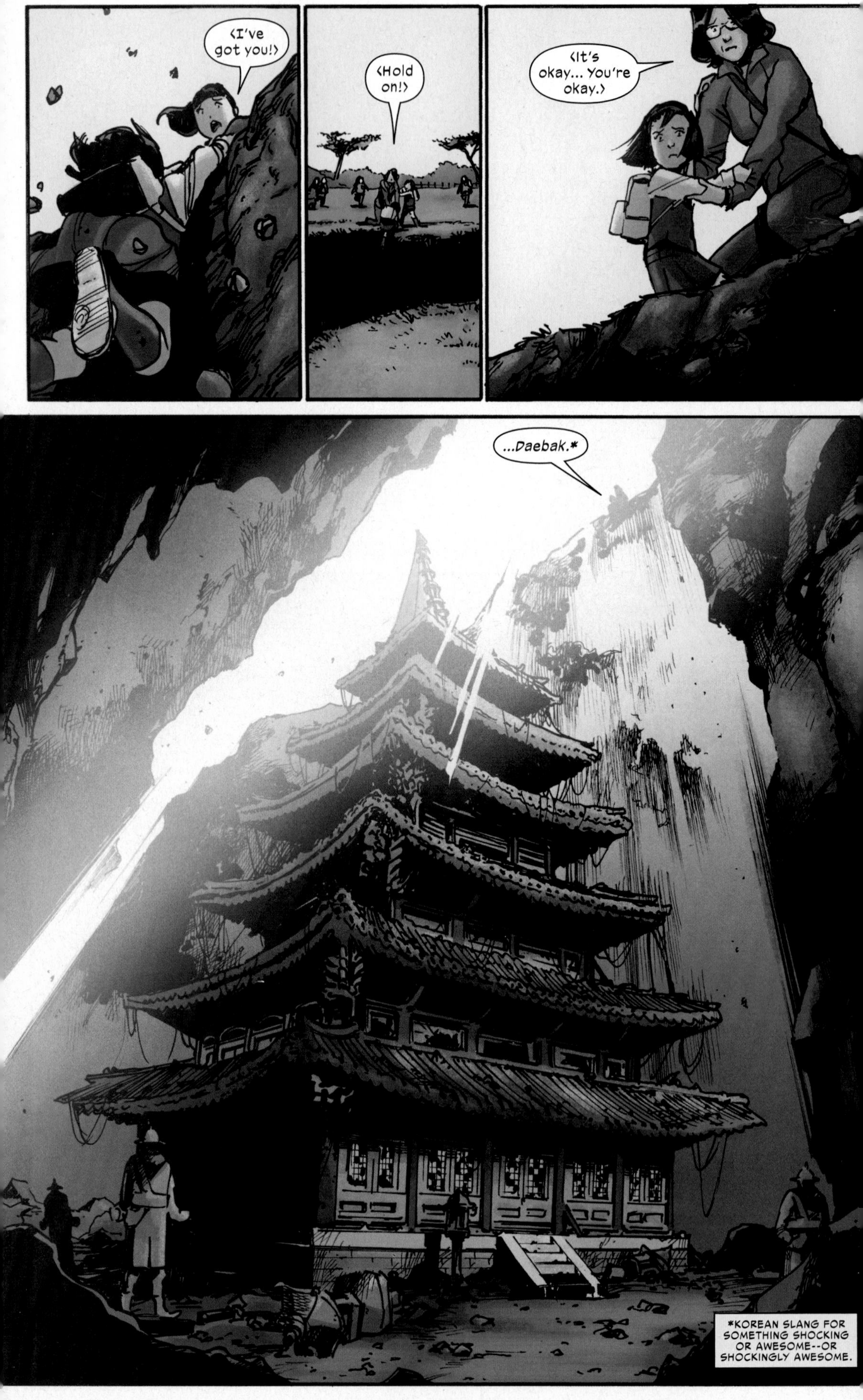

<I've got you!>
<Hold on!>
<It's okay... You're okay.>
...Daebak.*
*KOREAN SLANG FOR SOMETHING SHOCKING OR AWESOME--OR SHOCKINGLY AWESOME.

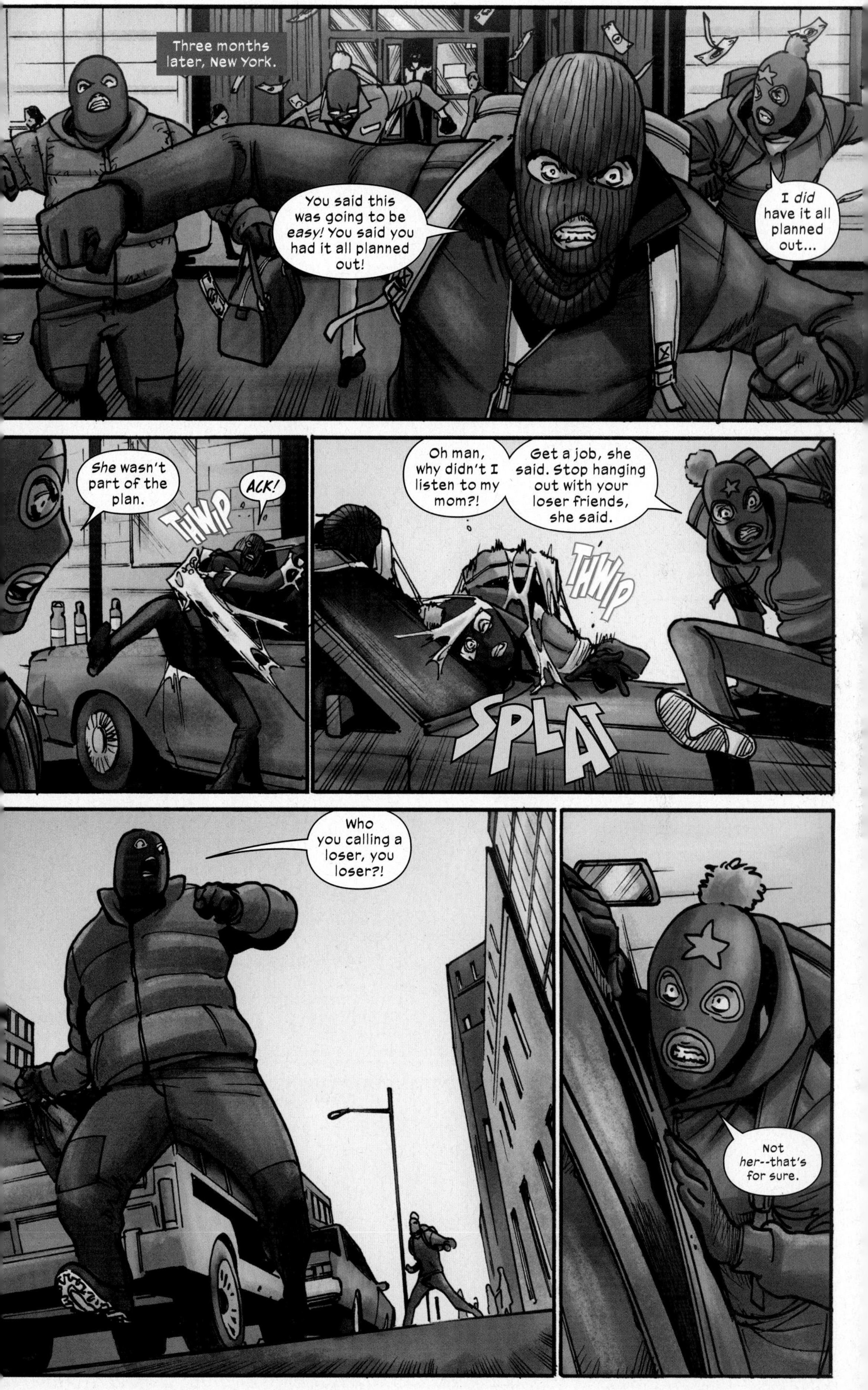
Three months later, New York.
You said this was going to be *easy!* You said you had it all planned out!
I *did* have it all planned out...
She wasn't part of the plan.
THWIP
ACK!
Oh man, why didn't I listen to my mom?!
Get a job, she said. Stop hanging out with your loser friends, she said.
THWIP
SPLAT
Who you calling a loser, you loser?!
Not *her*--that's for sure.

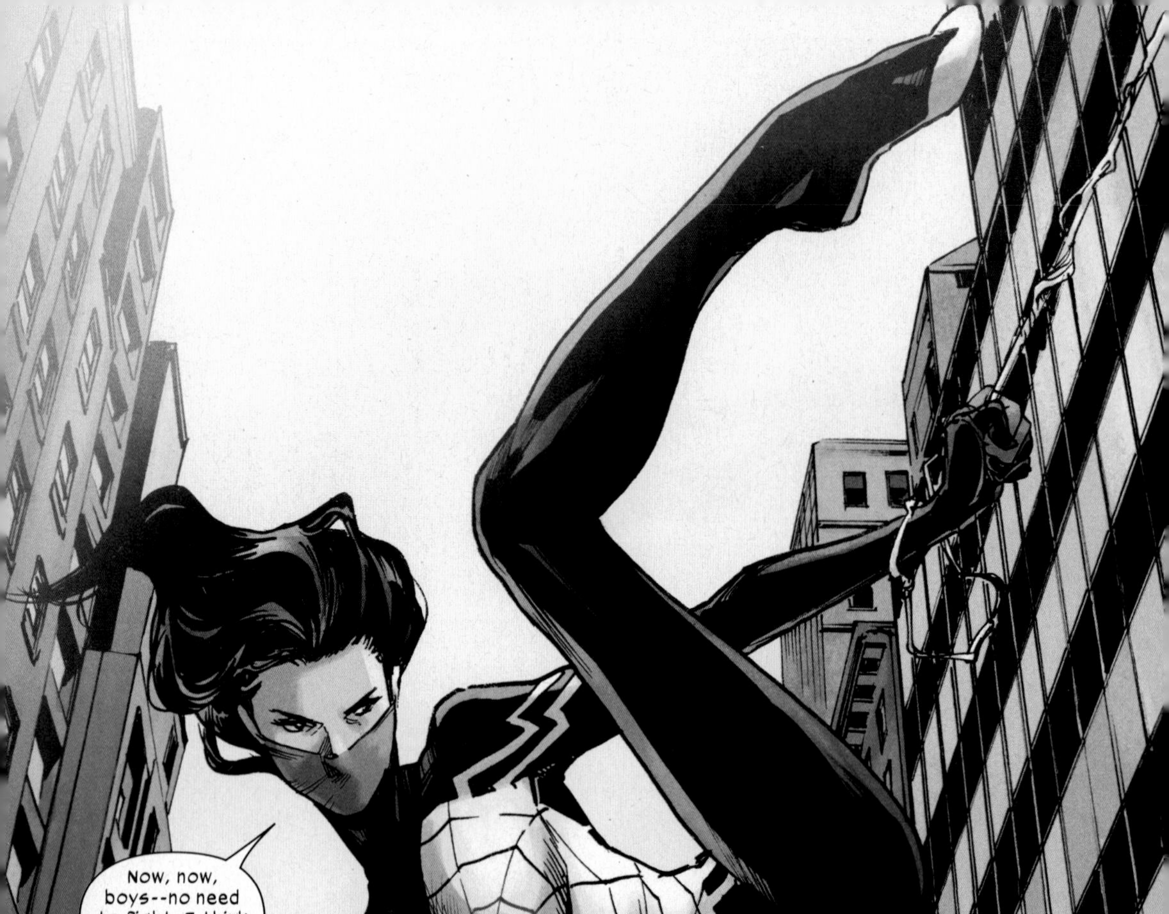
Now, now, boys--no need to fight. I think you're *all* losers here.

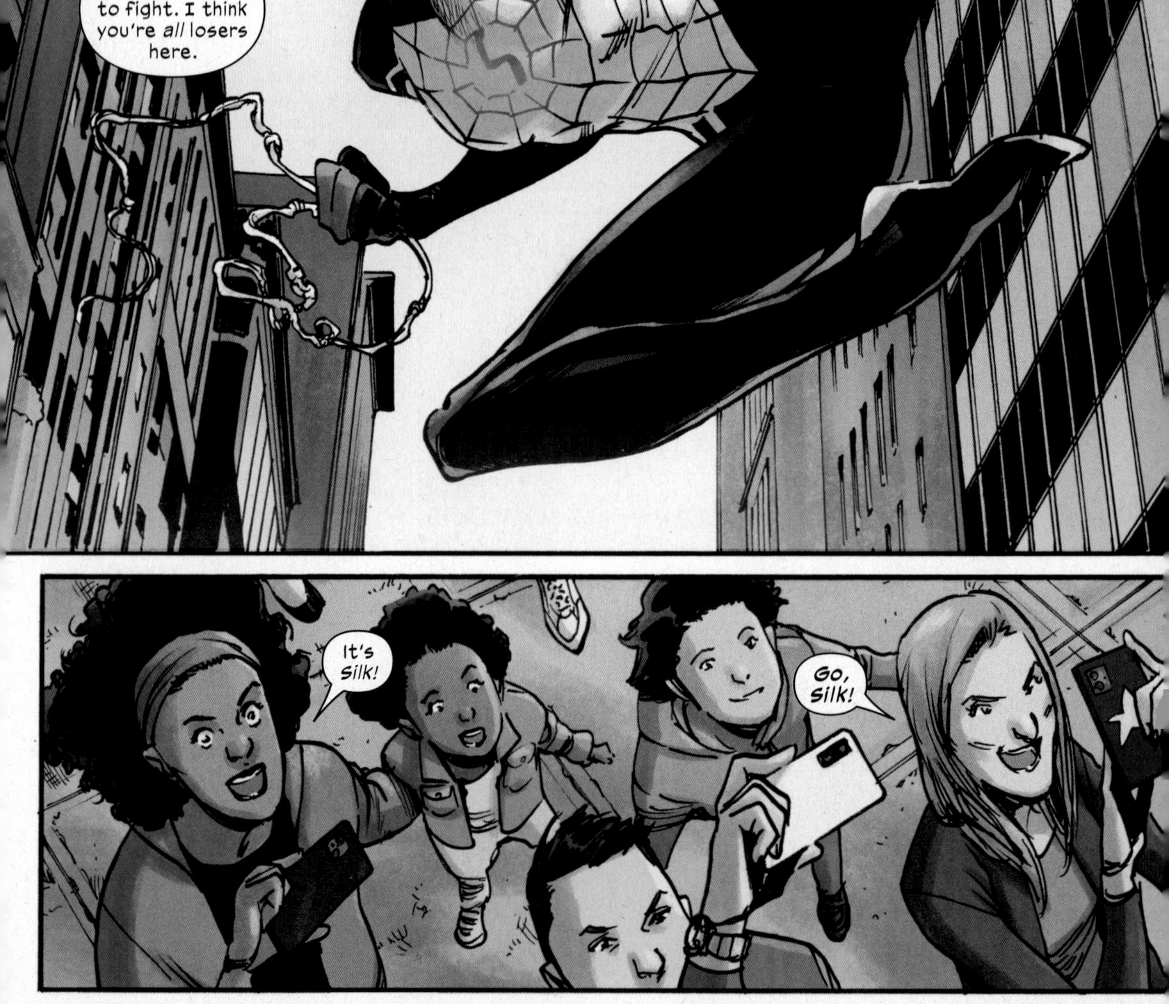
It's Silk!
Go, Silk!

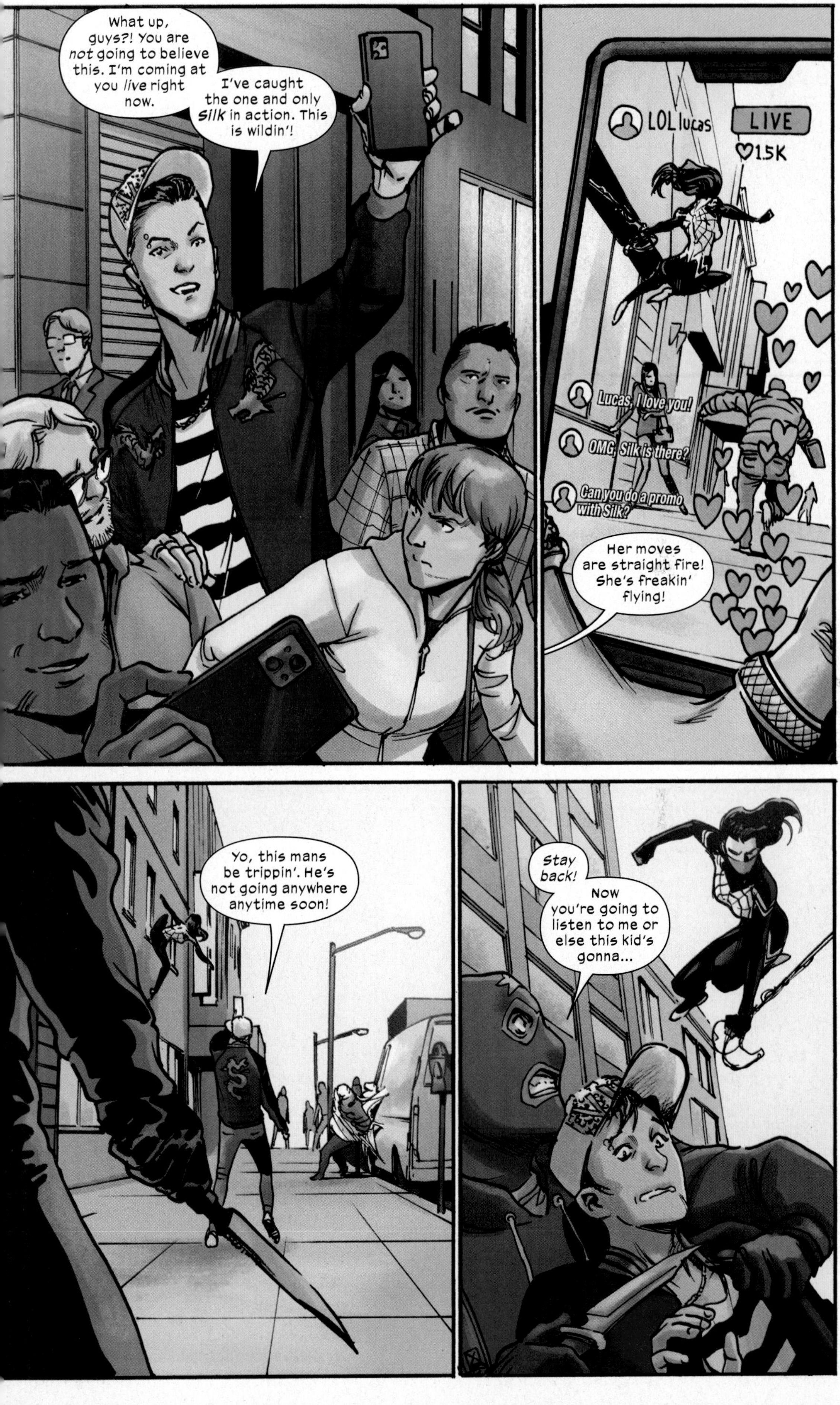
What up, guys?! You are *not* going to believe this. I'm coming at you *live* right now.
I've caught the one and only *Silk* in action. This is wildin'!
LOL lucas
LIVE
1.5K
Lucas, I love you!
OMG, Silk is there?
Can you do a promo with Silk?
Her moves are straight fire! She's freakin' flying!
Yo, this mans be trippin'. He's not going anywhere anytime soon!
Stay back!
Now you're going to listen to me or else this kid's gonna...

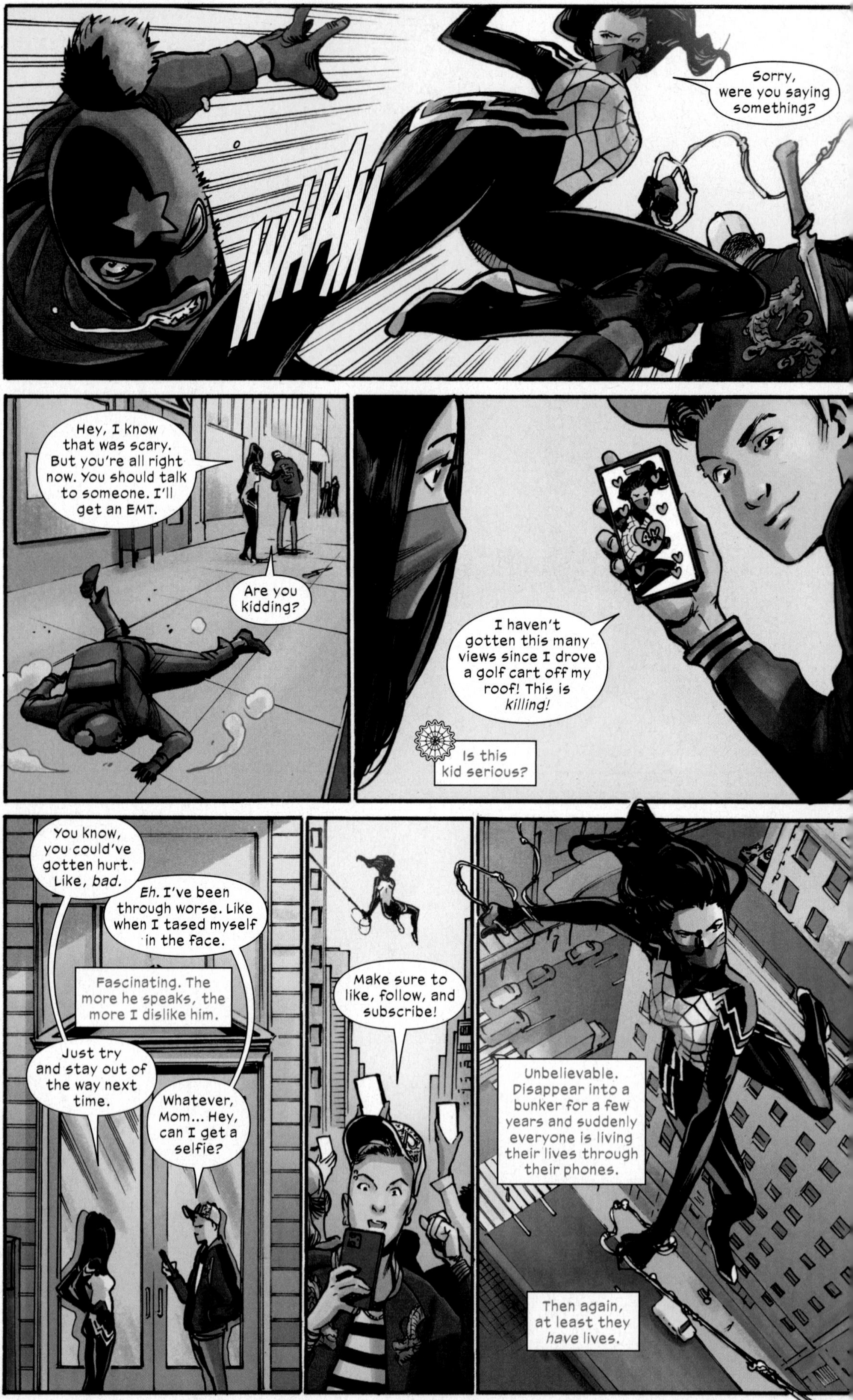

Sorry, were you saying something?
WHAM
Hey, I know that was scary. But you're all right now. You should talk to someone. I'll get an EMT.
Are you kidding?
I haven't gotten this many views since I drove a golf cart off my roof! This is *killing!*
Is this kid serious?
You know, you could've gotten hurt. Like, *bad.*
Eh. I've been through worse. Like when I tased myself in the face.
Fascinating. The more he speaks, the more I dislike him.
Just try and stay out of the way next time.
Whatever, Mom... Hey, can I get a selfie?
Make sure to like, follow, and subscribe!
Unbelievable. Disappear into a bunker for a few years and suddenly everyone is living their lives through their phones.
Then again, at least they *have* lives.

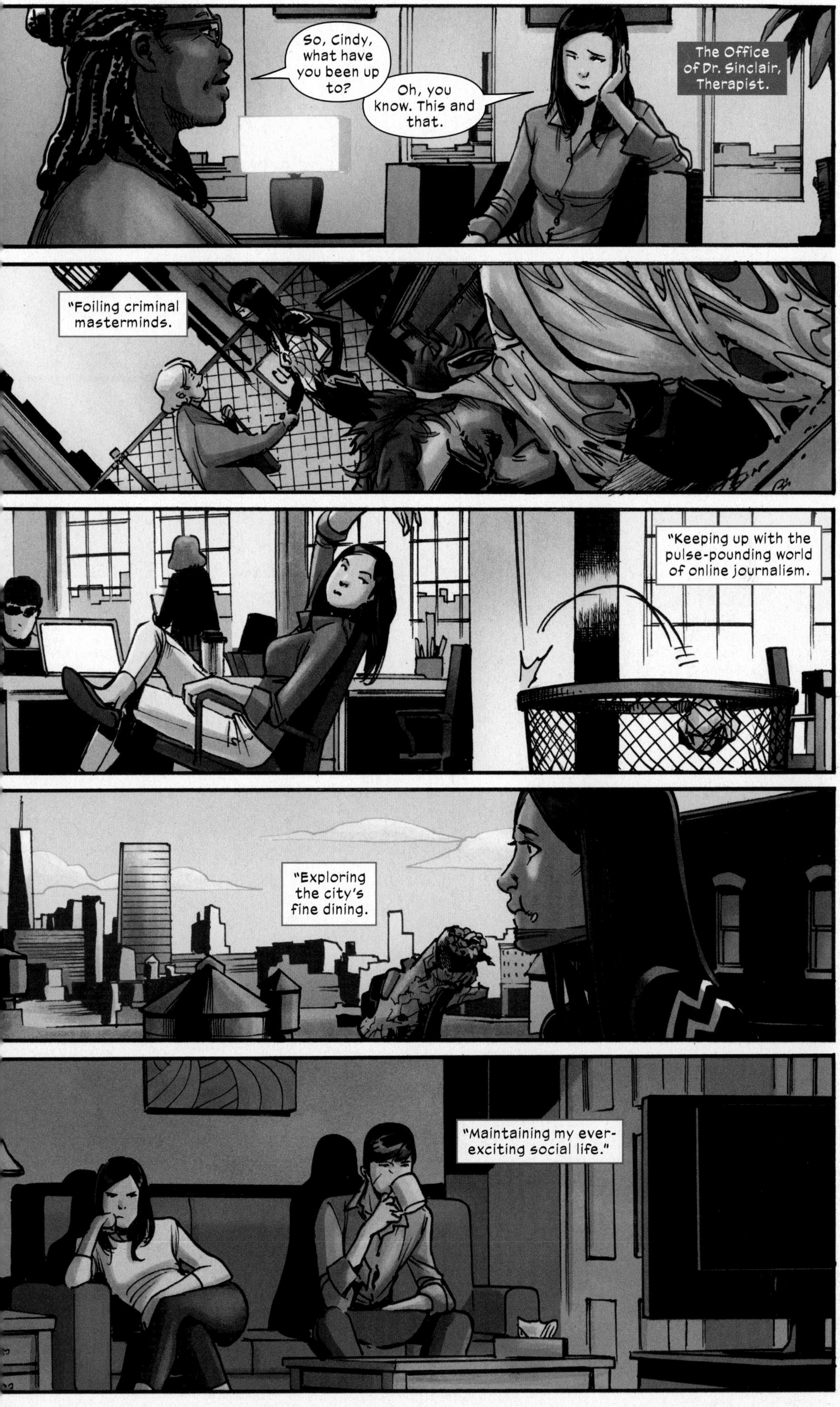
So, Cindy, what have you been up to?
Oh, you know. This and that.
The Office of Dr. Sinclair, Therapist.
"Foiling criminal masterminds.
"Keeping up with the pulse-pounding world of online journalism.
"Exploring the city's fine dining.
"Maintaining my ever-exciting social life."

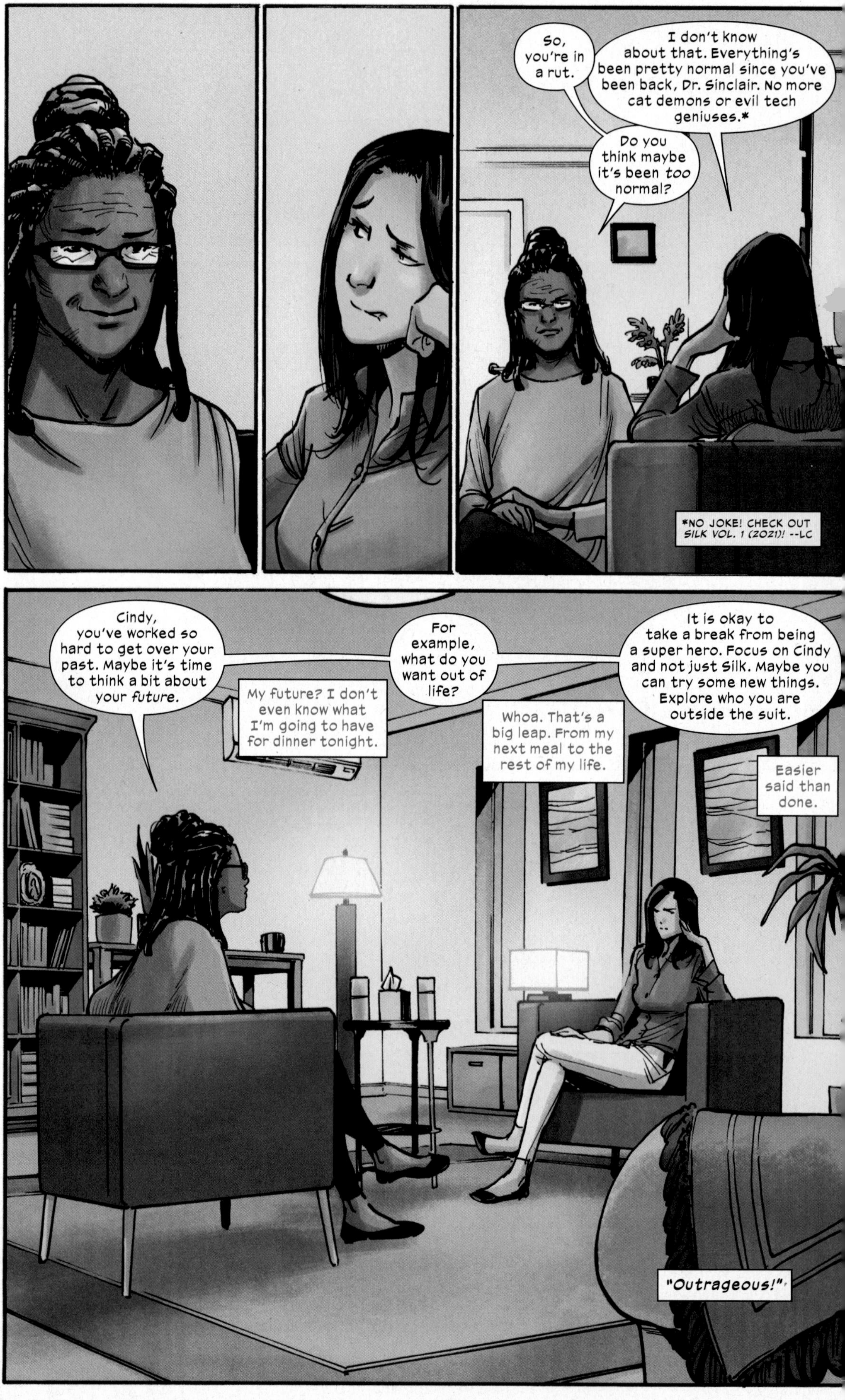
So, you're in a rut.
I don't know about that. Everything's been pretty normal since you've been back, Dr. Sinclair. No more cat demons or evil tech geniuses.*
Do you think maybe it's been *too* normal?
*NO JOKE! CHECK OUT *SILK VOL. 1 (2021)!* --LC
Cindy, you've worked so hard to get over your past. Maybe it's time to think a bit about your *future*.
My future? I don't even know what I'm going to have for dinner tonight.
For example, what do you want out of life?
Whoa. That's a big leap. From my next meal to the rest of my life.
It is okay to take a break from being a super hero. Focus on Cindy and not just Silk. Maybe you can try some new things. Explore who you are outside the suit.
Easier said than done.
"Outrageous!"

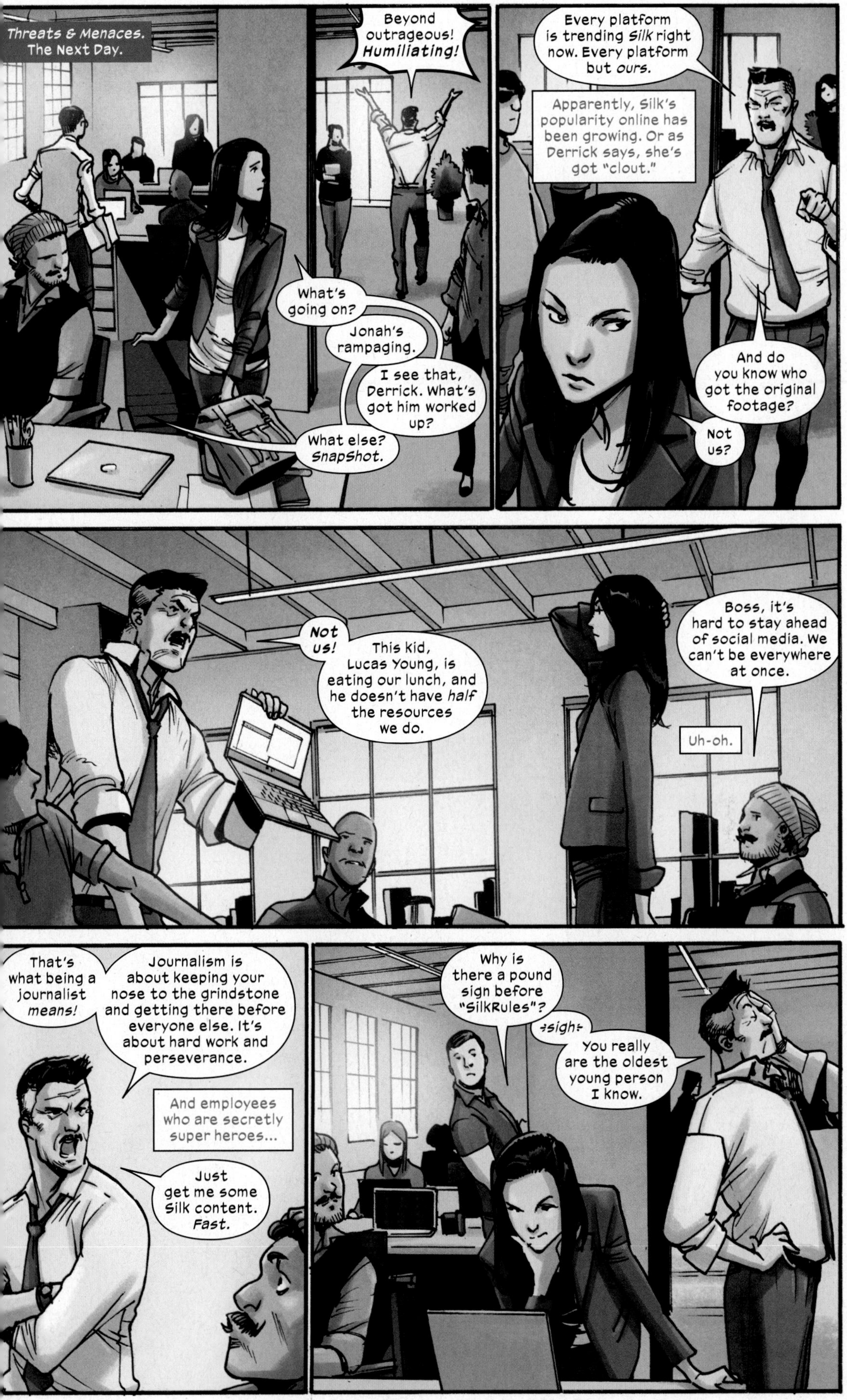
Threats & Menaces. The Next Day.
Beyond outrageous! Humiliating!
What's going on?
Jonah's rampaging.
I see that, Derrick. What's got him worked up?
What else? SnapShot.
Every platform is trending Silk right now. Every platform but ours.
Apparently, Silk's popularity online has been growing. Or as Derrick says, she's got "clout."
And do you know who got the original footage?
Not us?
Not us!
This kid, Lucas Young, is eating our lunch, and he doesn't have half the resources we do.
Boss, it's hard to stay ahead of social media. We can't be everywhere at once.
Uh-oh.
That's what being a journalist means!
Journalism is about keeping your nose to the grindstone and getting there before everyone else. It's about hard work and perseverance.
And employees who are secretly super heroes...
Just get me some Silk content. Fast.
Why is there a pound sign before "SilkRules"?
-sigh-
You really are the oldest young person I know.

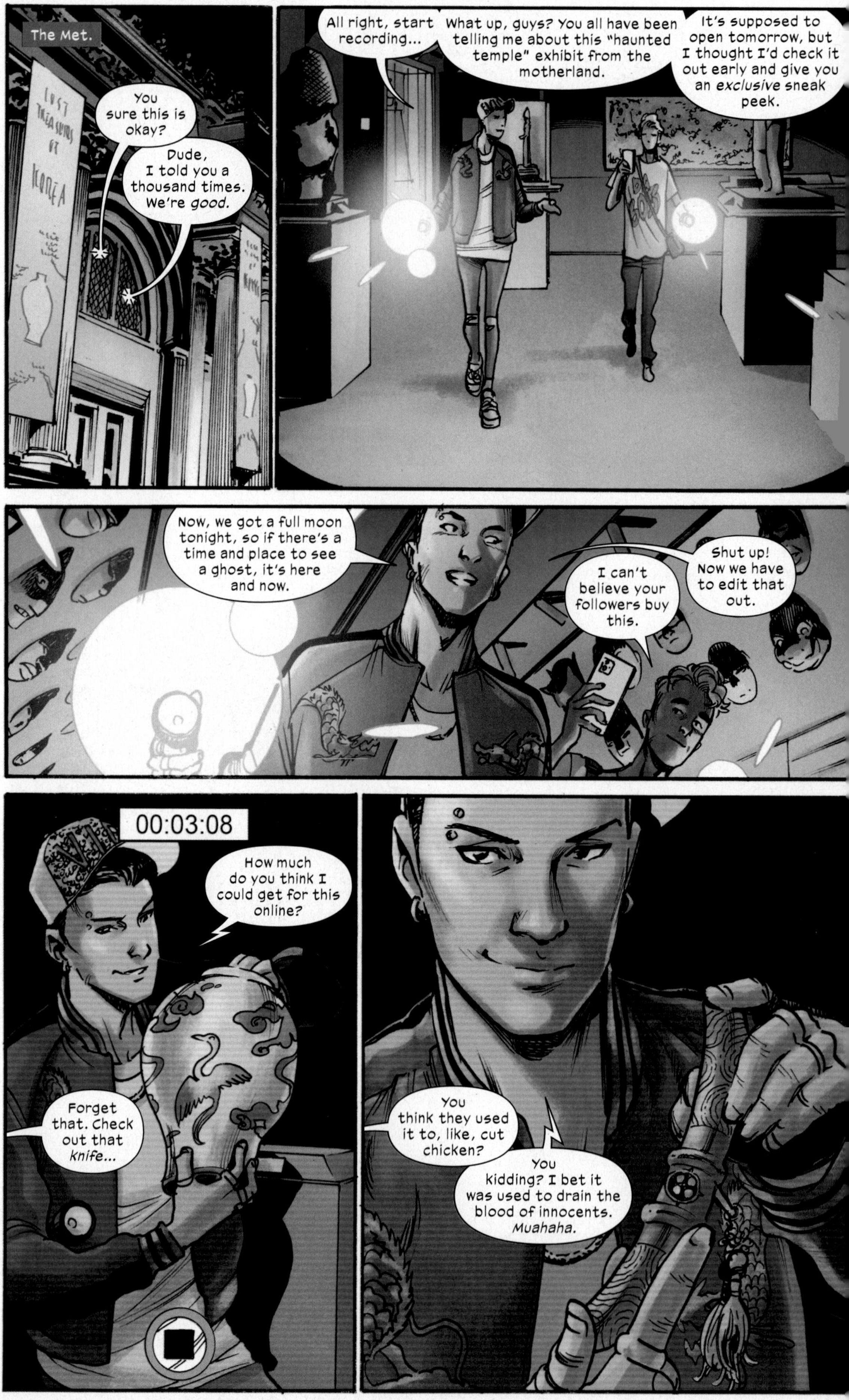
The Met.
You sure this is okay?
Dude, I told you a thousand times. We're *good.*
All right, start recording...
What up, guys? You all have been telling me about this "haunted temple" exhibit from the motherland.
It's supposed to open tomorrow, but I thought I'd check it out early and give you an *exclusive* sneak peek.
Now, we got a full moon tonight, so if there's a time and place to see a ghost, it's here and now.
I can't believe your followers buy this.
Shut up! Now we have to edit that out.
00:03:08
How much do you think I could get for this online?
Forget that. Check out that *knife...*
You think they used it to, like, cut chicken?
You kidding? I bet it was used to drain the blood of innocents. *Muahaha.*

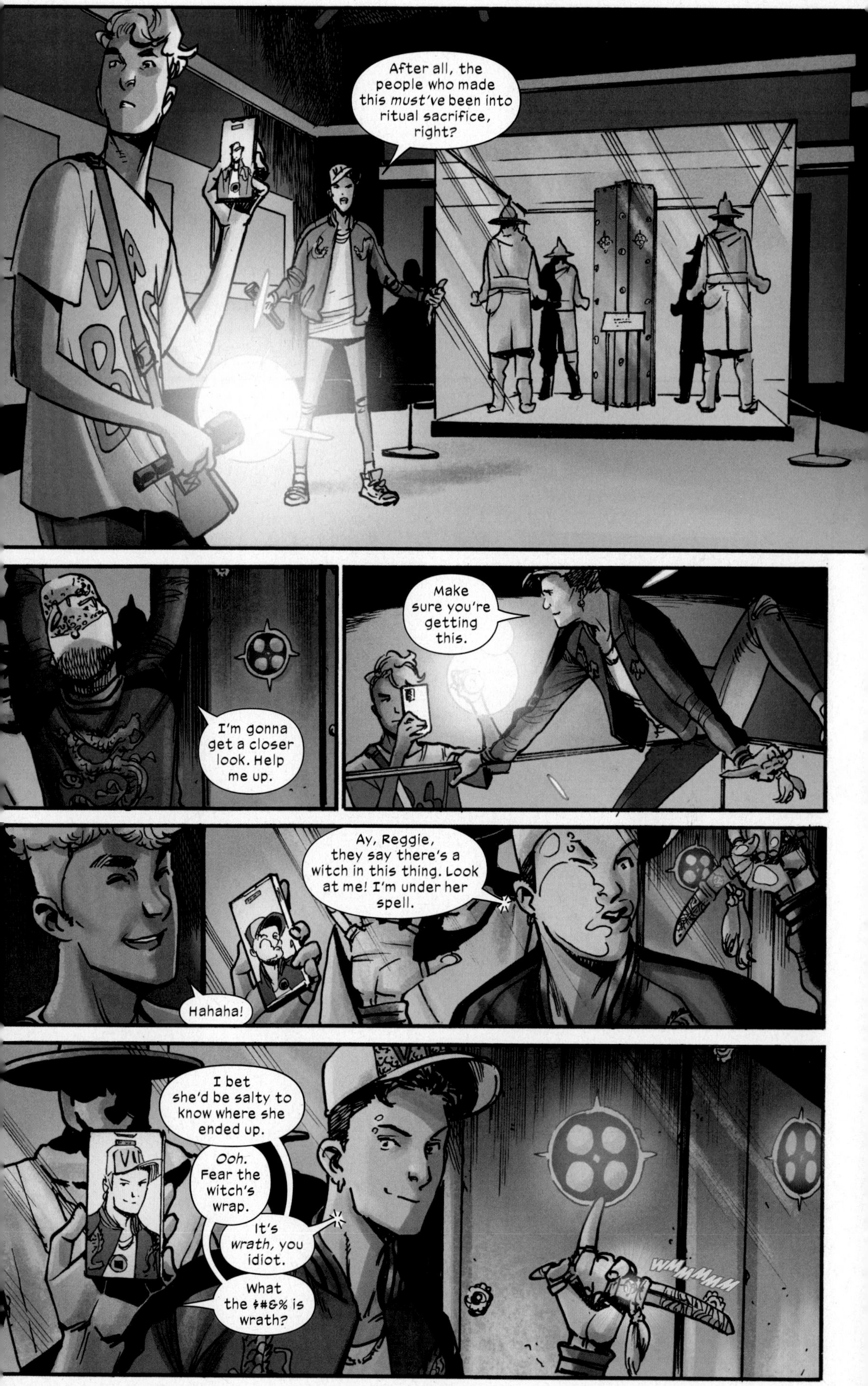
After all, the people who made this *must've* been into ritual sacrifice, right?
I'm gonna get a closer look. Help me up.
Make sure you're getting this.
Ay, Reggie, they say there's a witch in this thing. Look at me! I'm under her spell.
Hahaha!
I bet she'd be salty to know where she ended up.
Ooh. Fear the witch's wrap.
It's *wrath,* you idiot.
What the $#&% is wrath?
WMMMMMM

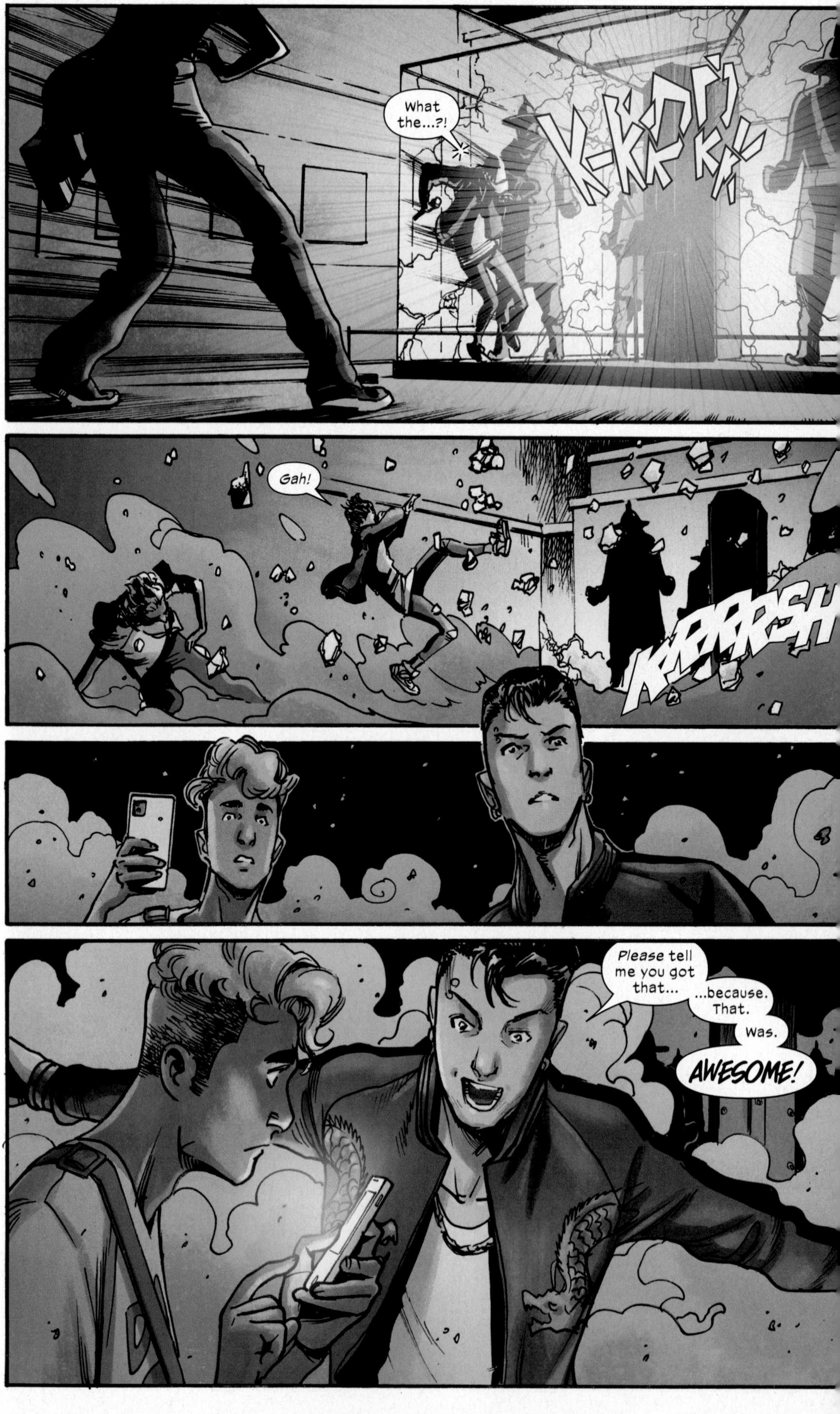
What the...?!
K-KRRAK
Gah!
KRRRSH
Please tell me you got that...
...because.
That.
Was.
AWESOME!

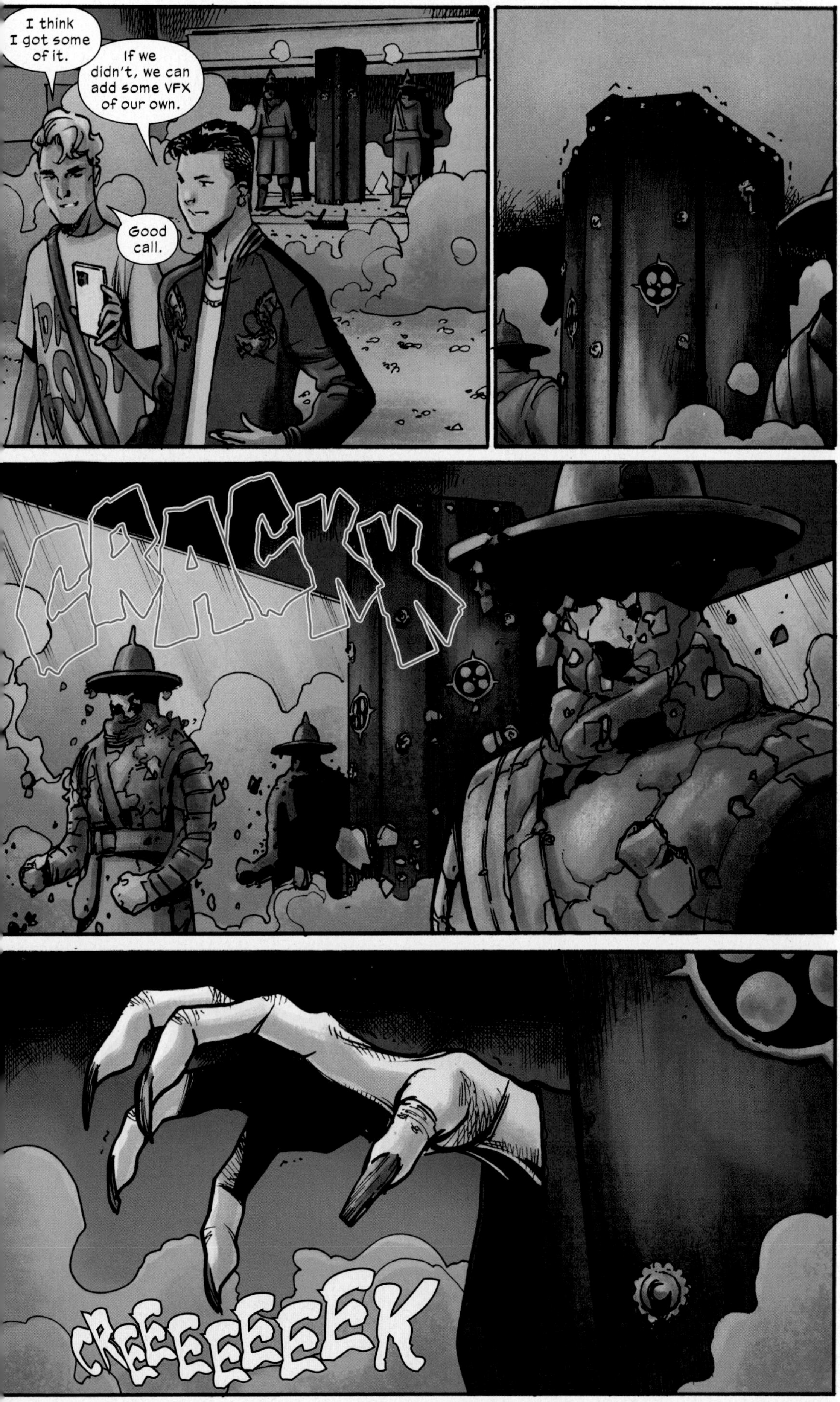
I think I got some of it.
If we didn't, we can add some VFX of our own.
Good call.
CRACKK
CREEEEEEEK

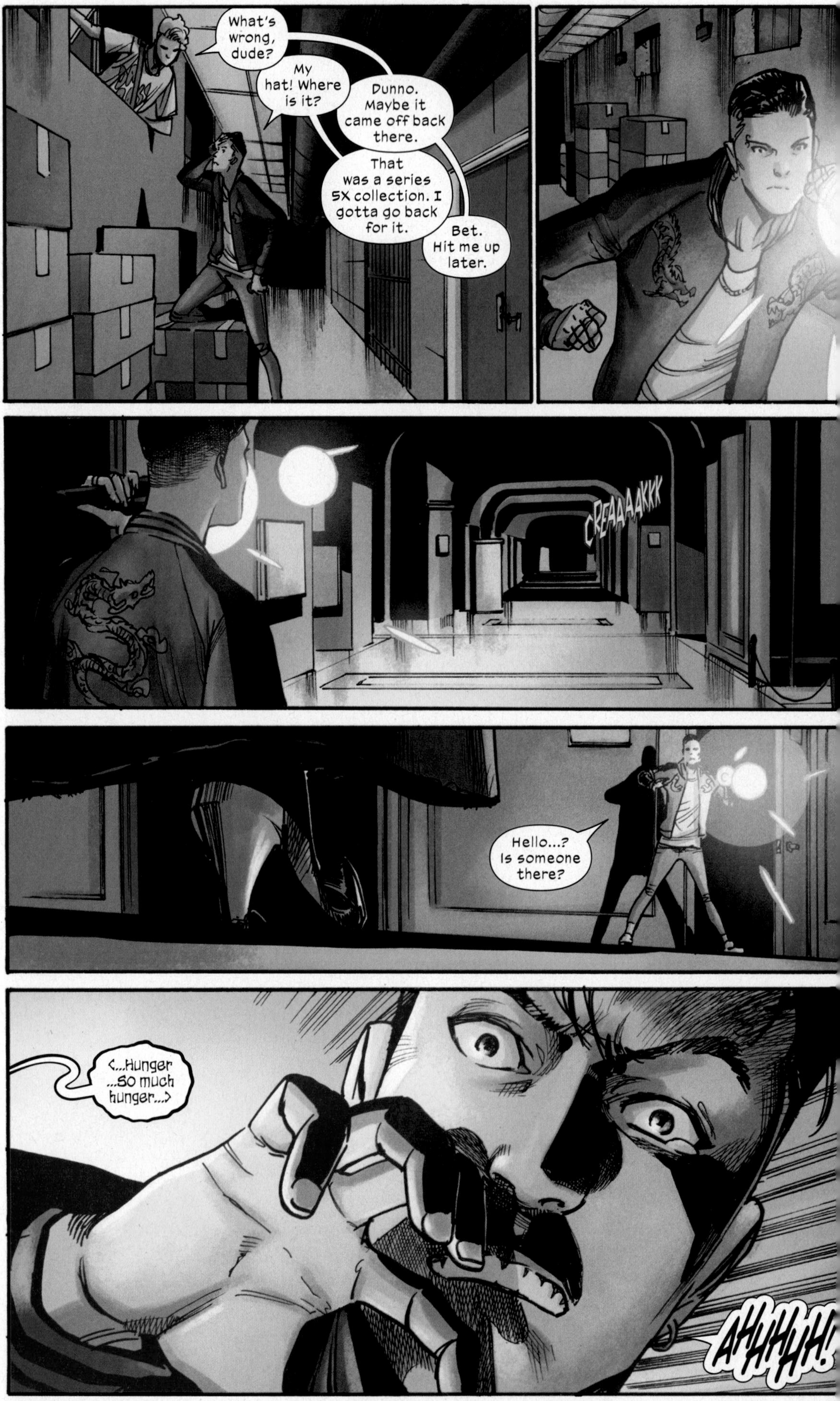
What's wrong, dude?
My hat! Where is it?
Dunno. Maybe it came off back there.
That was a series 5X collection. I gotta go back for it.
Bet. Hit me up later.
CREAAAAKKK
Hello...? Is someone there?
<...Hunger ...so much hunger...>
AHHHH!

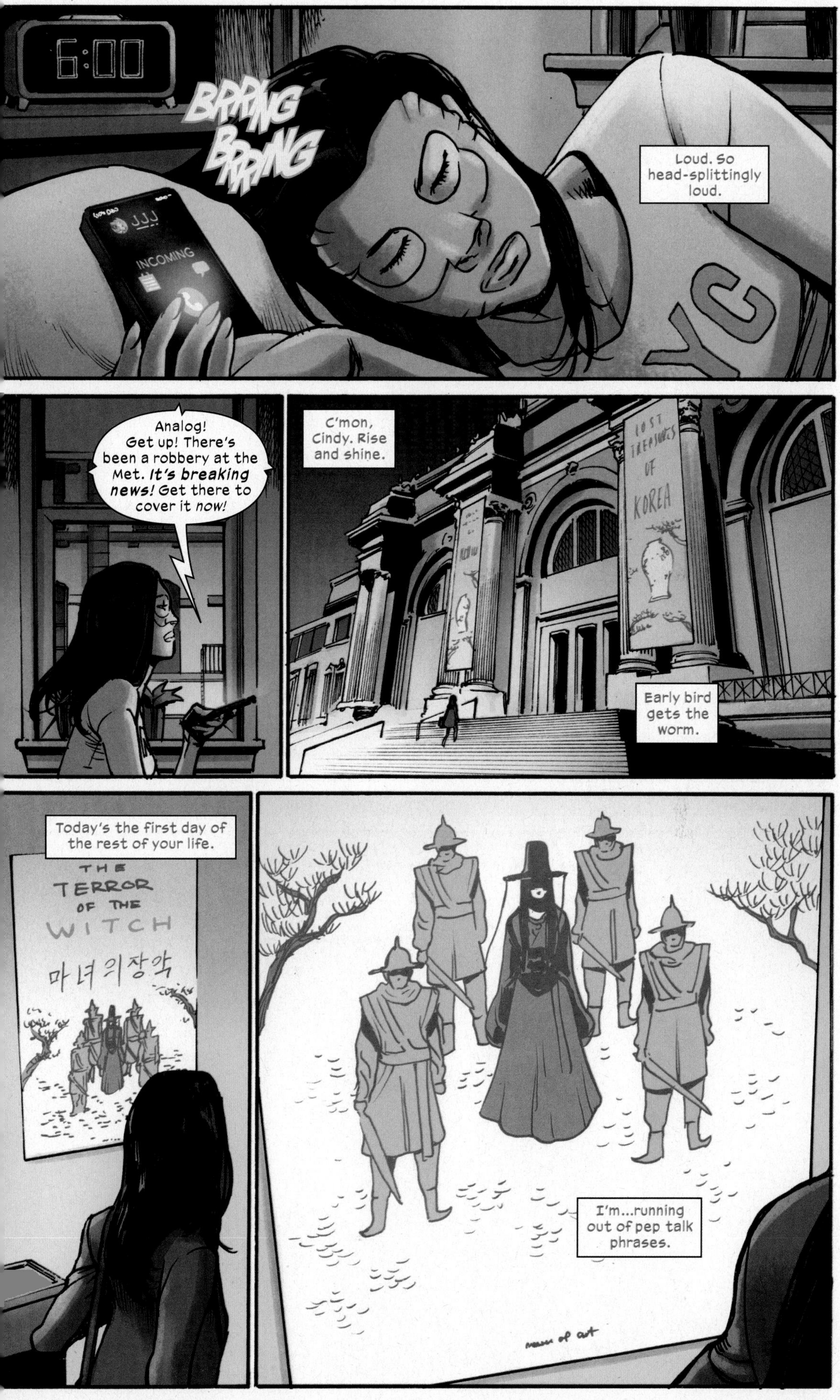
6:00
BRRING
BRRING
JJJ
INCOMING
Loud. So head-splittingly loud.
Analog! Get up! There's been a robbery at the Met. *It's breaking news!* Get there to cover it *now!*
C'mon, Cindy. Rise and shine.
LOST TREASURES OF KOREA
Early bird gets the worm.
Today's the first day of the rest of your life.
THE TERROR OF THE WITCH
마녀의장악
I'm...running out of pep talk phrases.

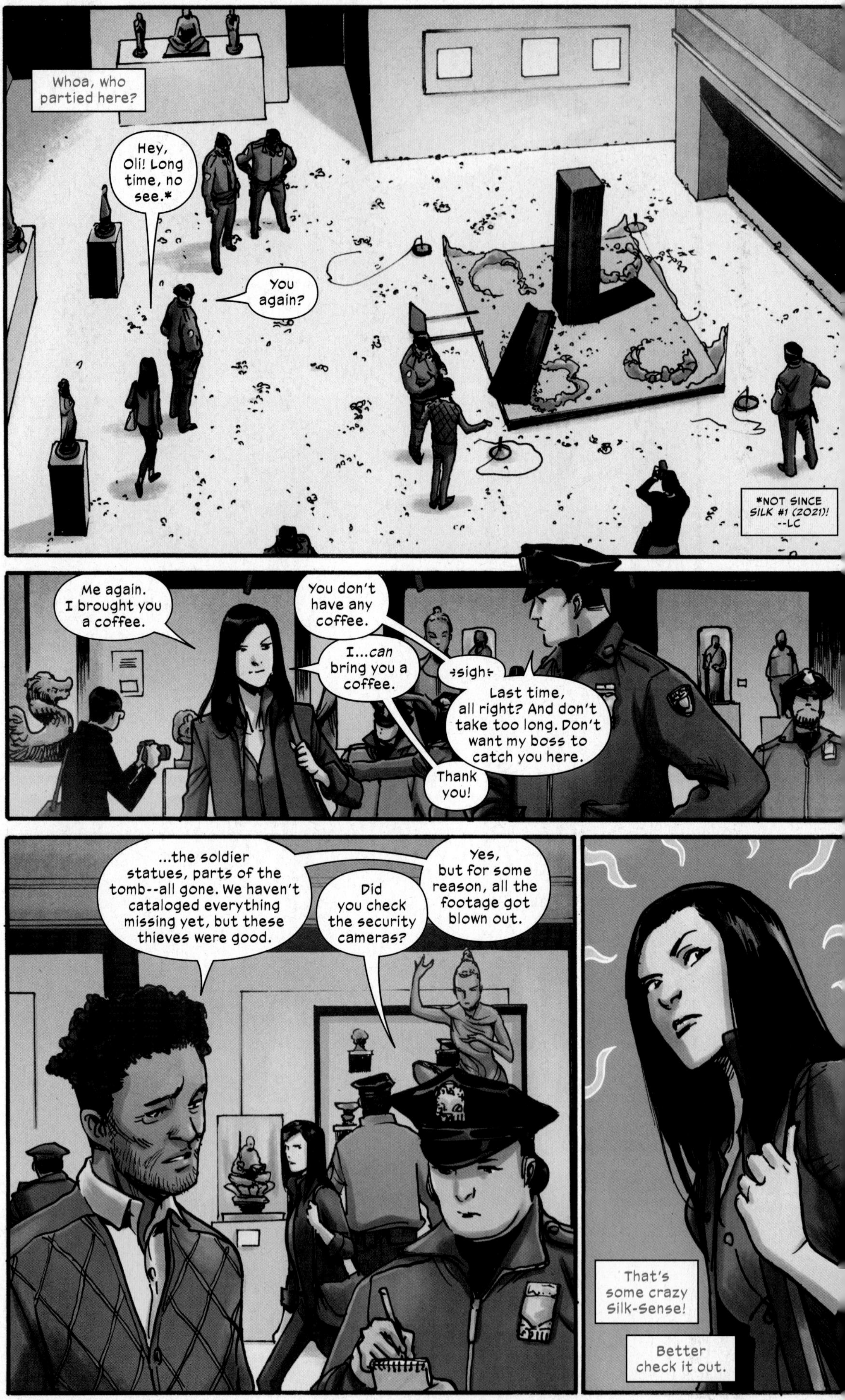
Whoa, who partied here?
Hey, Oli! Long time, no see.*
You again?
*NOT SINCE SILK #1 (2021)! --LC
Me again. I brought you a coffee.
You don't have any coffee.
I...*can* bring you a coffee.
-sigh-
Last time, all right? And don't take too long. Don't want my boss to catch you here.
Thank you!
...the soldier statues, parts of the tomb--all gone. We haven't cataloged everything missing yet, but these thieves were good.
Did you check the security cameras?
Yes, but for some reason, all the footage got blown out.
That's some crazy Silk-Sense!
Better check it out.

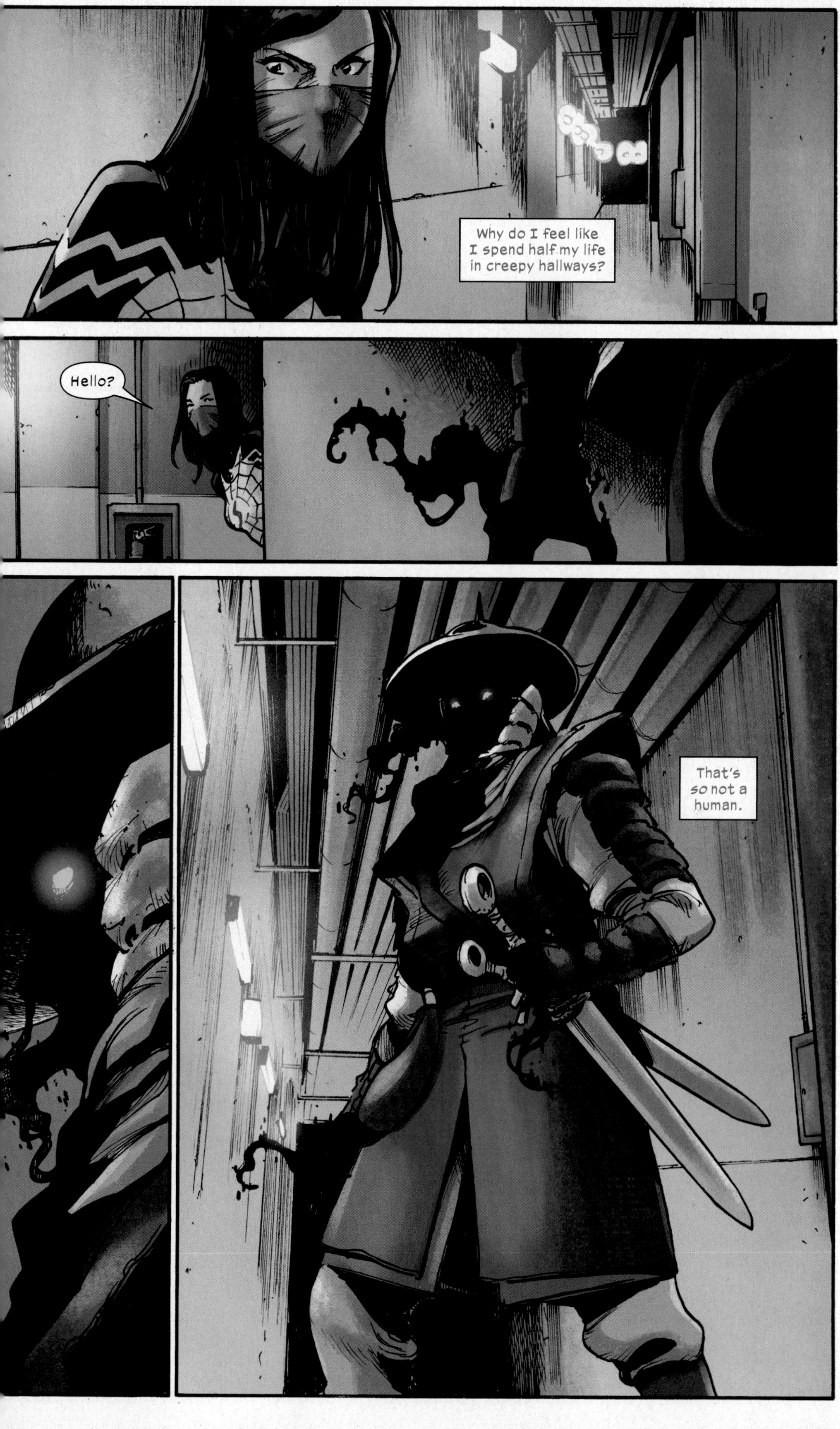
Why do I feel like I spend half my life in creepy hallways?
Hello?
That's so not a human.

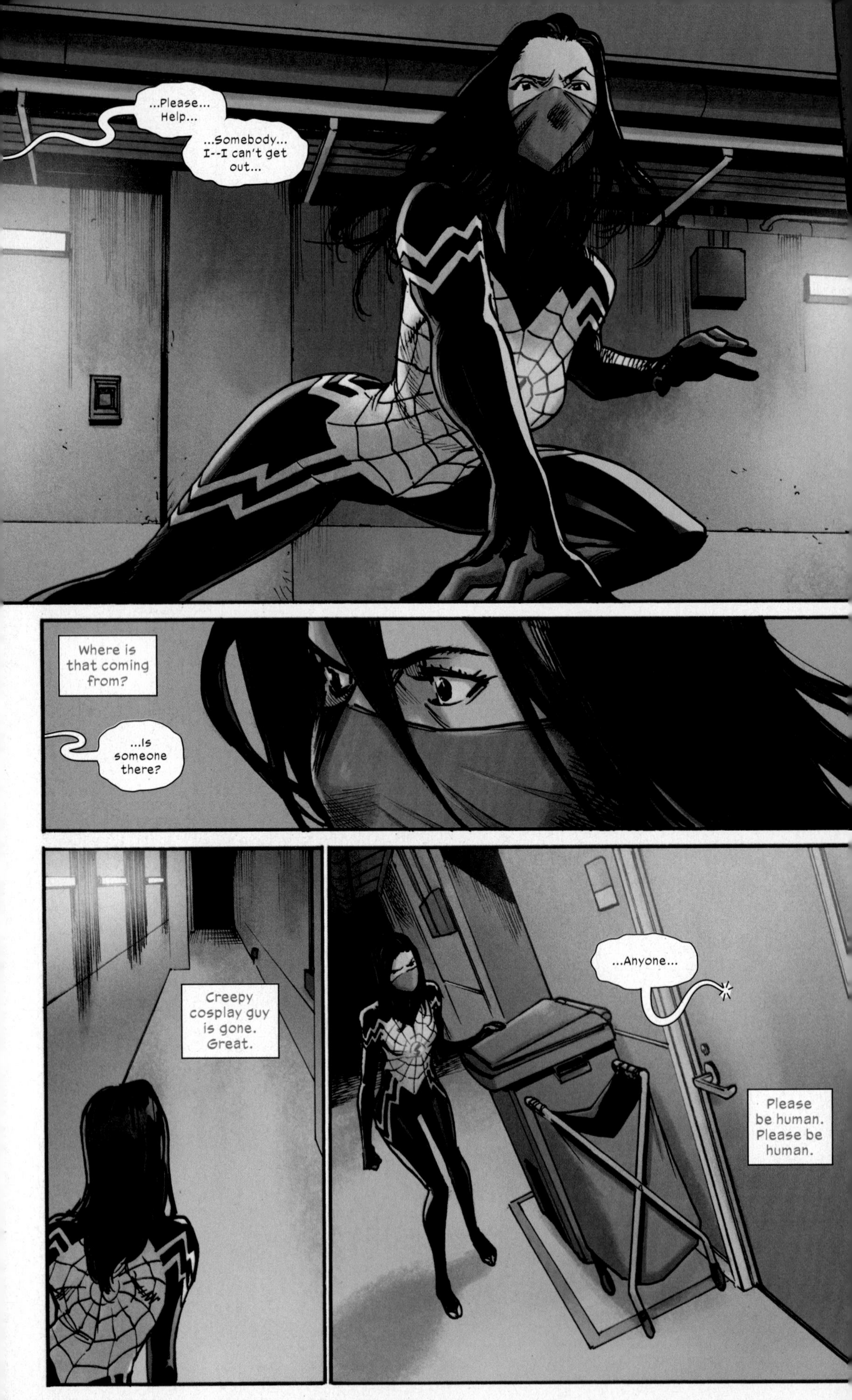
...Please... Help...
...Somebody... I--I can't get out...
Where is that coming from?
...Is someone there?
Creepy cosplay guy is gone. Great.
...Anyone...
Please be human. Please be human.

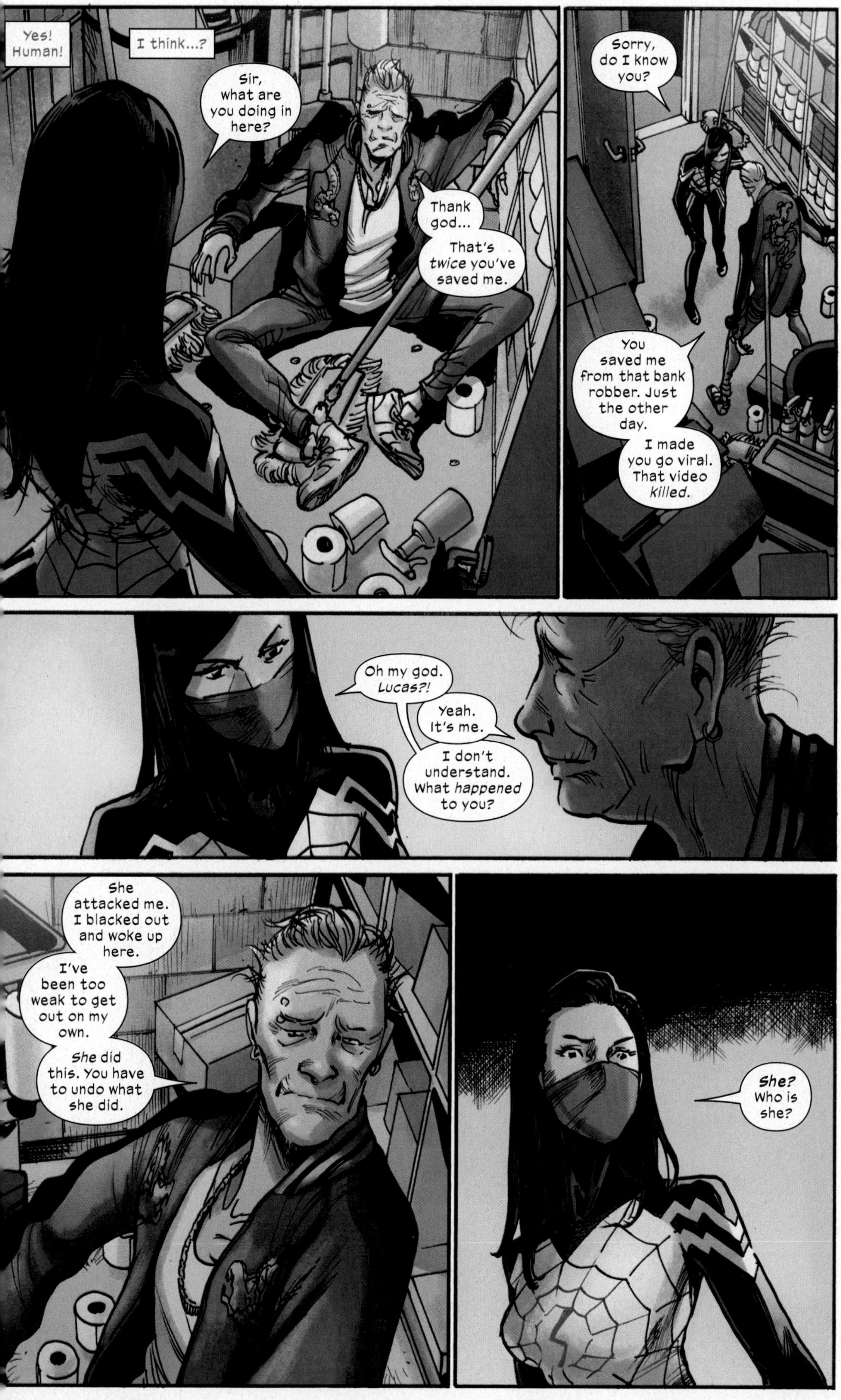

Yes! Human!
I think...?
Sir, what are you doing in here?
Thank god...
That's *twice* you've saved me.
Sorry, do I know you?
You saved me from that bank robber. Just the other day.
I made you go viral. That video *killed*.
Oh my god. *Lucas?!*
Yeah. It's me.
I don't understand. What *happened* to you?
She attacked me. I blacked out and woke up here.
I've been too weak to get out on my own.
She did this. You have to undo what she did.
She? Who is she?

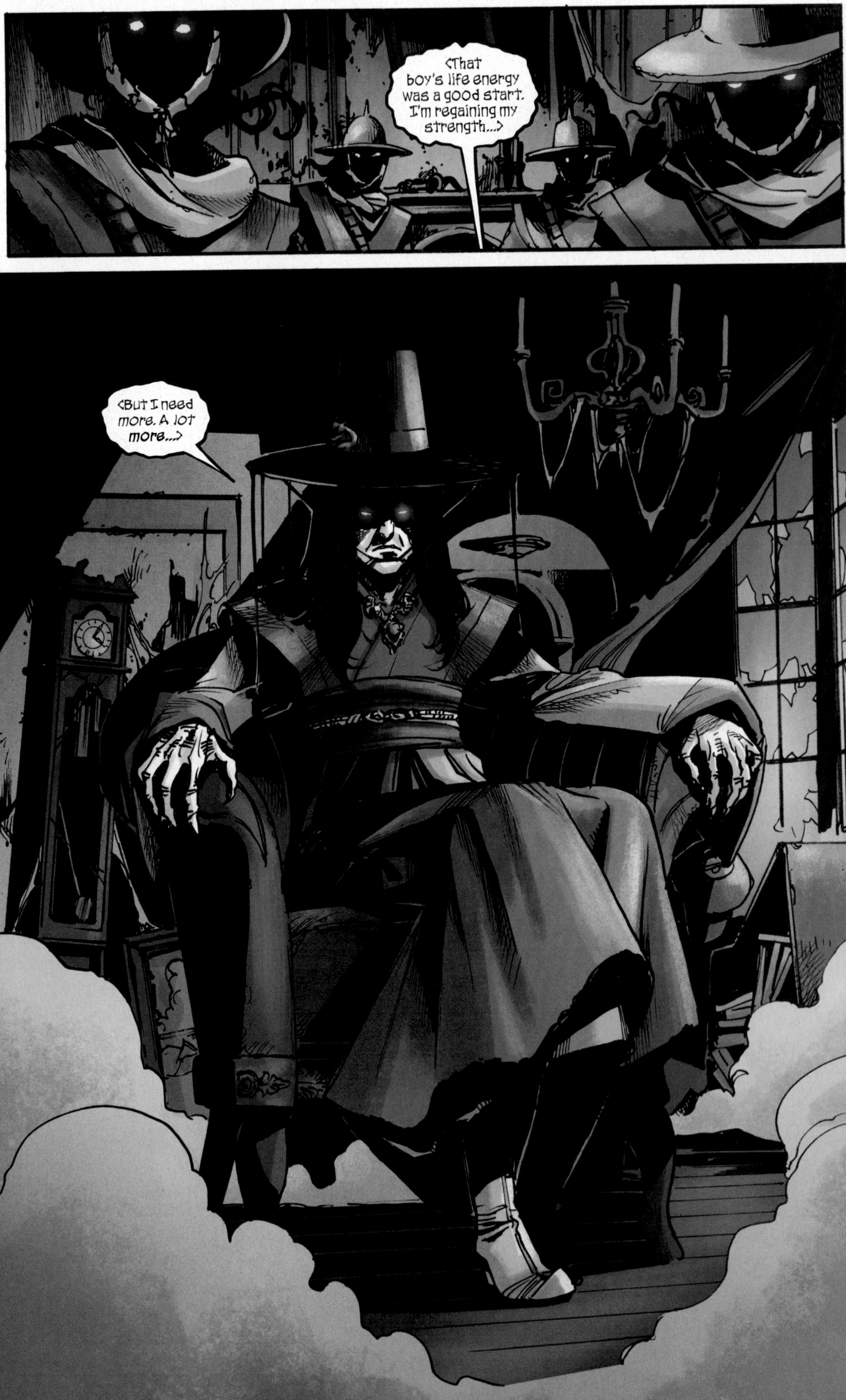
<That boy's life energy was a good start. I'm regaining my strength...>
<But I need more. A lot more...>

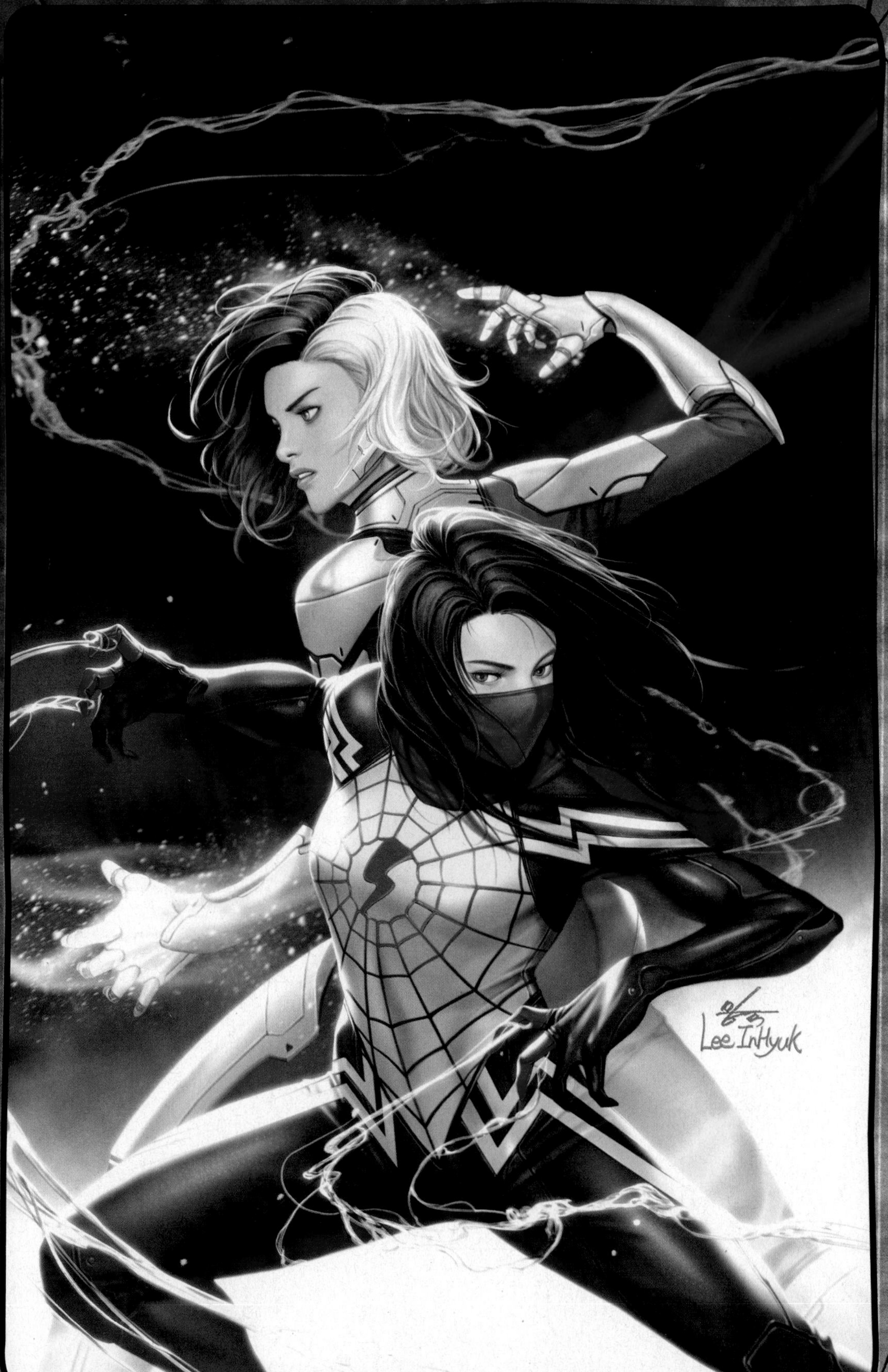
Lee InHyuk

SILK #2

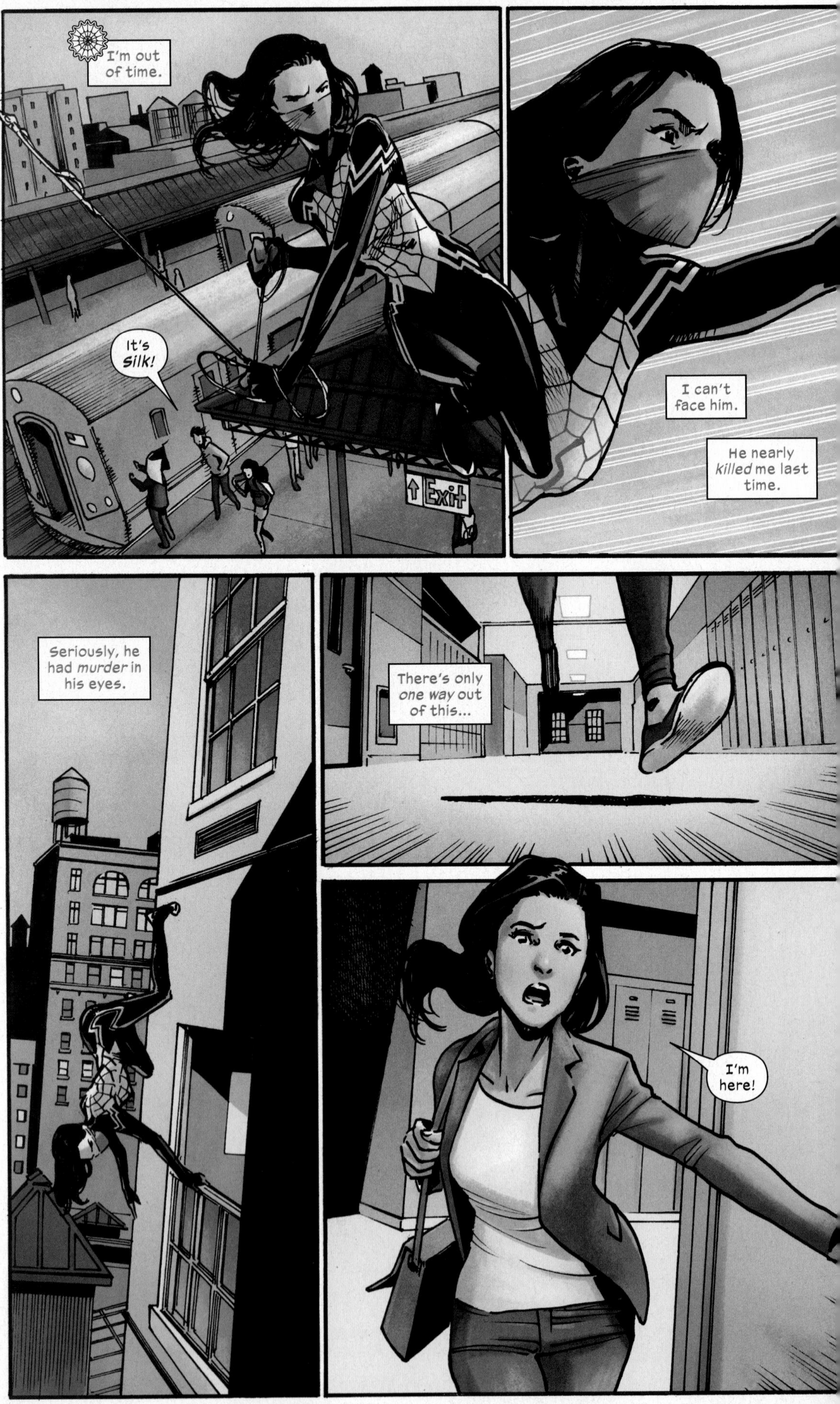
I'm out of time.
It's *Silk!*
Exit
I can't face him.
He nearly *killed* me last time.
Seriously, he had *murder* in his eyes.
There's only *one way* out of this...
I'm here!

Late *again*, Ms. Moon.

I thought I was very clear about my expectations the last *two* times you were tardy. As I've said before, pottery requires *commitment*...

LICENSE TO KILN

So it turns out I'm not the Picasso of pottery.

I'm also not the Picasso of cooking. Or woodworking. Or meditating.

I don't even know if this is what Dr. Sinclair meant when she said to "find myself."

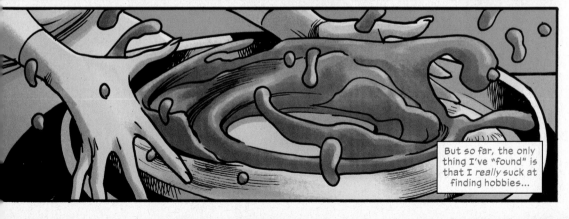

But so far, the only thing I've "found" is that I *really* suck at finding hobbies...

In my defense, it's been difficult to focus on anything other than this crazy mystery...

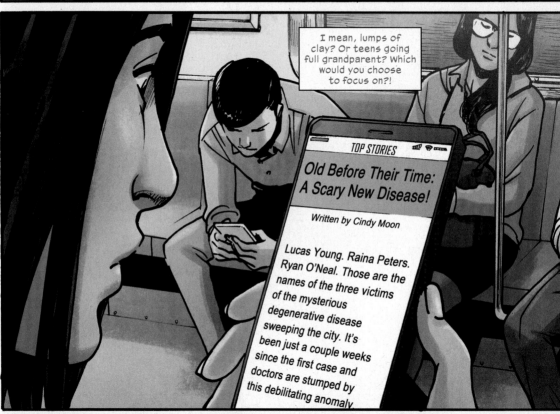

I mean, lumps of clay? Or teens going full grandparent? Which would you choose to focus on?!

TOP STORIES

Old Before Their Time: A Scary New Disease!

Written by Cindy Moon

Lucas Young. Raina Peters. Ryan O'Neal. Those are the names of the three victims of the mysterious degenerative disease sweeping the city. It's been just a couple weeks since the first case and doctors are stumped by this debilitating anomaly.

DING!

Luna Snow

Emailed you two tickets for tonight!
Come. It'll be fun!

Note to self. Try to make it to Luna's concert.

Second note to self. Seriously. She's your friend.

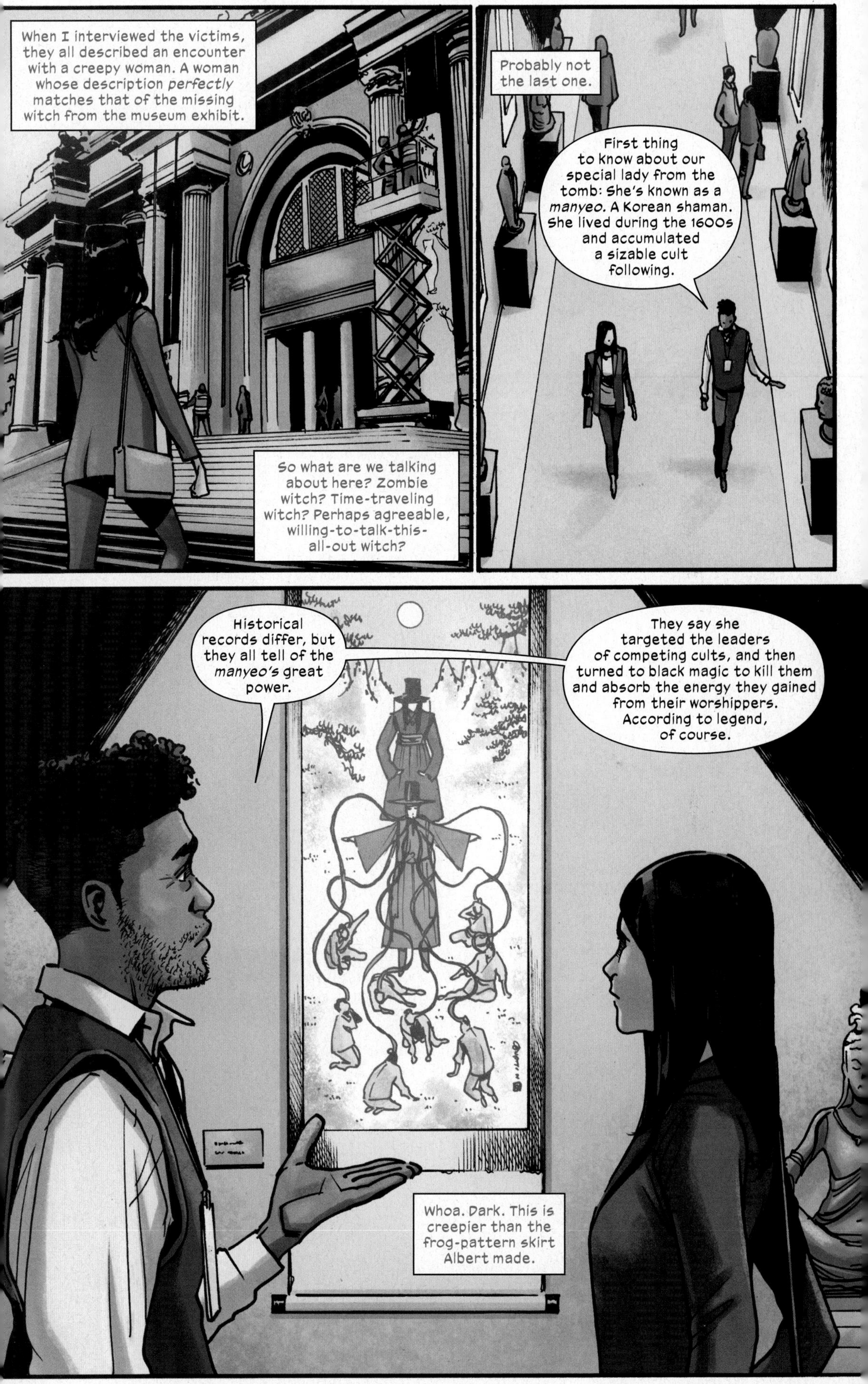

When I interviewed the victims, they all described an encounter with a creepy woman. A woman whose description *perfectly* matches that of the missing witch from the museum exhibit.
So what are we talking about here? Zombie witch? Time-traveling witch? Perhaps agreeable, willing-to-talk-this-all-out witch?
Probably not the last one.
First thing to know about our special lady from the tomb: She's known as a *manyeo.* A Korean shaman. She lived during the 1600s and accumulated a sizable cult following.
Historical records differ, but they all tell of the *manyeo's* great power.
They say she targeted the leaders of competing cults, and then turned to black magic to kill them and absorb the energy they gained from their worshippers. According to legend, of course.
Whoa. Dark. This is creepier than the frog-pattern skirt Albert made.

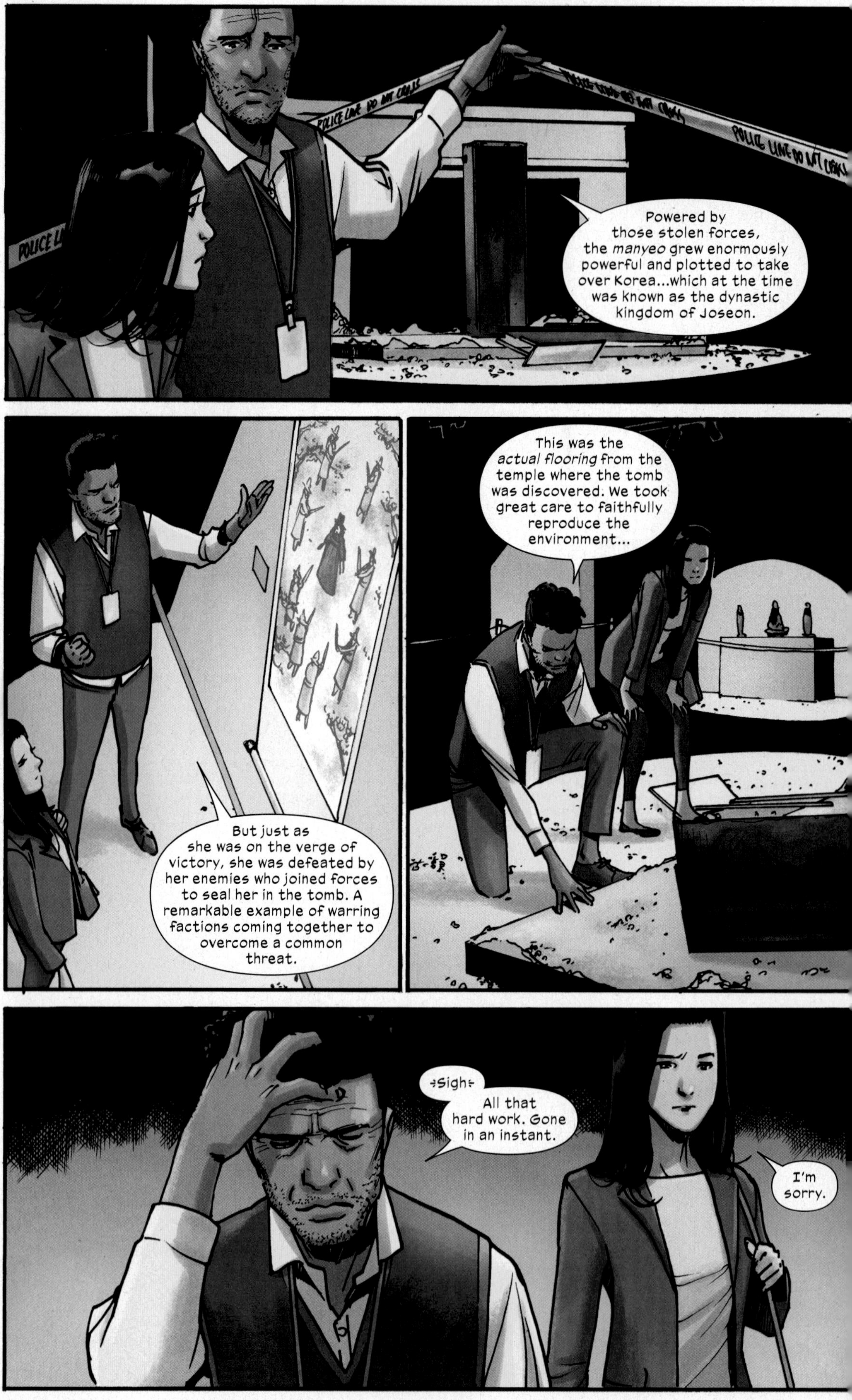

POLICE LINE DO NOT CROSS
Powered by those stolen forces, the *manyeo* grew enormously powerful and plotted to take over Korea...which at the time was known as the dynastic kingdom of Joseon.
But just as she was on the verge of victory, she was defeated by her enemies who joined forces to seal her in the tomb. A remarkable example of warring factions coming together to overcome a common threat.
This was the *actual flooring* from the temple where the tomb was discovered. We took great care to faithfully reproduce the environment...
-Sigh-
All that hard work. Gone in an instant.
I'm sorry.

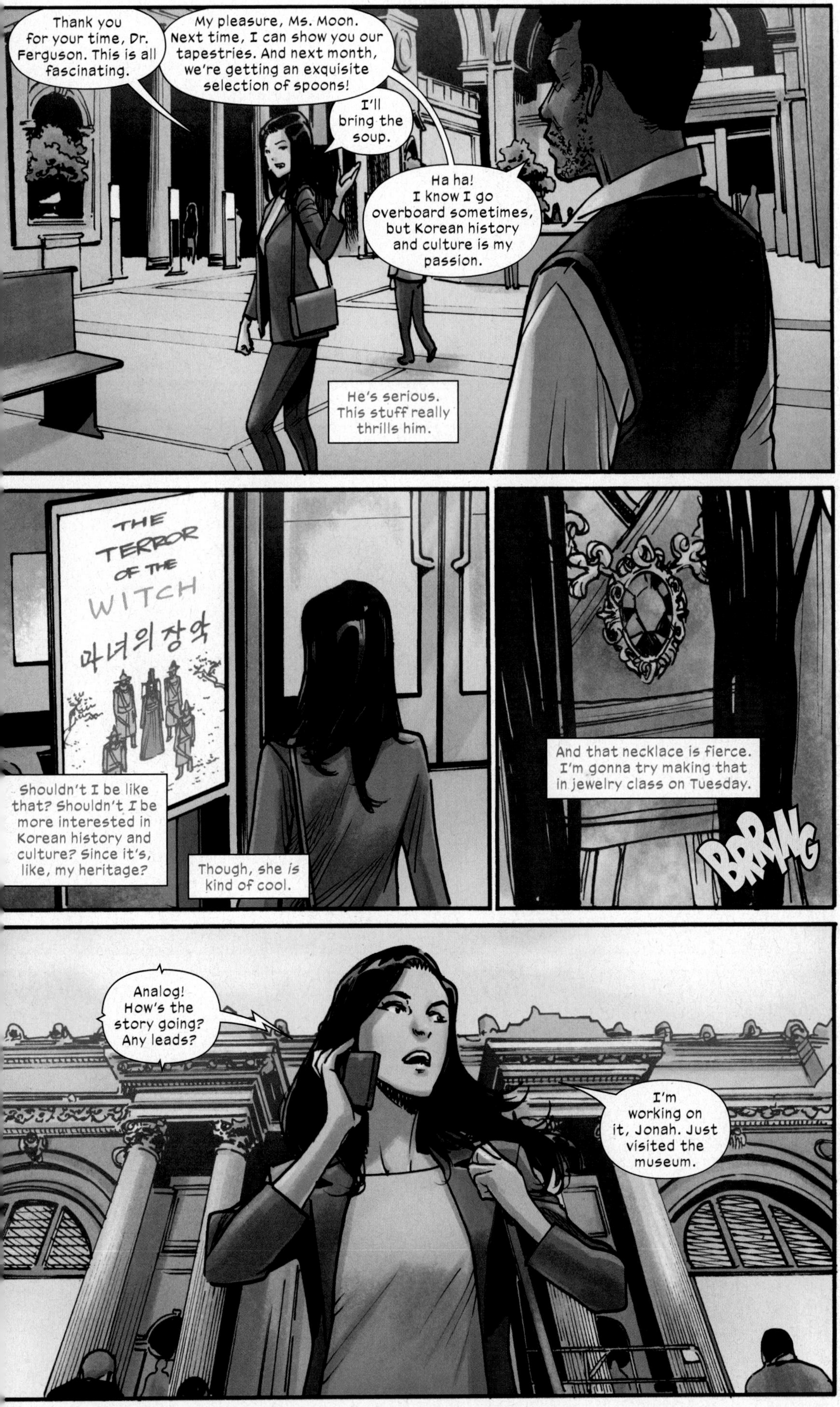
Thank you for your time, Dr. Ferguson. This is all fascinating.
My pleasure, Ms. Moon. Next time, I can show you our tapestries. And next month, we're getting an exquisite selection of spoons!
I'll bring the soup.
Ha ha! I know I go overboard sometimes, but Korean history and culture is my passion.
He's serious. This stuff really thrills him.
THE TERROR OF THE WITCH
마녀의 장악
Shouldn't I be like that? Shouldn't I be more interested in Korean history and culture? Since it's, like, my heritage?
Though, she is kind of cool.
And that necklace is fierce. I'm gonna try making that in jewelry class on Tuesday.
BRRING
Analog! How's the story going? Any leads?
I'm working on it, Jonah. Just visited the museum.

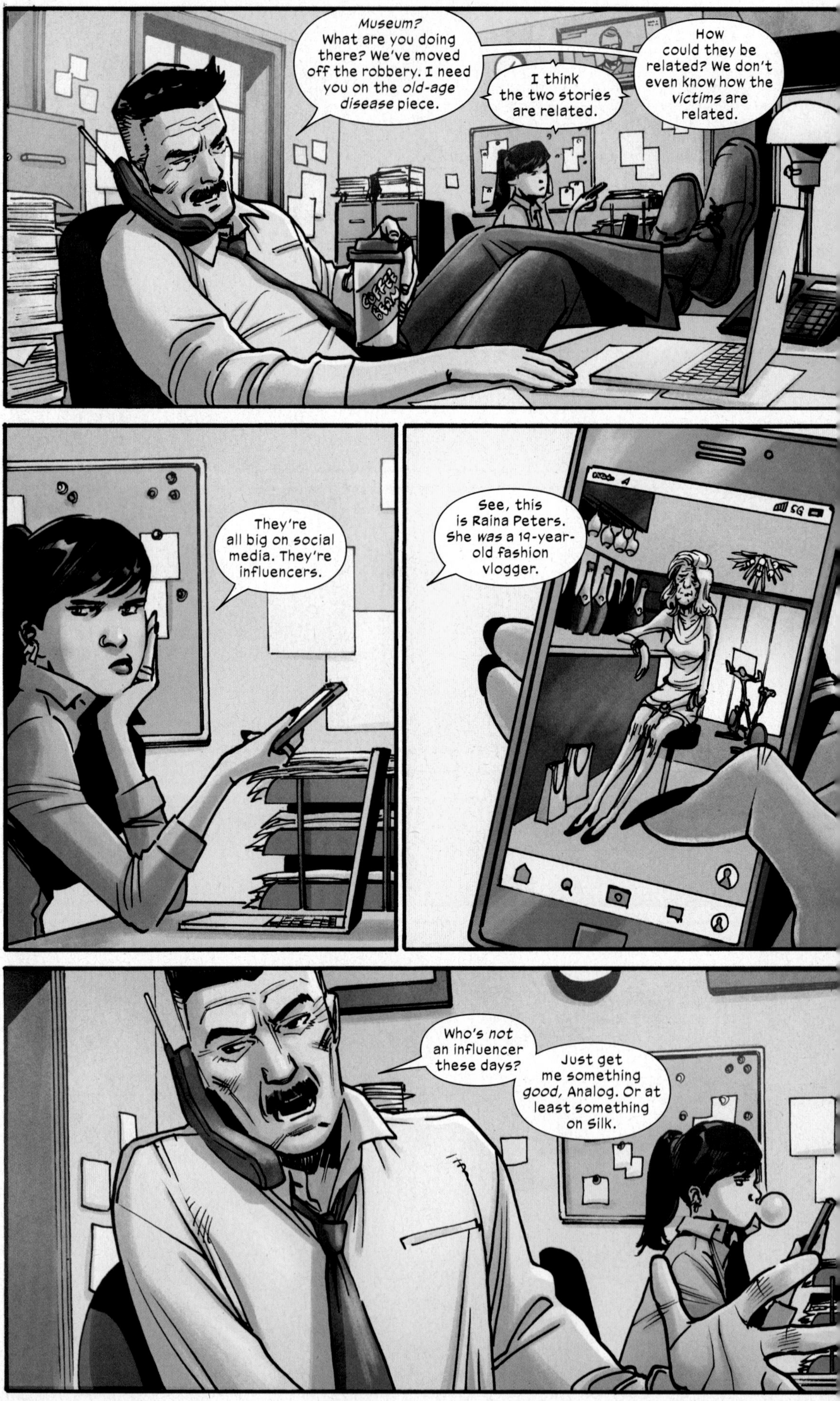
Museum? What are you doing there? We've moved off the robbery. I need you on the old-age disease piece.
I think the two stories are related.
How could they be related? We don't even know how the victims are related.
They're all big on social media. They're influencers.
See, this is Raina Peters. She was a 19-year-old fashion vlogger.
Who's not an influencer these days?
Just get me something good, Analog. Or at least something on Silk.

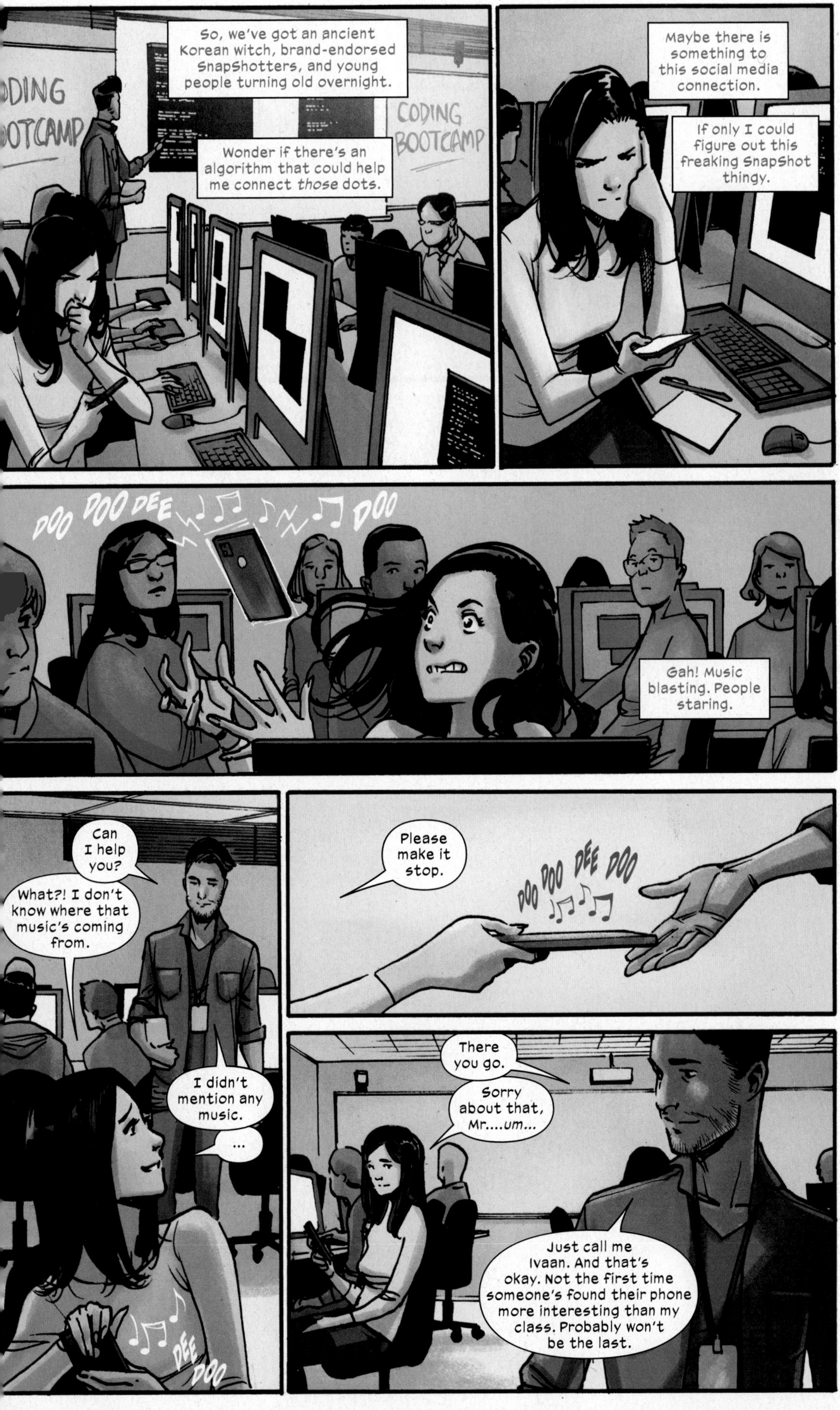

So, we've got an ancient Korean witch, brand-endorsed SnapShotters, and young people turning old overnight.
Wonder if there's an algorithm that could help me connect *those* dots.
CODING BOOTCAMP
Maybe there is something to this social media connection.
If only I could figure out this freaking SnapShot thingy.
DOO DOO DEE DOO
Gah! Music blasting. People staring.
Can I help you?
What?! I don't know where that music's coming from.
I didn't mention any music.
...
DEE DOO
Please make it stop.
DOO DOO DEE DOO
There you go.
Sorry about that, Mr....*um*...
Just call me Ivaan. And that's okay. Not the first time someone's found their phone more interesting than my class. Probably won't be the last.

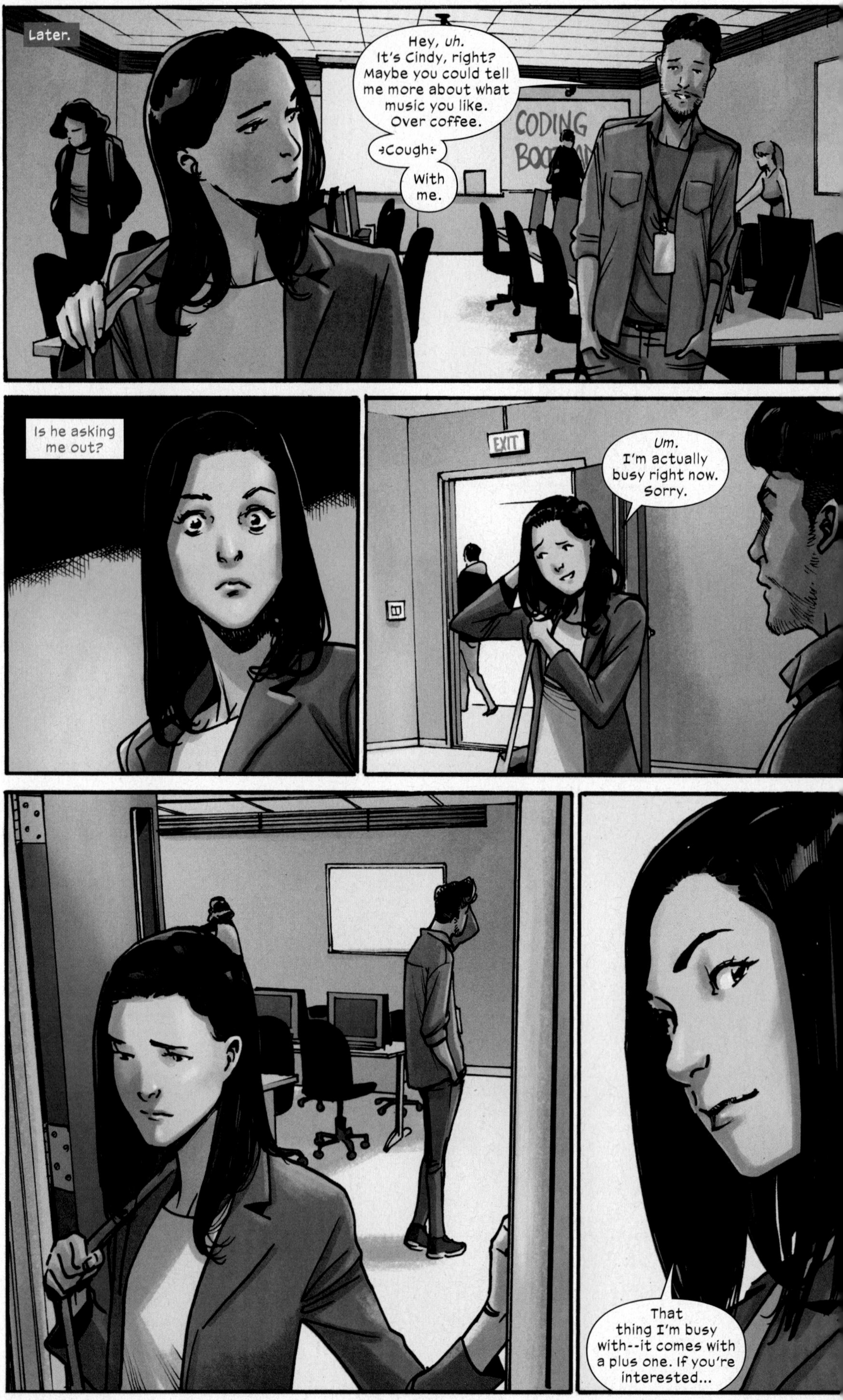
Later.
Hey, uh. It's Cindy, right? Maybe you could tell me more about what music you like. Over coffee.
Cough
With me.
CODING BOO
Is he asking me out?
EXIT
Um. I'm actually busy right now. Sorry.
That thing I'm busy with--it comes with a plus one. If you're interested...

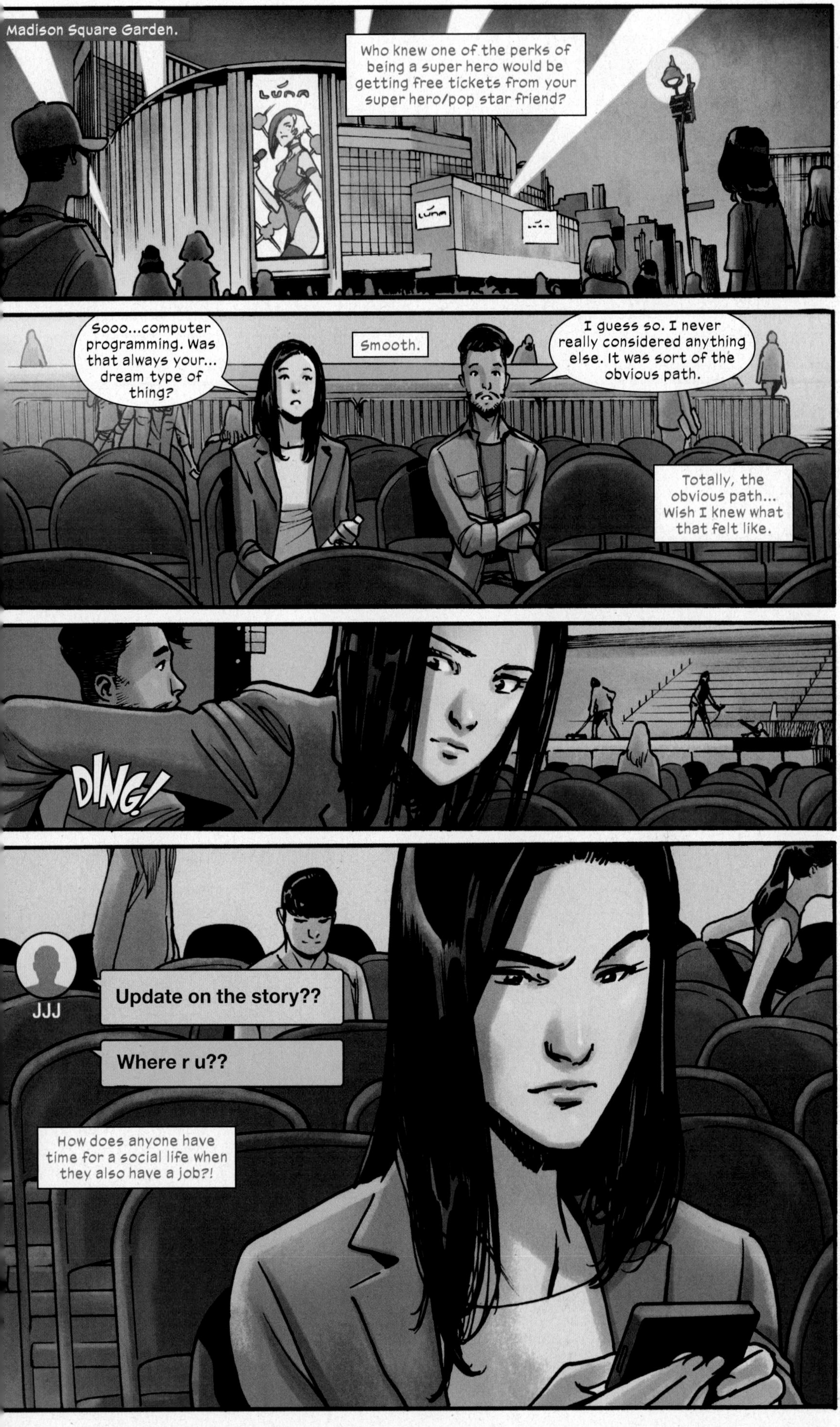
Madison Square Garden.
Who knew one of the perks of being a super hero would be getting free tickets from your super hero/pop star friend?
LUNA
Sooo...computer programming. Was that always your... dream type of thing?
Smooth.
I guess so. I never really considered anything else. It was sort of the obvious path.
Totally, the obvious path... Wish I knew what that felt like.
DING!
JJJ
Update on the story??
Where r u??
How does anyone have time for a social life when they also have a job?!

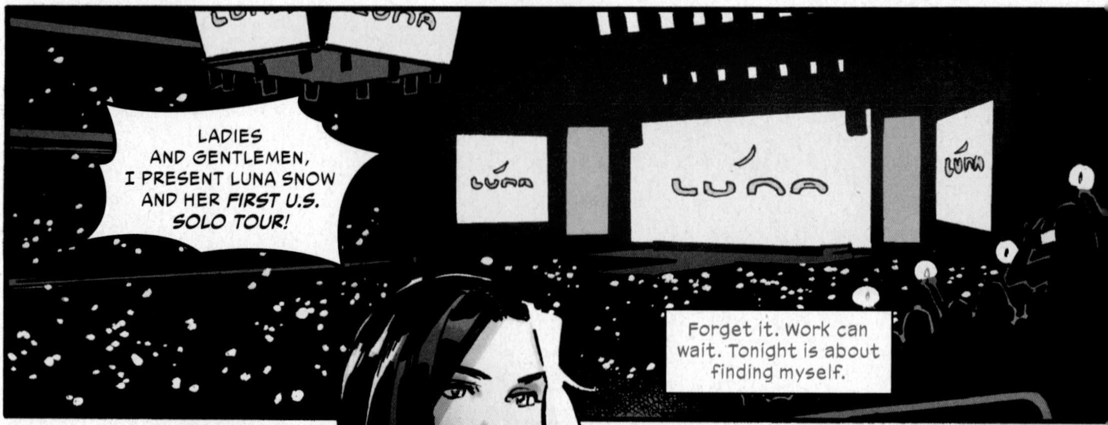
LADIES AND GENTLEMEN, I PRESENT LUNA SNOW AND HER *FIRST U.S.* SOLO TOUR!
LÚNA
LÚNA
LÚNA
LÚNA
Forget it. Work can wait. Tonight is about finding myself.

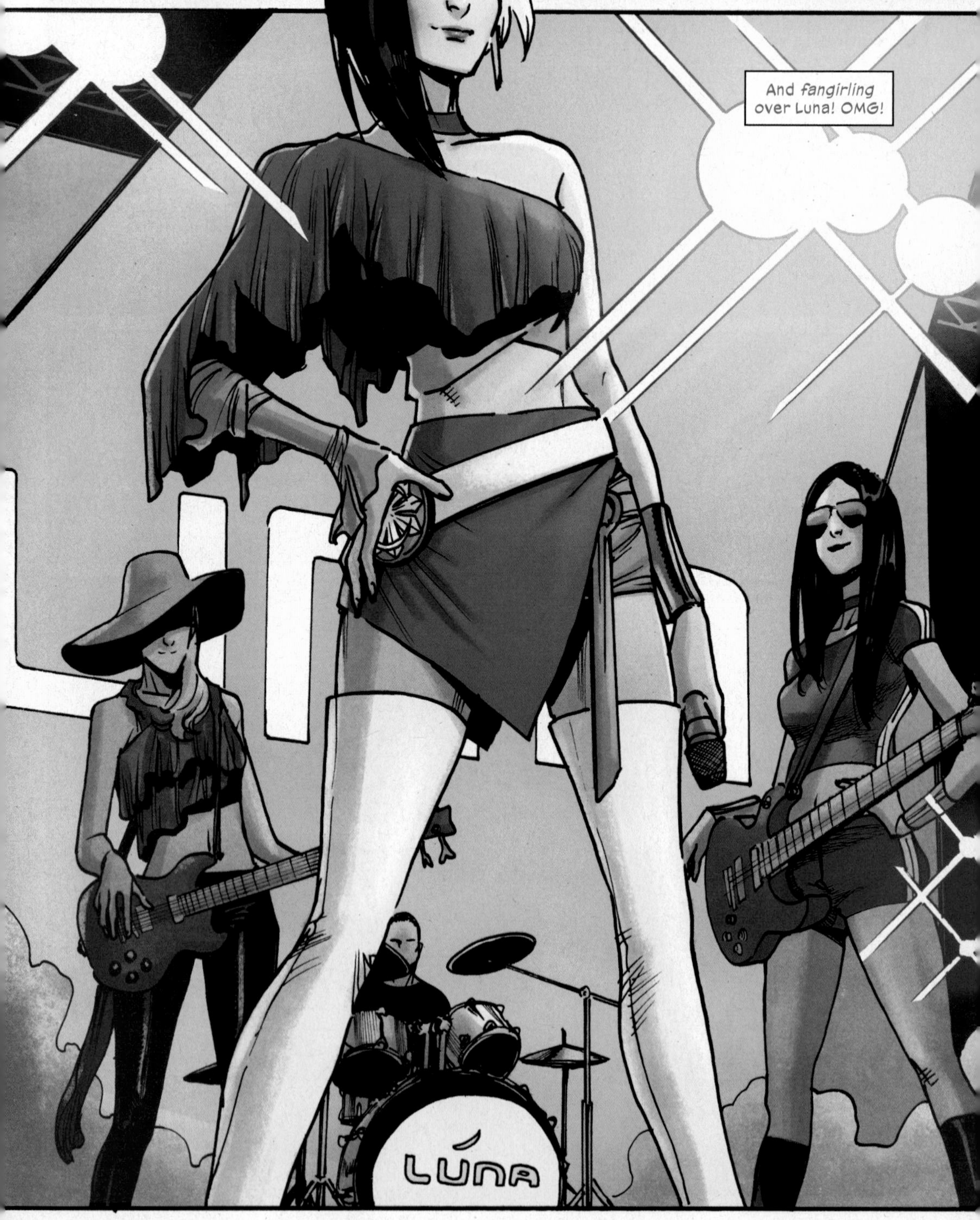
And *fangirling* over Luna! OMG!
LÚNA

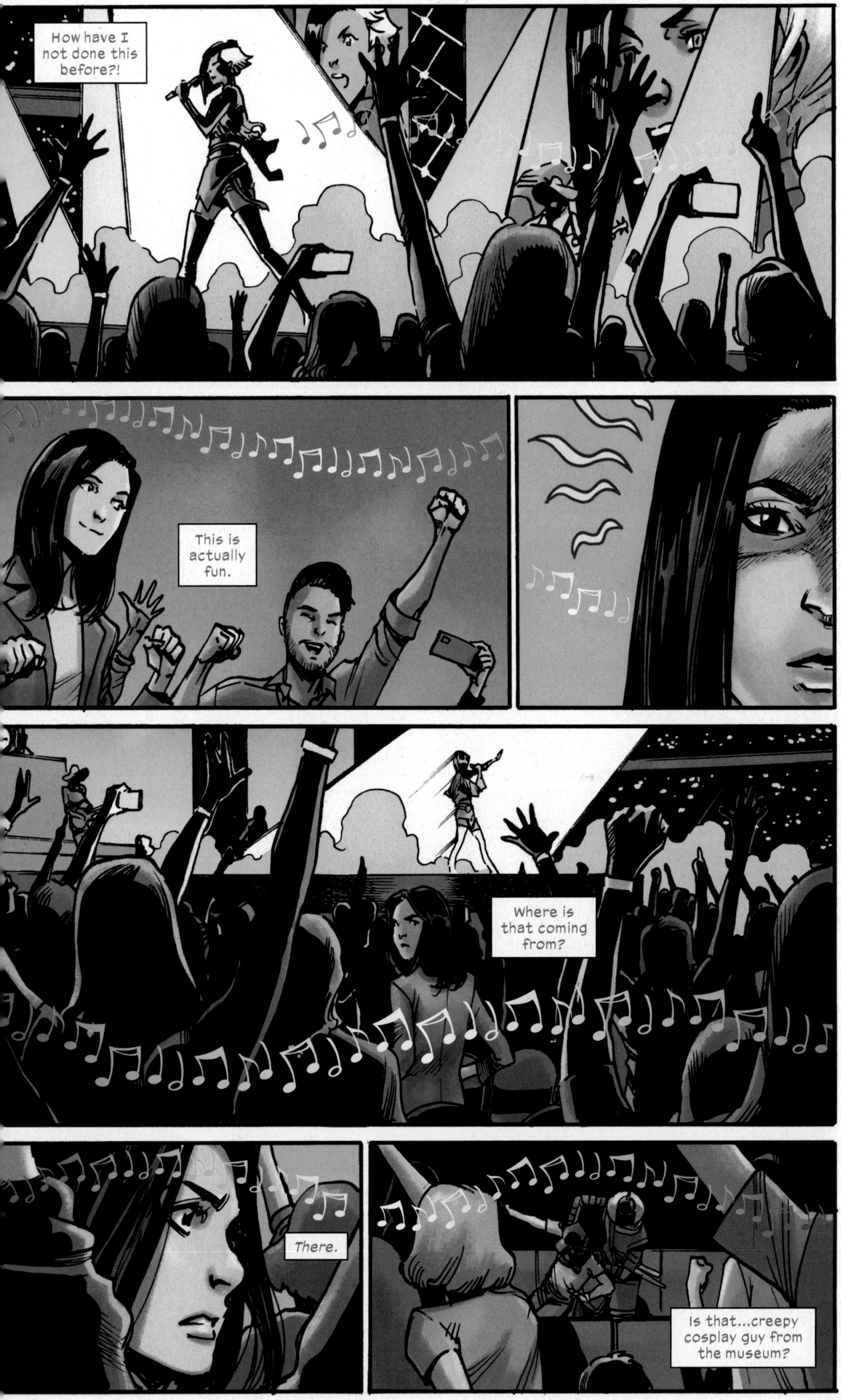
How have I not done this before?!
This is actually fun.
Where is that coming from?
There.
Is that...creepy cosplay guy from the museum?

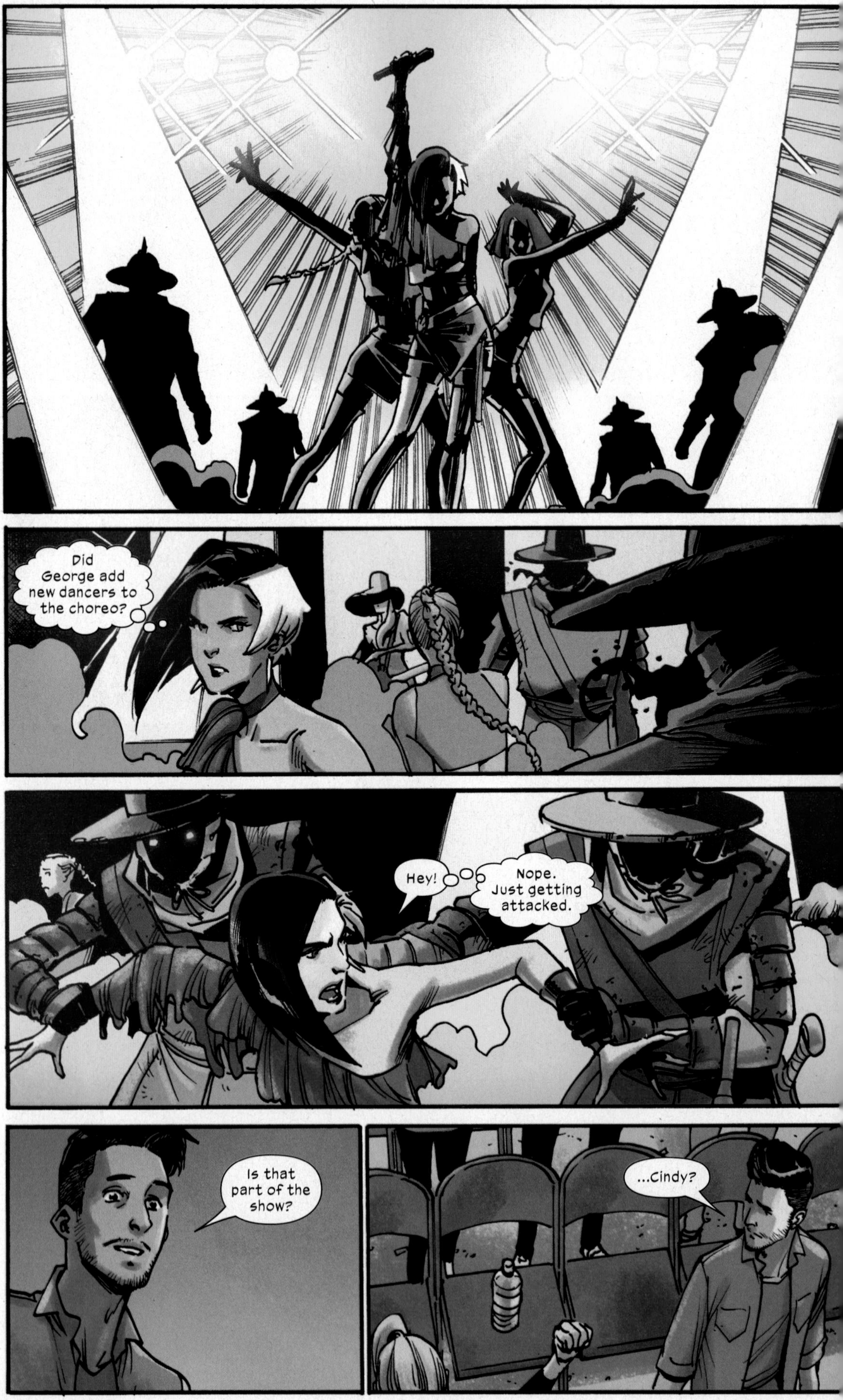
Did George add new dancers to the choreo?
Hey!
Nope. Just getting attacked.
Is that part of the show?
...Cindy?

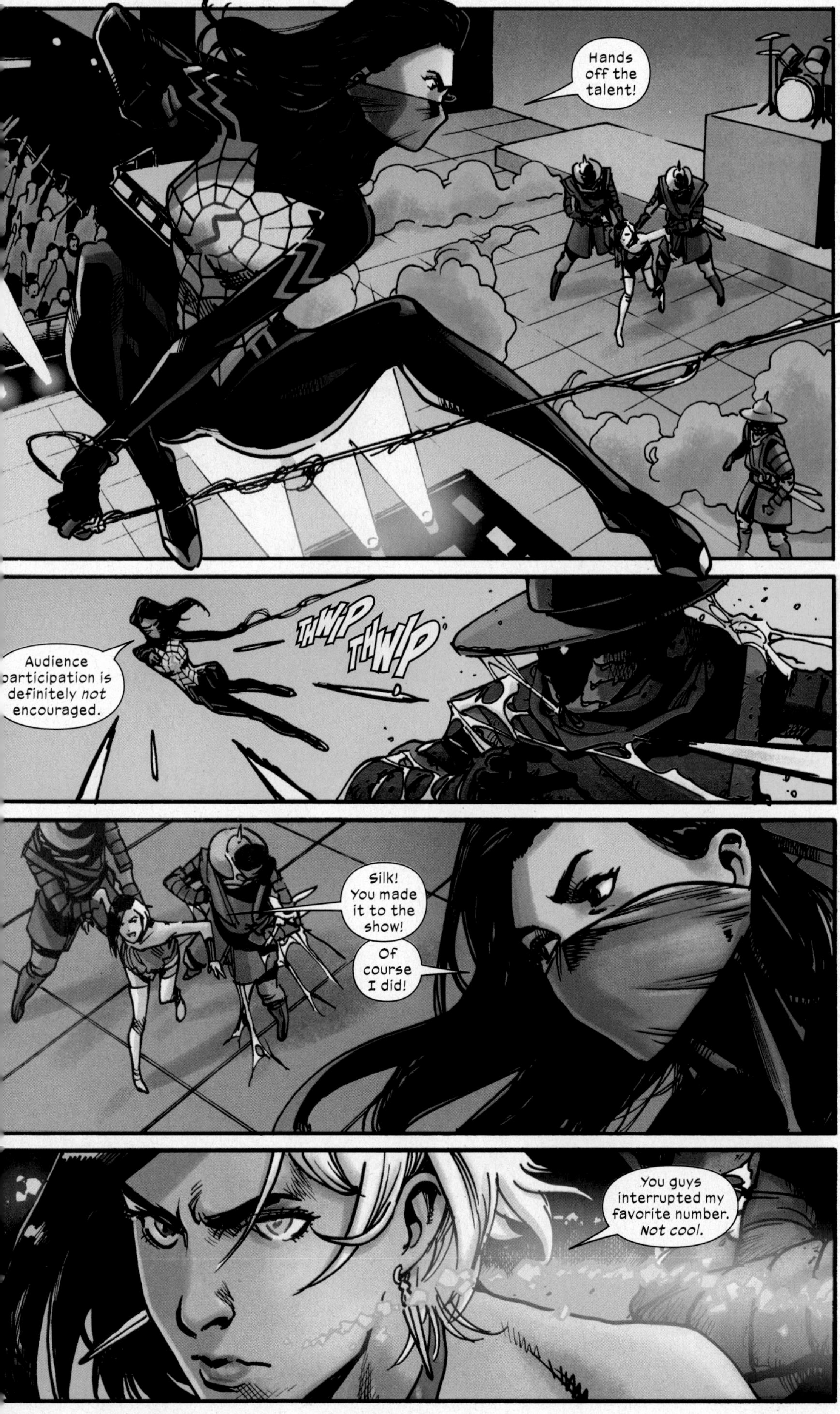
Hands off the talent!
THWIP THWIP
Audience participation is definitely *not* encouraged.
Silk! You made it to the show!
Of course I did!
You guys interrupted my favorite number. *Not cool.*

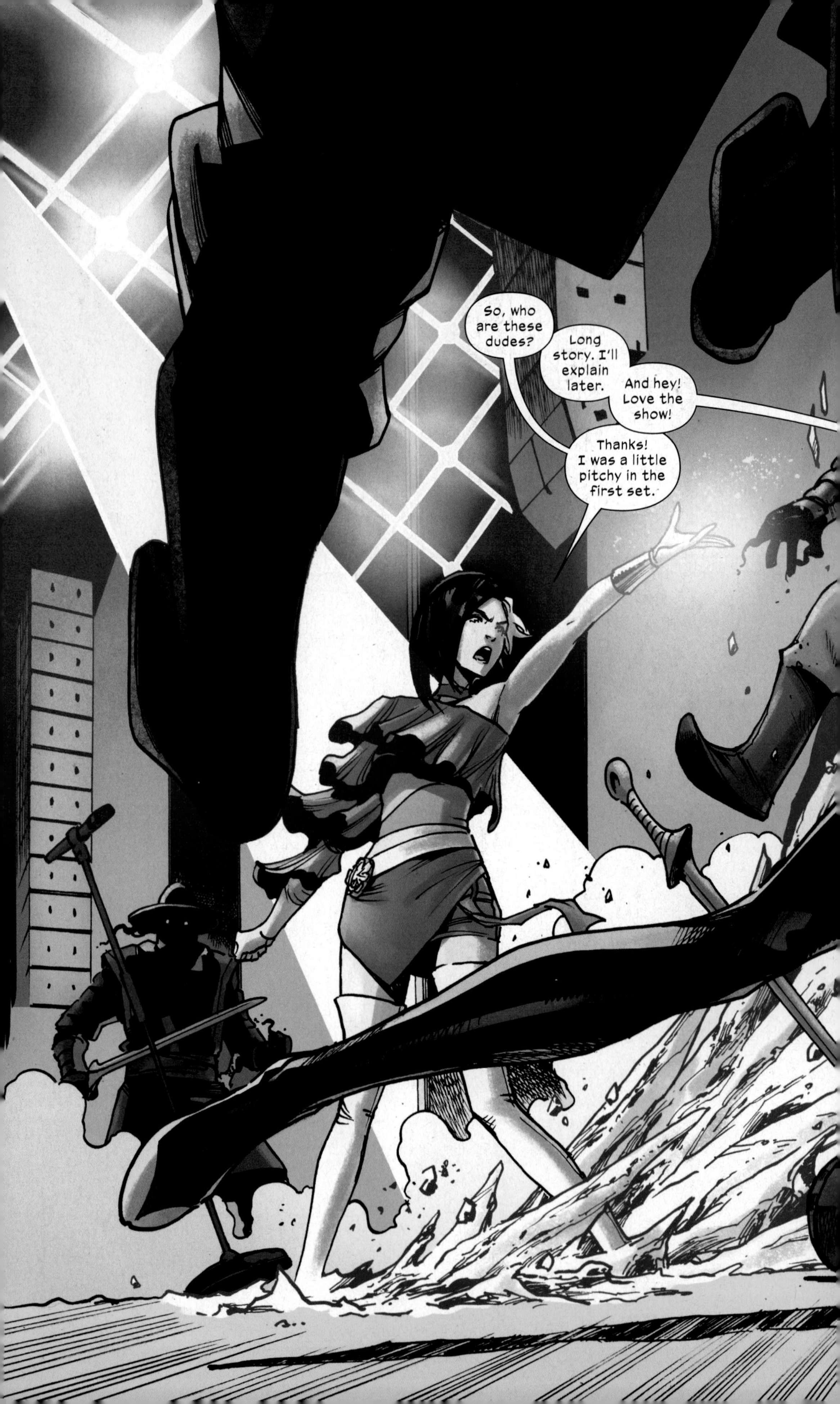
So, who are these dudes?
Long story. I'll explain later.
And hey! Love the show!
Thanks! I was a little pitchy in the first set.

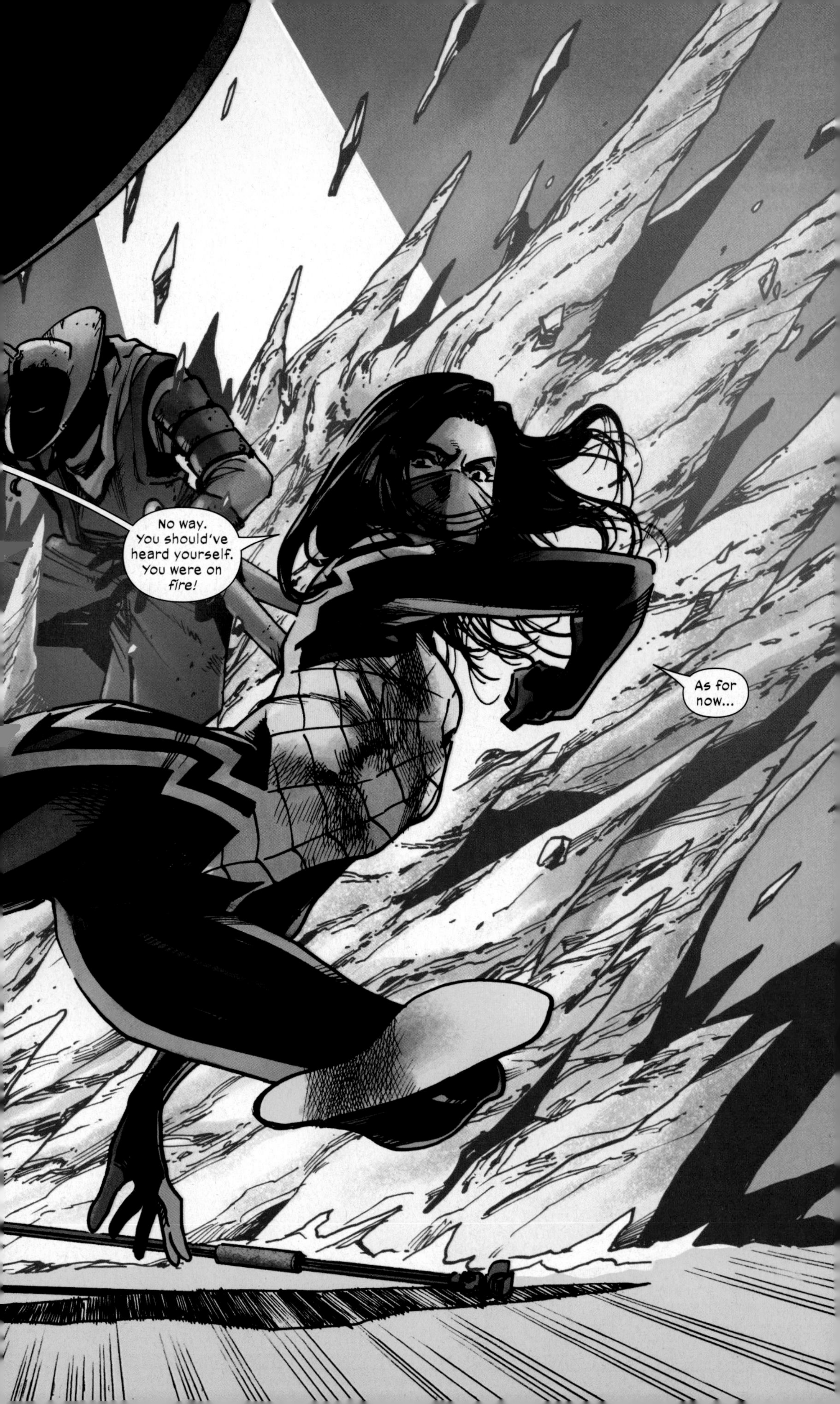
No way. You should've heard yourself. You were on fire!
As for now...

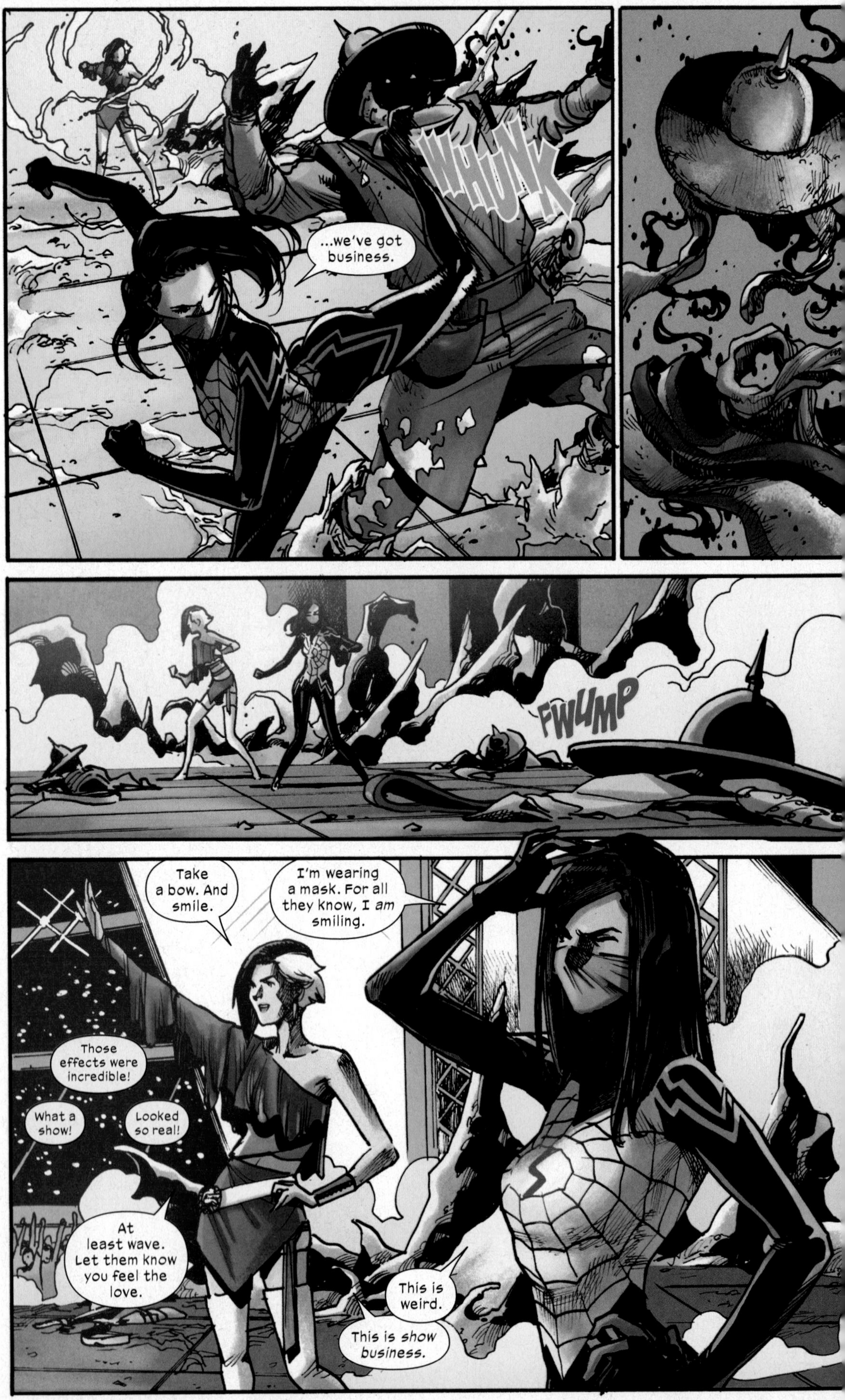
WHUNK
...we've got business.
FWUMP
Take a bow. And smile.
I'm wearing a mask. For all they know, I *am* smiling.
Those effects were incredible!
What a show!
Looked so real!
At least wave. Let them know you feel the love.
This is weird.
This is *show business.*

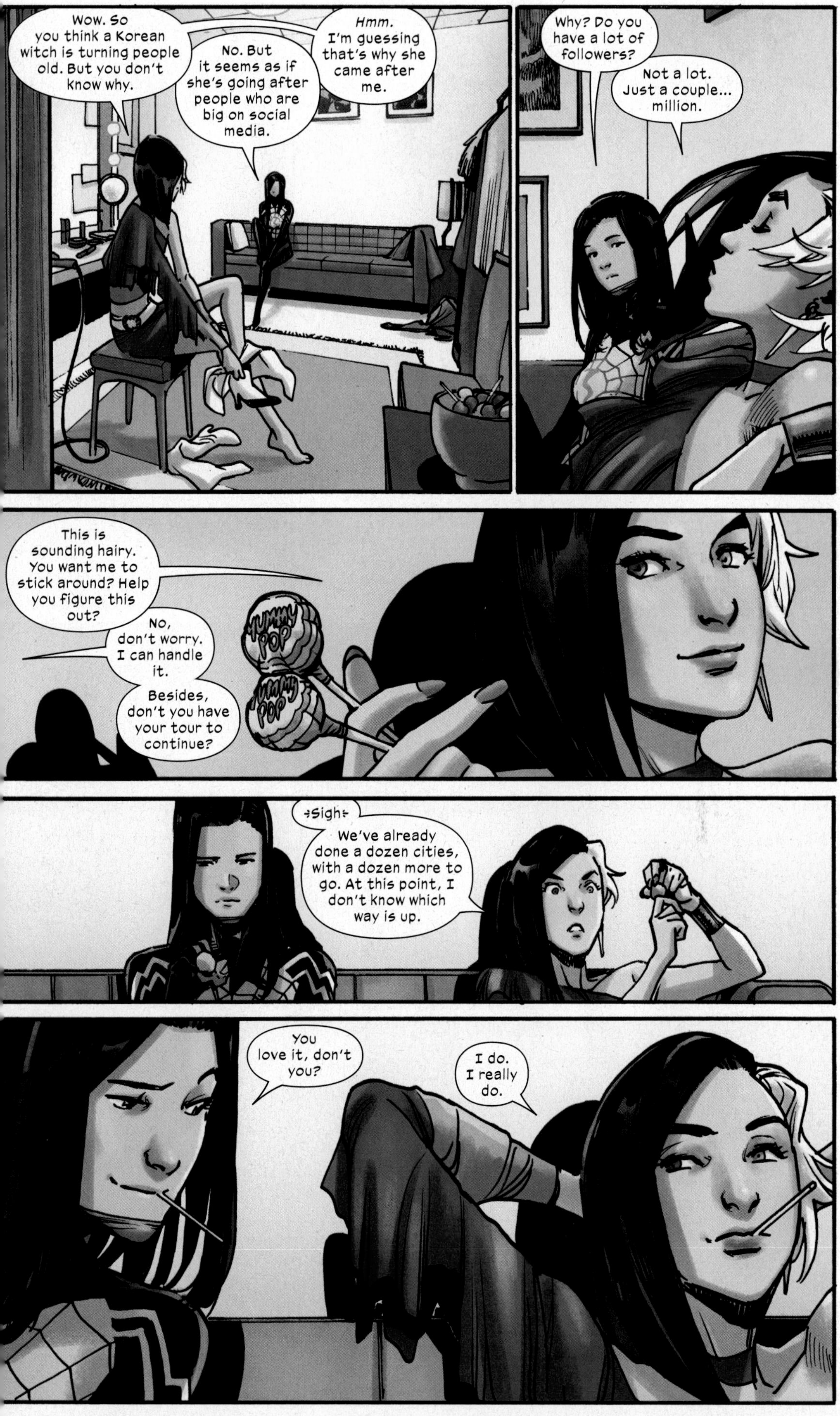
Wow. So you think a Korean witch is turning people old. But you don't know why.
No. But it seems as if she's going after people who are big on social media.
Hmm. I'm guessing that's why she came after me.
Why? Do you have a lot of followers?
Not a lot. Just a couple... million.
This is sounding hairy. You want me to stick around? Help you figure this out?
No, don't worry. I can handle it.
Besides, don't you have your tour to continue?
YUMMY POP
YUMMY POP
-Sigh-
We've already done a dozen cities, with a dozen more to go. At this point, I don't know which way is up.
You love it, don't you?
I do. I really do.

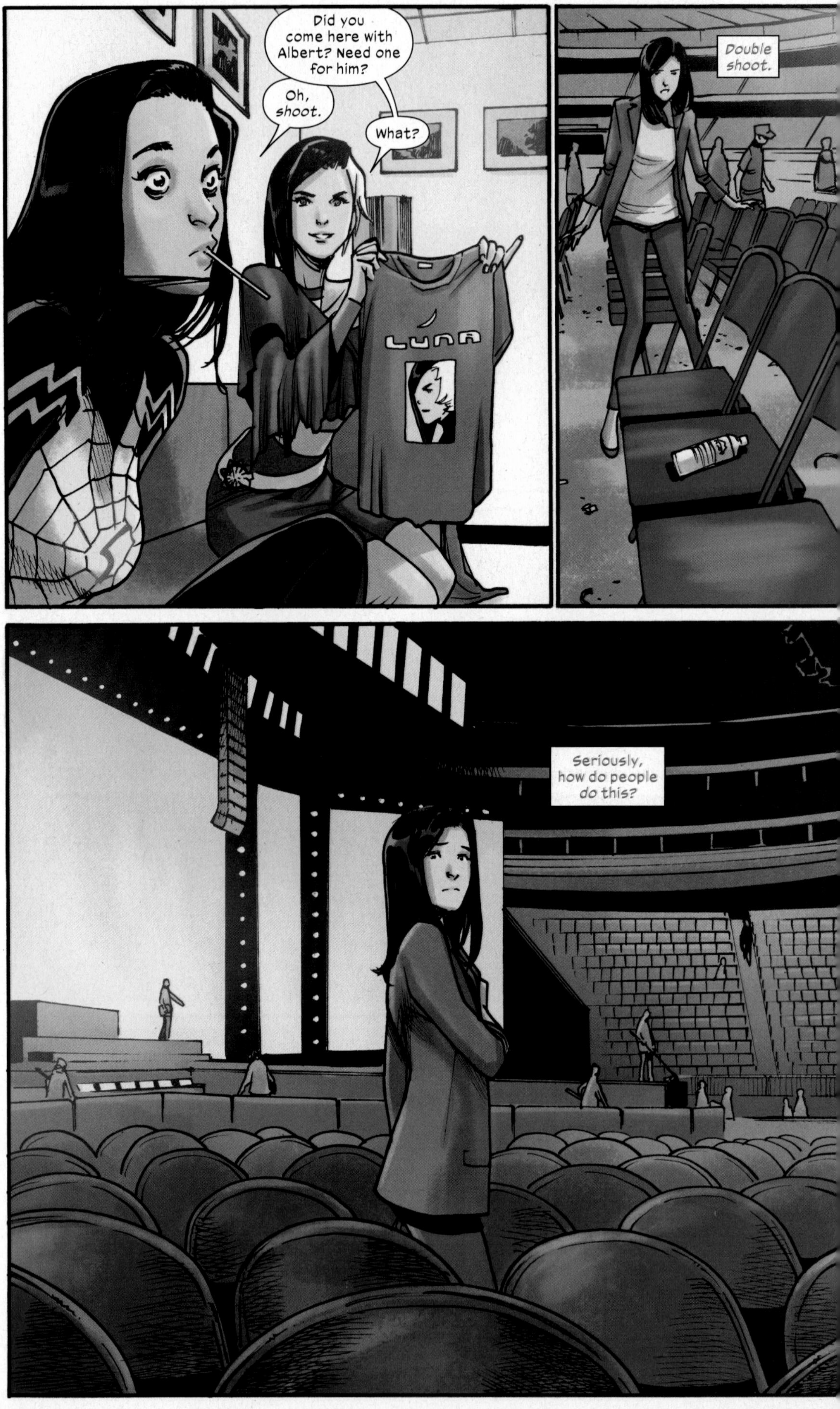
Did you come here with Albert? Need one for him?
Oh, shoot.
What?
LUNA
Double shoot.
Seriously, how do people do this?

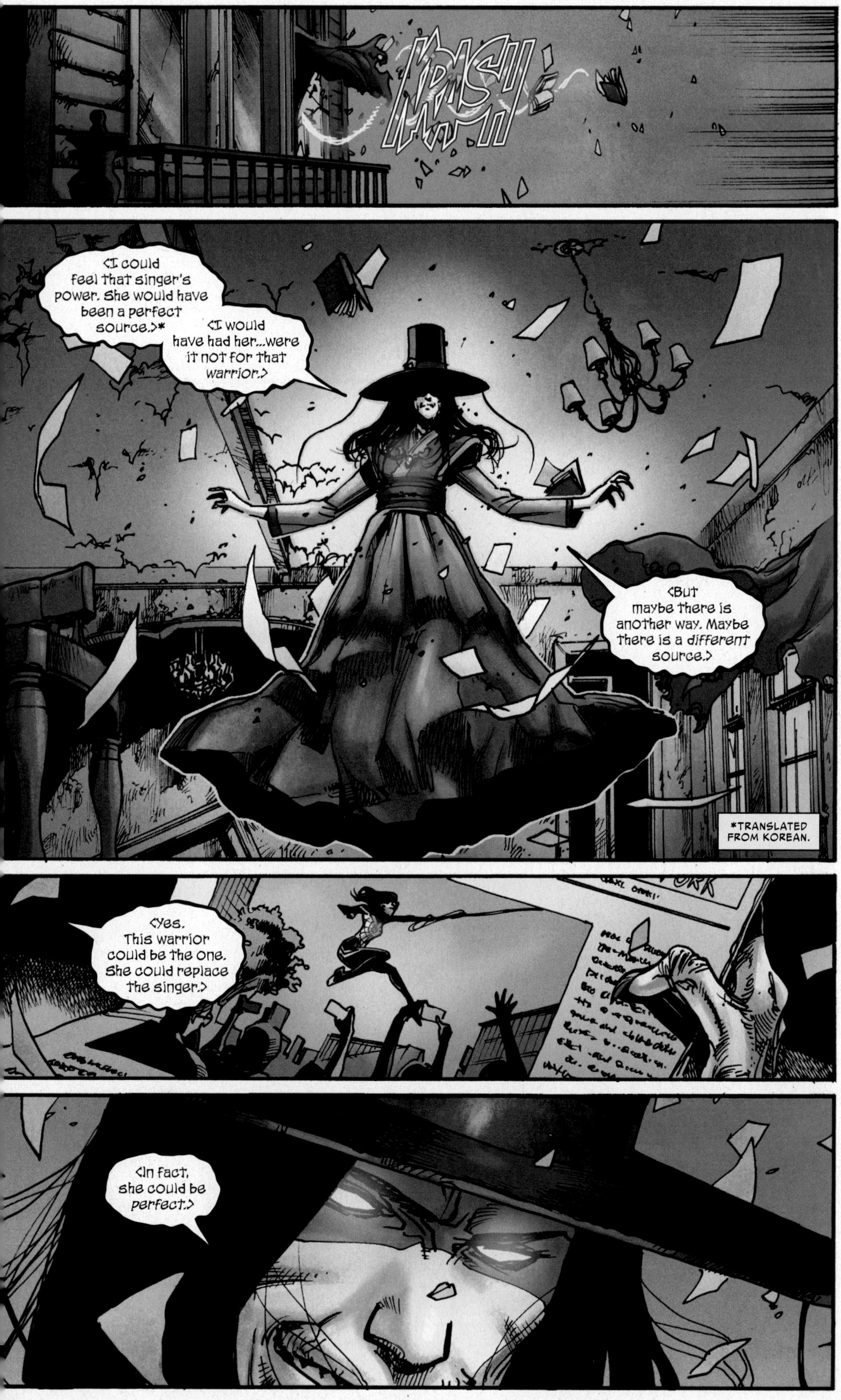
KRASH
<I could feel that singer's power. She would have been a perfect source.>*
<I would have had her...were it not for that warrior.>
<But maybe there is another way. Maybe there is a different source.>
*TRANSLATED FROM KOREAN.
<Yes. This warrior could be the one. She could replace the singer.>
<In fact, she could be perfect.>

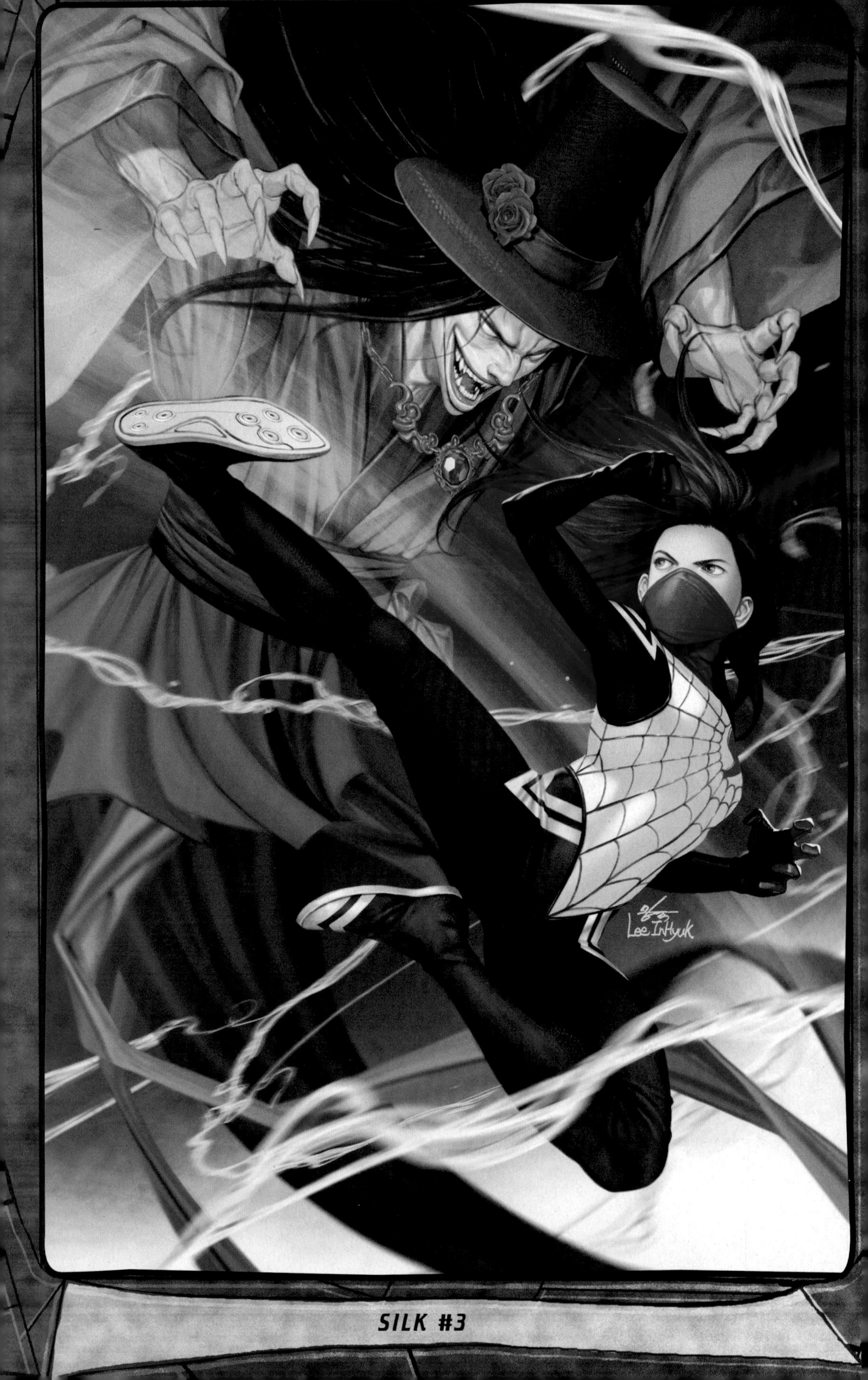
Lee InHyuk

SILK #3

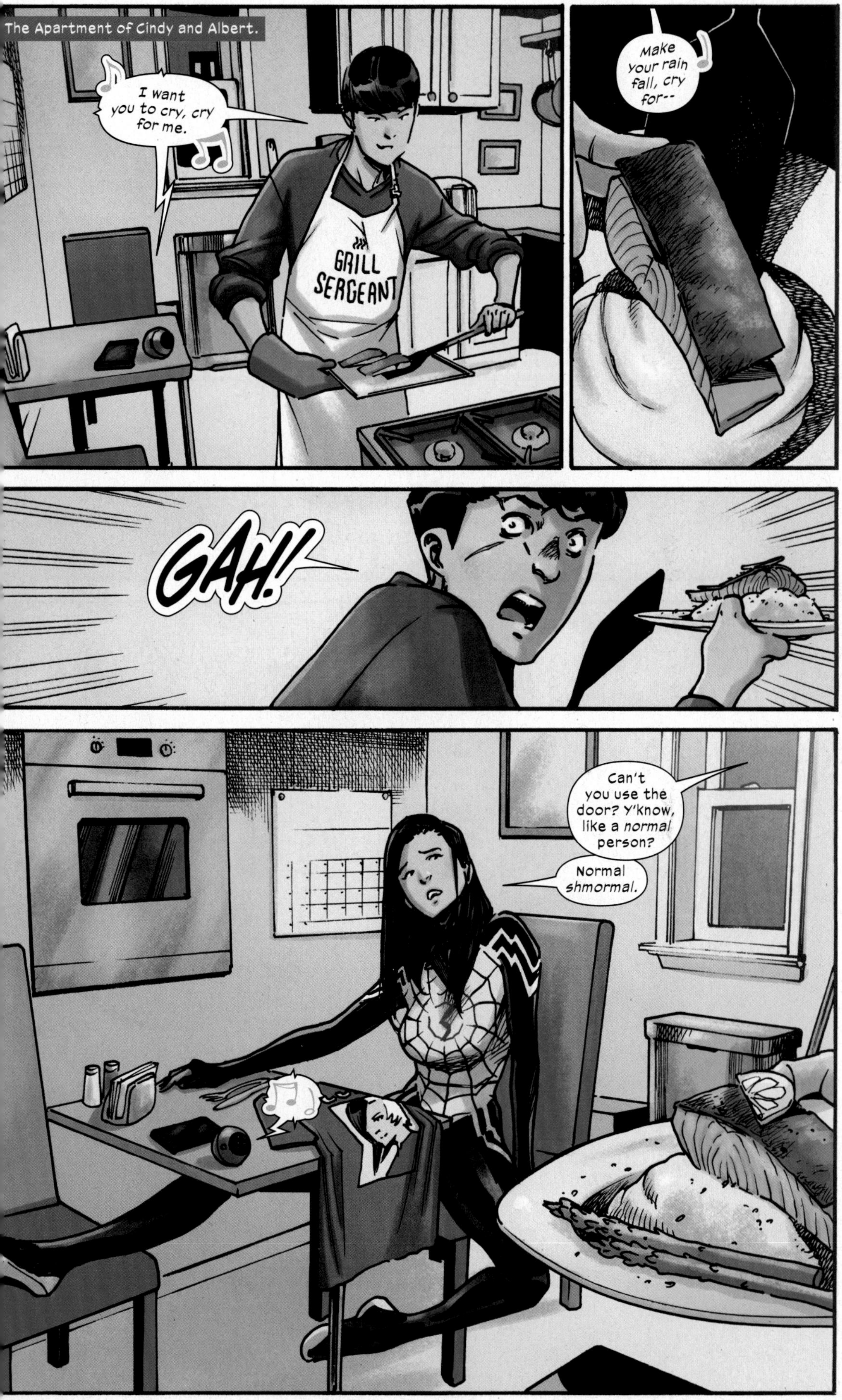

The Apartment of Cindy and Albert.
I want you to cry, cry for me.
GRILL SERGEANT
Make your rain fall, cry for--
GAH!
Can't you use the door? Y'know, like a *normal* person?
Normal *shmormal.*

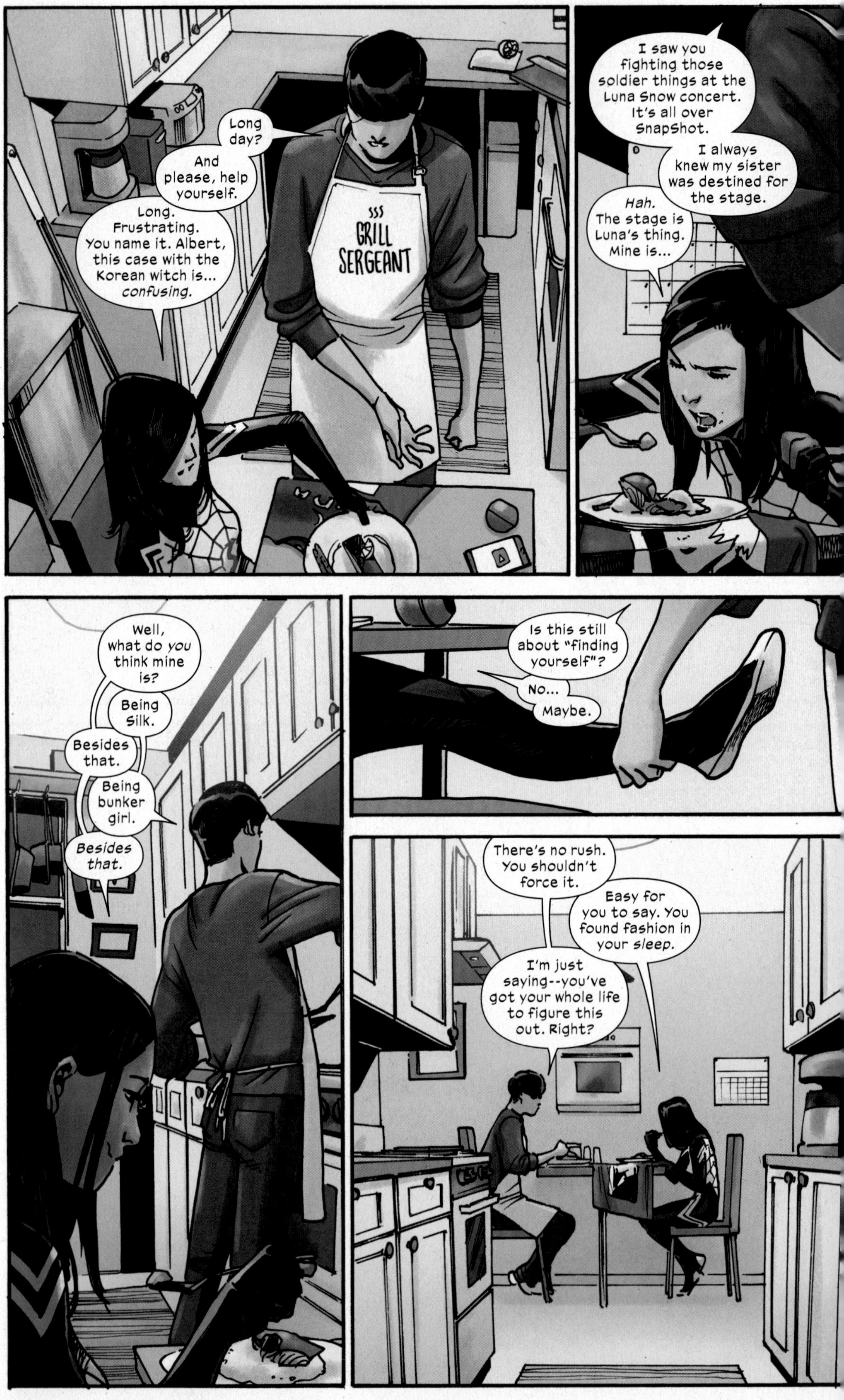

Long day?
And please, help yourself.
Long. Frustrating. You name it. Albert, this case with the Korean witch is... *confusing.*
SSS GRILL SERGEANT
I saw you fighting those soldier things at the Luna Snow concert. It's all over SnapShot.
I always knew my sister was destined for the stage.
Hah. The stage is Luna's thing. Mine is...
Well, what do *you* think mine is?
Being Silk.
Besides that.
Being bunker girl.
Besides that.
Is this still about "finding yourself"?
No...
Maybe.
There's no rush. You shouldn't force it.
Easy for you to say. You found fashion in your *sleep.*
I'm just saying--you've got your whole life to figure this out. Right?

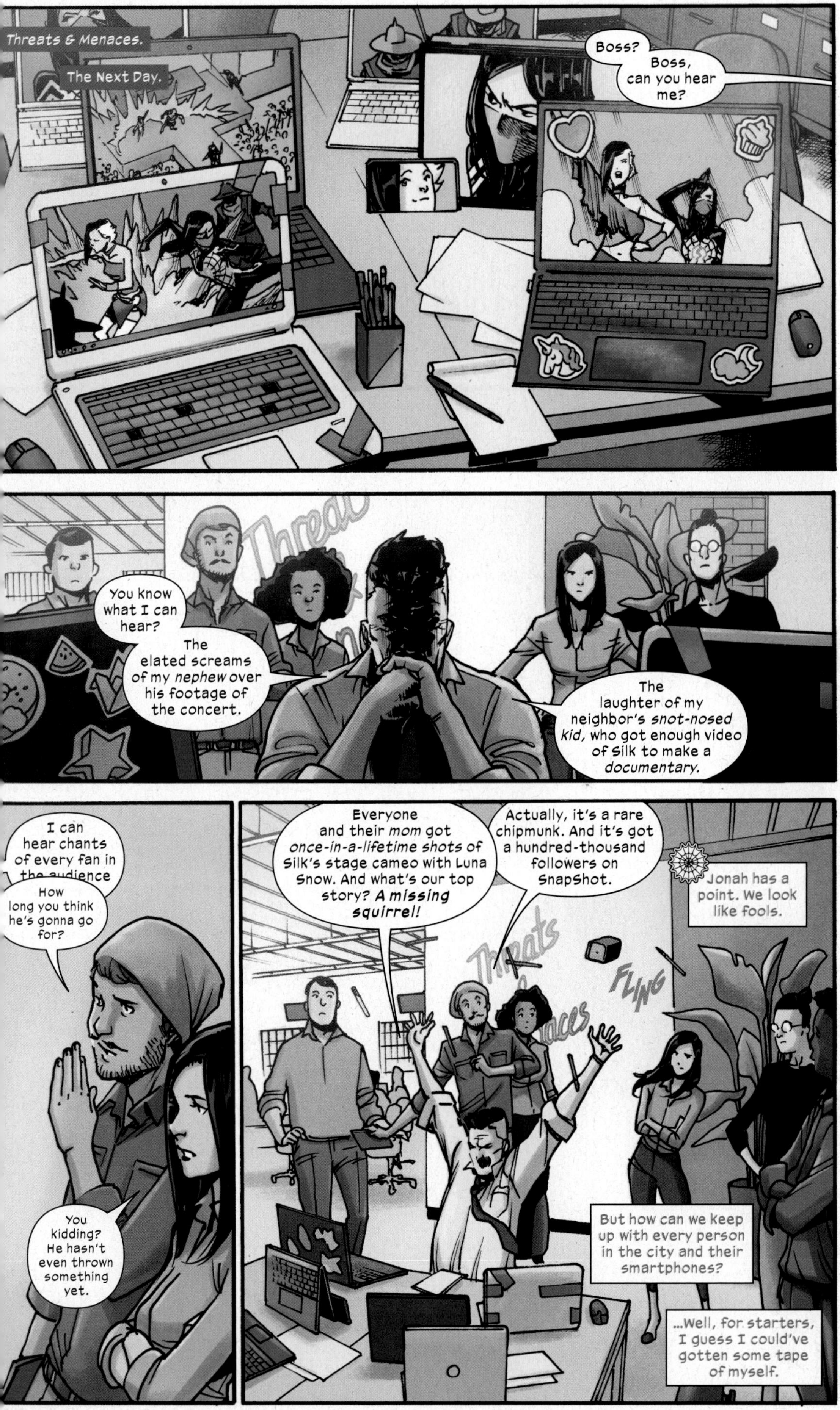
Threats & Menaces.
The Next Day.
Boss? Boss, can you hear me?
You know what I can hear?
The elated screams of my *nephew* over his footage of the concert.
The laughter of my neighbor's *snot-nosed kid,* who got enough video of Silk to make a *documentary.*
I can hear chants of every fan in the audience
How long you think he's gonna go for?
You kidding? He hasn't even thrown something yet.
Everyone and their *mom* got *once-in-a-lifetime shots* of Silk's stage cameo with Luna Snow. And what's our top story? **A missing squirrel!**
Actually, it's a rare chipmunk. And it's got a hundred-thousand followers on SnapShot.
Jonah has a point. We look like fools.
FLING
But how can we keep up with every person in the city and their smartphones?
...Well, for starters, I guess I could've gotten some tape of myself.

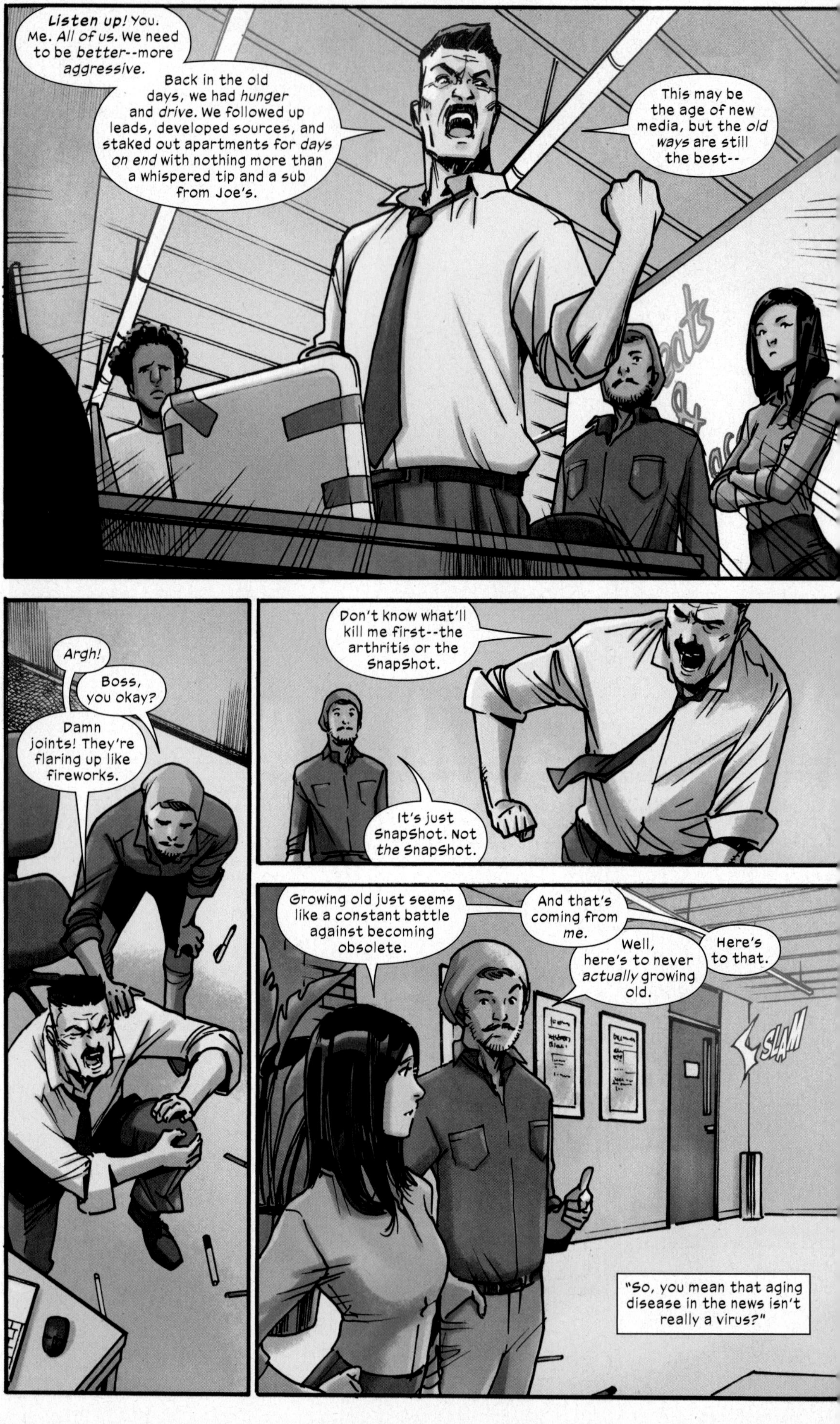
Listen up! You. Me. All of us. We need to be better--more aggressive.
Back in the old days, we had hunger and drive. We followed up leads, developed sources, and staked out apartments for days on end with nothing more than a whispered tip and a sub from Joe's.
This may be the age of new media, but the old ways are still the best--
Argh!
Boss, you okay?
Damn joints! They're flaring up like fireworks.
Don't know what'll kill me first--the arthritis or the SnapShot.
It's just SnapShot. Not the SnapShot.
Growing old just seems like a constant battle against becoming obsolete.
And that's coming from me.
Well, here's to never actually growing old.
Here's to that.
SLAM
"So, you mean that aging disease in the news isn't really a virus?"

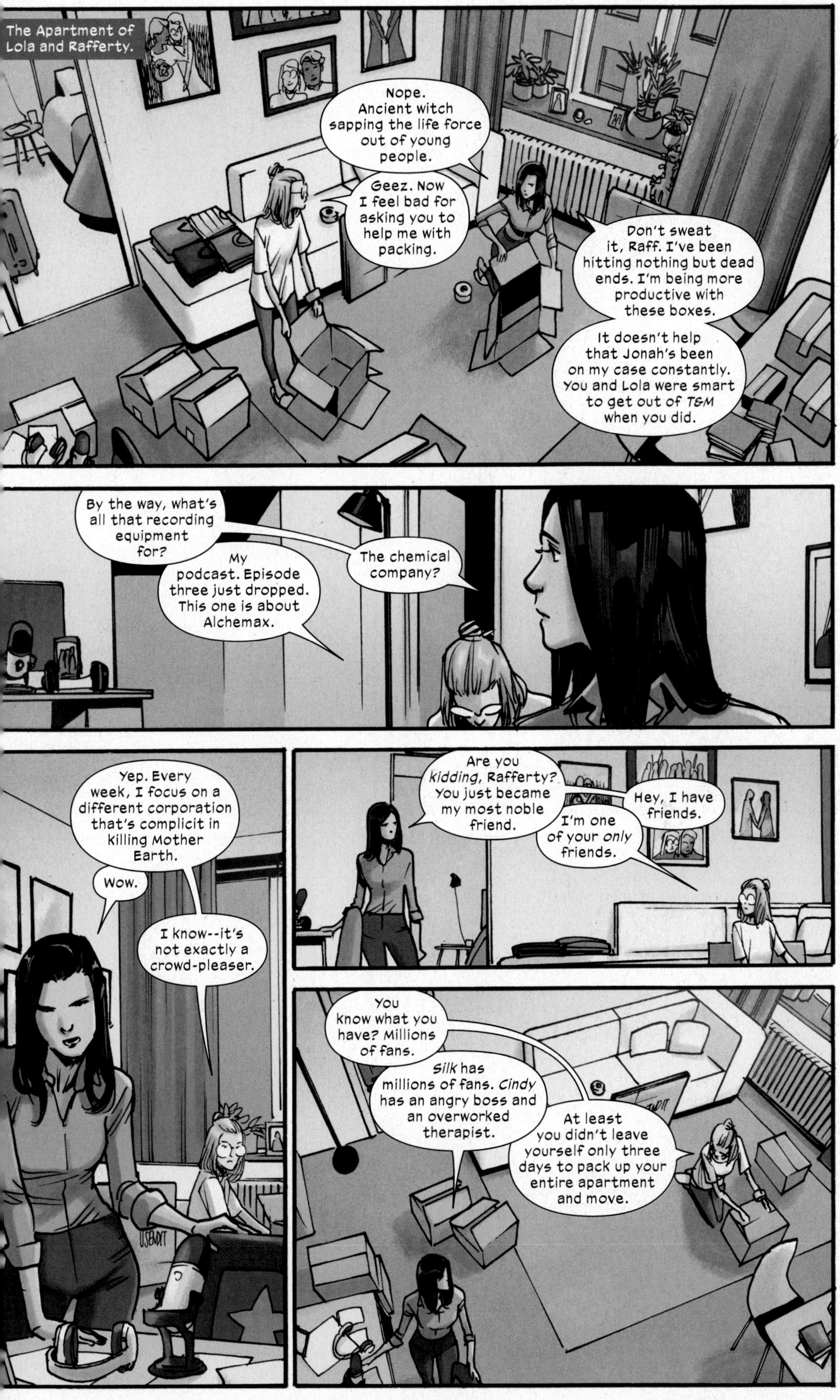
The Apartment of Lola and Rafferty.
Nope. Ancient witch sapping the life force out of young people.
Geez. Now I feel bad for asking you to help me with packing.
Don't sweat it, Raff. I've been hitting nothing but dead ends. I'm being more productive with these boxes.
It doesn't help that Jonah's been on my case constantly. You and Lola were smart to get out of T&M when you did.
By the way, what's all that recording equipment for?
My podcast. Episode three just dropped. This one is about Alchemax.
The chemical company?
Yep. Every week, I focus on a different corporation that's complicit in killing Mother Earth.
Wow.
I know--it's not exactly a crowd-pleaser.
Are you kidding, Rafferty? You just became my most noble friend.
Hey, I have friends.
I'm one of your only friends.
You know what you have? Millions of fans.
Silk has millions of fans. Cindy has an angry boss and an overworked therapist.
At least you didn't leave yourself only three days to pack up your entire apartment and move.

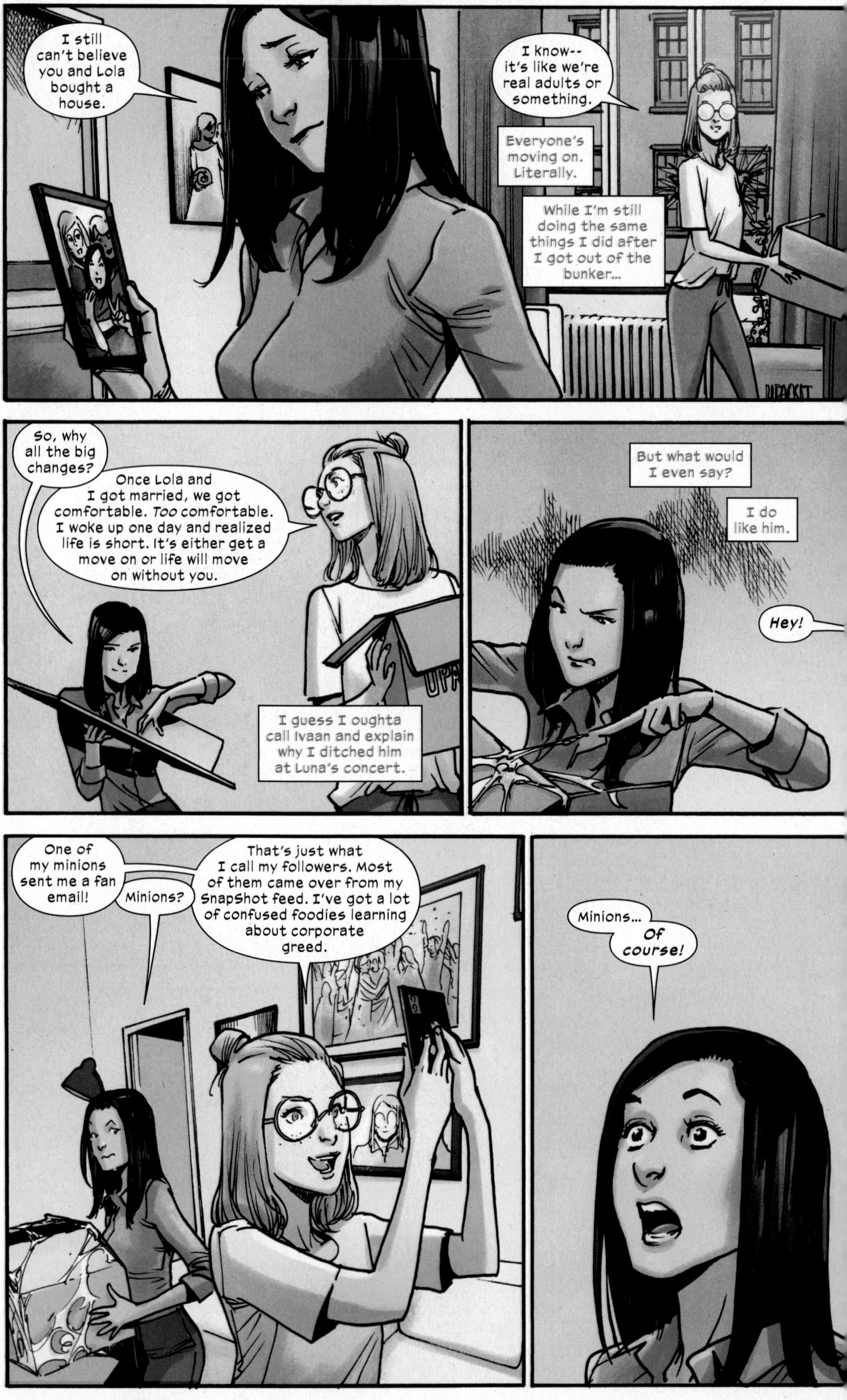

I still can't believe you and Lola bought a house.
I know-- it's like we're real adults or something.
Everyone's moving on. Literally.
While I'm still doing the same things I did after I got out of the bunker...
So, why all the big changes?
Once Lola and I got married, we got comfortable. *Too* comfortable. I woke up one day and realized life is short. It's either get a move on or life will move on without you.
I guess I oughta call Ivaan and explain why I ditched him at Luna's concert.
But what would I even say?
I do like him.
Hey!
One of my minions sent me a fan email!
Minions?
That's just what I call my followers. Most of them came over from my SnapShot feed. I've got a lot of confused foodies learning about corporate greed.
Minions... *Of course!*

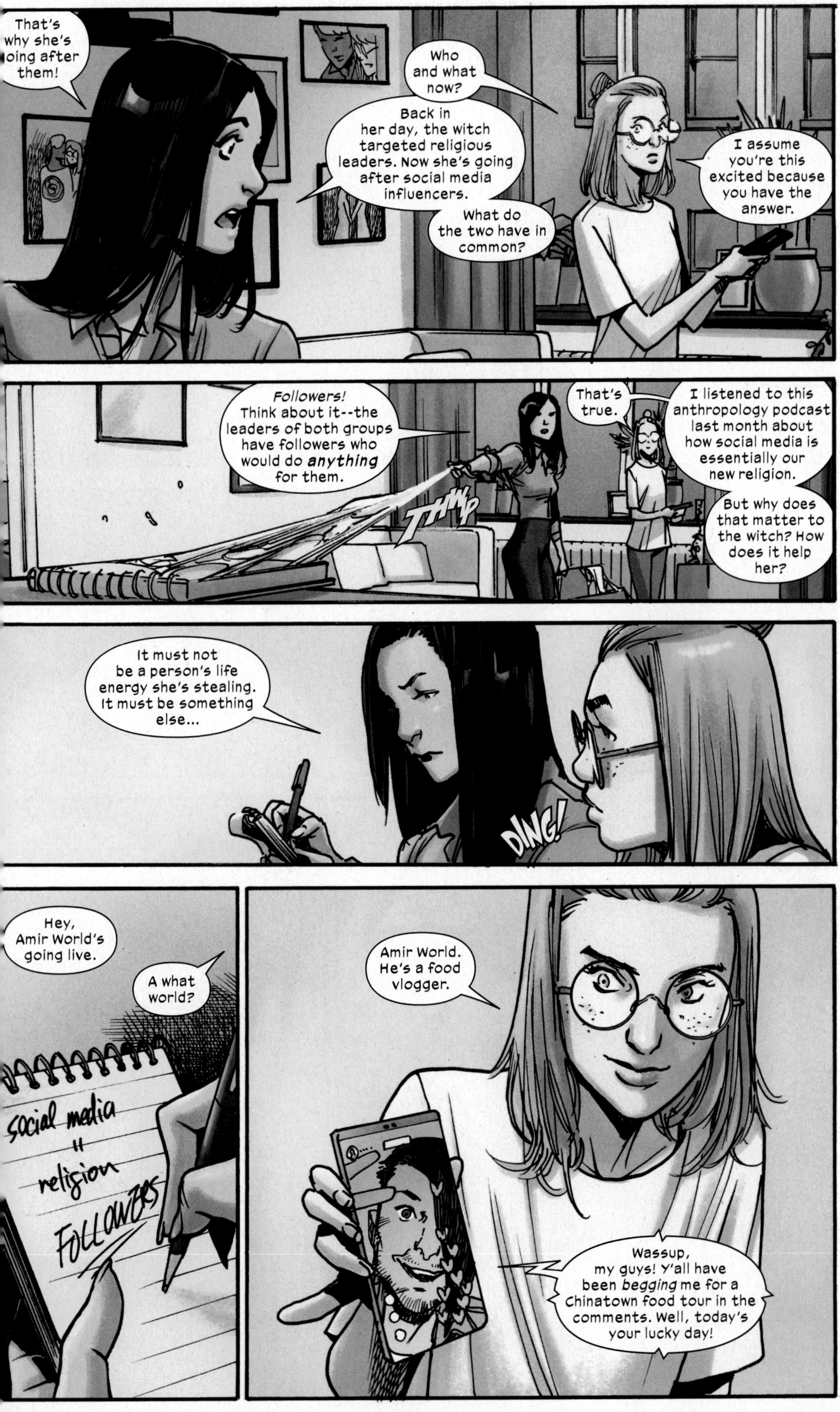
That's why she's going after them!
Who and what now?
Back in her day, the witch targeted religious leaders. Now she's going after social media influencers.
What do the two have in common?
I assume you're this excited because you have the answer.
Followers! Think about it--the leaders of both groups have followers who would do *anything* for them.
THWP
That's true.
I listened to this anthropology podcast last month about how social media is essentially our new religion.
But why does that matter to the witch? How does it help her?
It must not be a person's life energy she's stealing. It must be something else...
DING!
Hey, Amir World's going live.
A what world?
social media
=
religion
FOLLOWERS
Amir World. He's a food vlogger.
Wassup, my guys! Y'all have been *begging* me for a Chinatown food tour in the comments. Well, today's your lucky day!

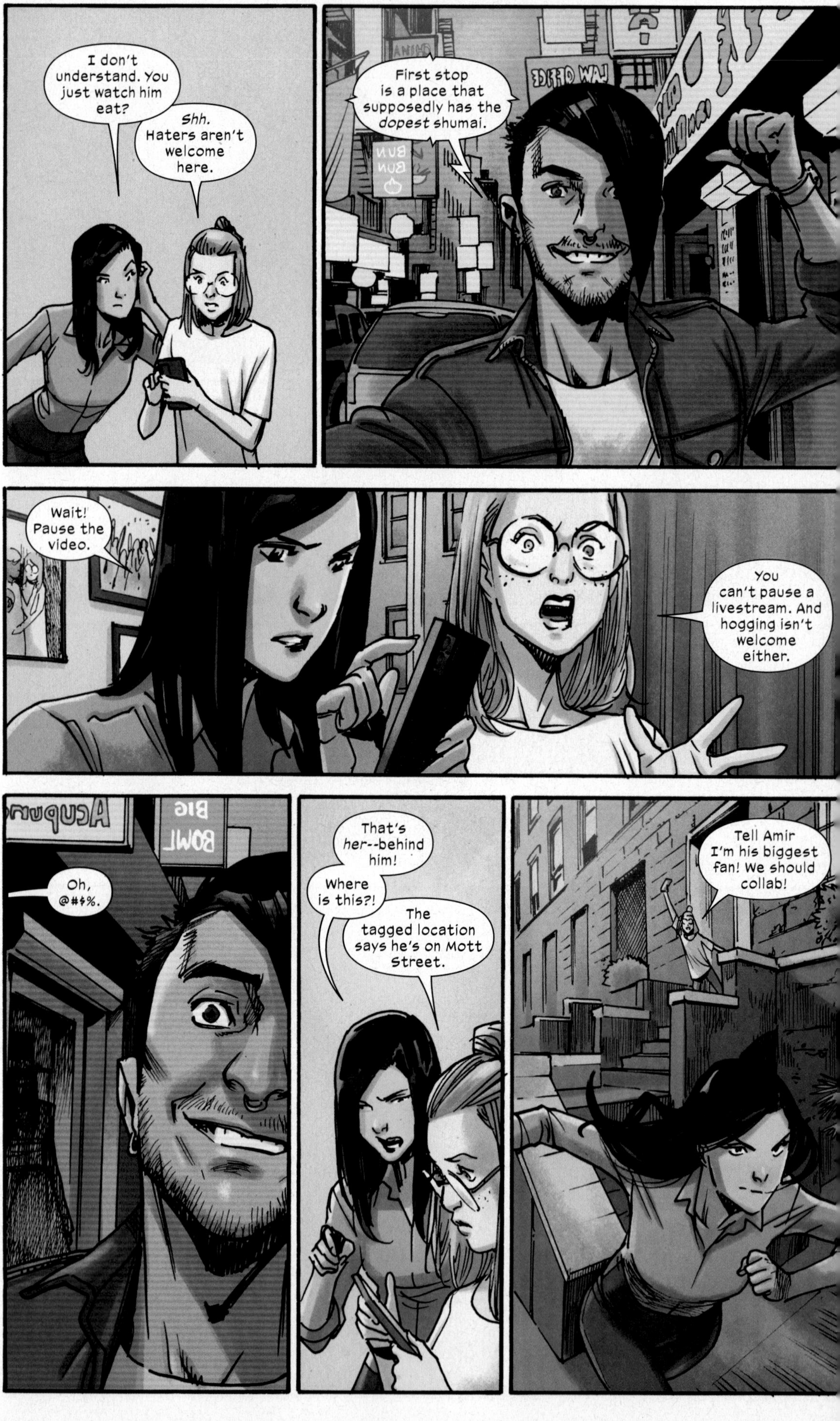

I don't understand. You just watch him eat?
Shh. Haters aren't welcome here.
First stop is a place that supposedly has the *dopest* shumai.
LAW OFFICE
BUN BUN
Wait! Pause the video.
You can't pause a livestream. And hogging isn't welcome either.
BIG BOWL
Oh, @#$%.
That's *her*--behind him!
Where is this?!
The tagged location says he's on Mott Street.
Tell Amir I'm his biggest fan! We should collab!

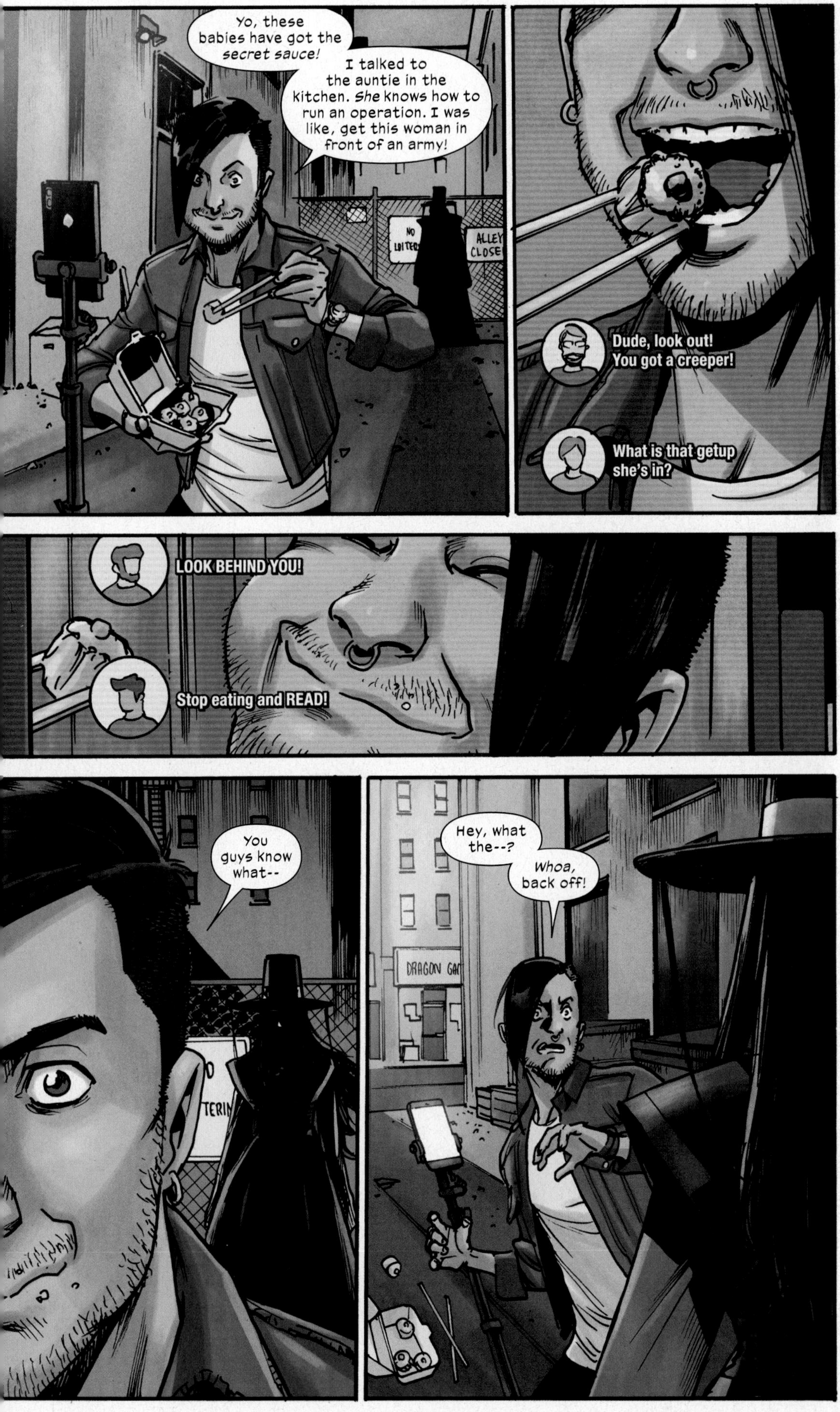

Yo, these babies have got the *secret sauce!*
I talked to the auntie in the kitchen. *She* knows how to run an operation. I was like, get this woman in front of an army!
NO LOITERI
ALLEY CLOSE
Dude, look out! You got a creeper!
What is that getup she's in?
LOOK BEHIND YOU!
Stop eating and READ!
You guys know what--
TERIN
Hey, what the--?
Whoa, back off!
DRAGON GA

AHHHH!
TOMATO SAUCE
TOMATO SAUCE
I'm too late.
Hhhhnn...
<Finally, I have you, warrior.>*
*TRANSLATED FROM KOREAN.
Warrior? Oh, she's talking about me.

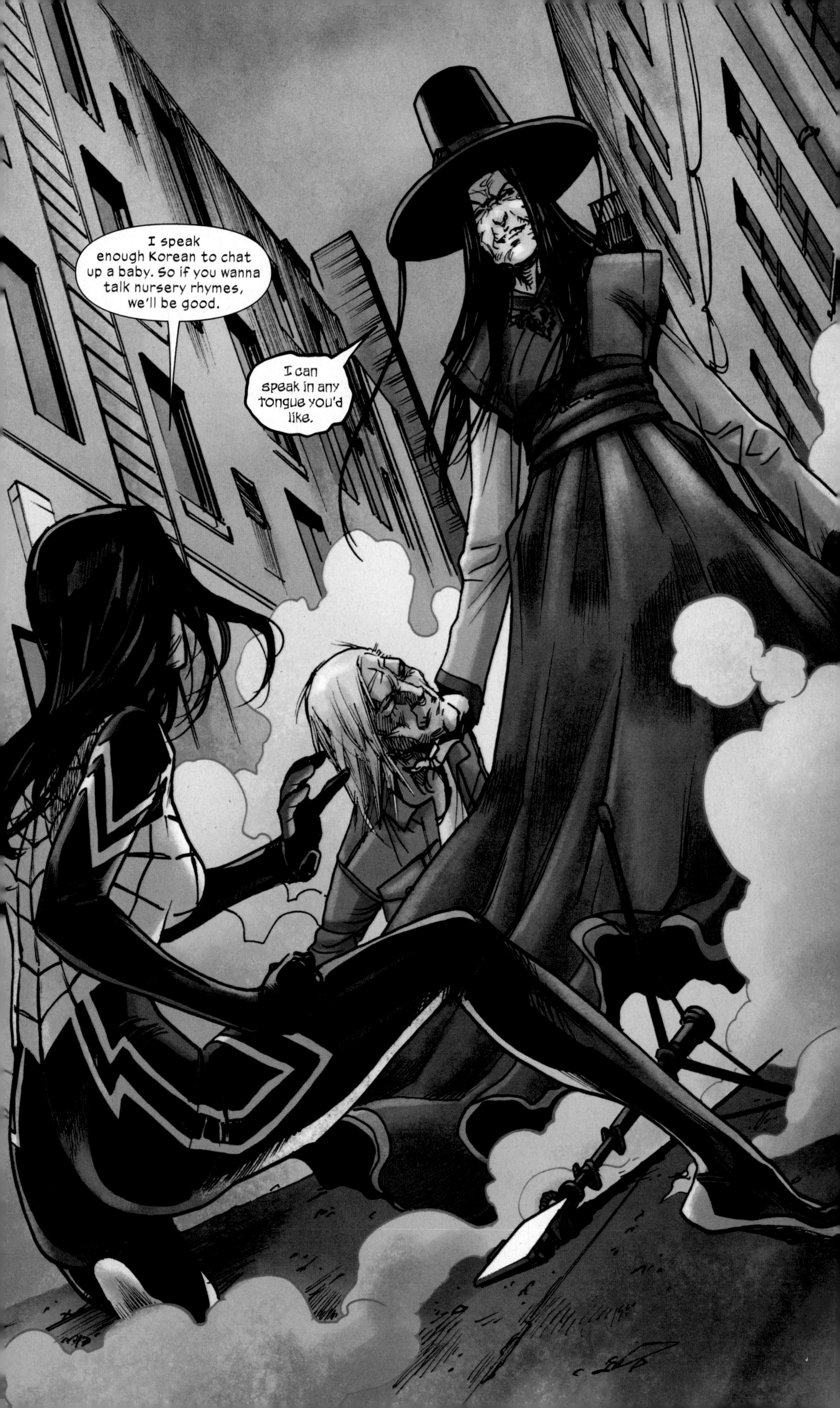
I speak enough Korean to chat up a baby. So if you wanna talk nursery rhymes, we'll be good.
I can speak in any tongue you'd like.

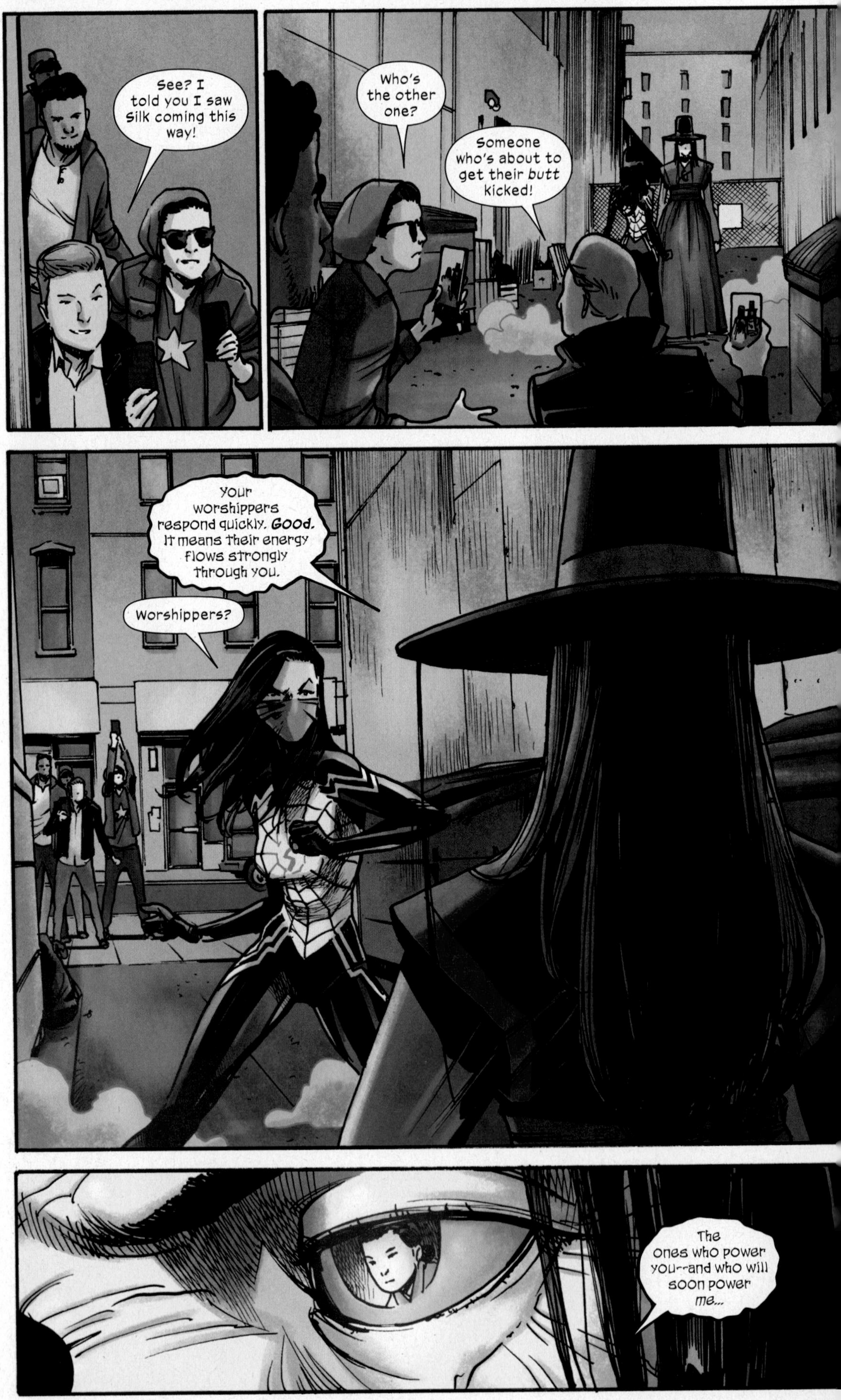
See? I told you I saw Silk coming this way!
Who's the other one?
Someone who's about to get their *butt* kicked!
Your worshippers respond quickly. **Good.** It means their energy flows strongly through you.
Worshippers?
The ones who power you--and who will soon power *me...*

"When I was a child, I learned that I was born with a gift."

"I could transfer *life energy* between organisms."

"My village was a poor one. We grew up on a diet of dirt and illness."

⟨Bless you, Songi.⟩

"Some people turned to me to heal their sick, even if it meant sacrificing their own life force."

"But many saw my actions differently."

⟨You commit crimes against nature. Be gone!⟩

"I was banished from my home. Everywhere I went, people deemed my abilities evil."

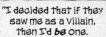

"I decided that if they saw me as a villain, then I'd *be* one."

"People pour their lives into the figures they love--shamans, demagogues, heroes."

"When that love turns to *obsession* and *delirium*, it turns into an energy I can *feed* on."

"I'd wait for leaders to grow fat on adoration. Then I'd strike and take their *worship energy* for myself.

"Only then did I feel what *true power* was. It allowed me to reach new heights. I could control objects, raise spirits, cast spells.

"I raised four loyal warriors.

"I traversed the country, tracking down congregations, building my strength, biding my time.

"As I neared my goal, the men who *feared* me banded together and persecuted me tirelessly.

"They thought they rid the world of me. But they merely *banished* me from their era. Now, in this time, I have a *second chance*. And here, things are different...

"Here, one small screen can funnel the love of thousands upon thousands of supporters.

"It's so *efficient*

Make sure to lik follow, an subscrib

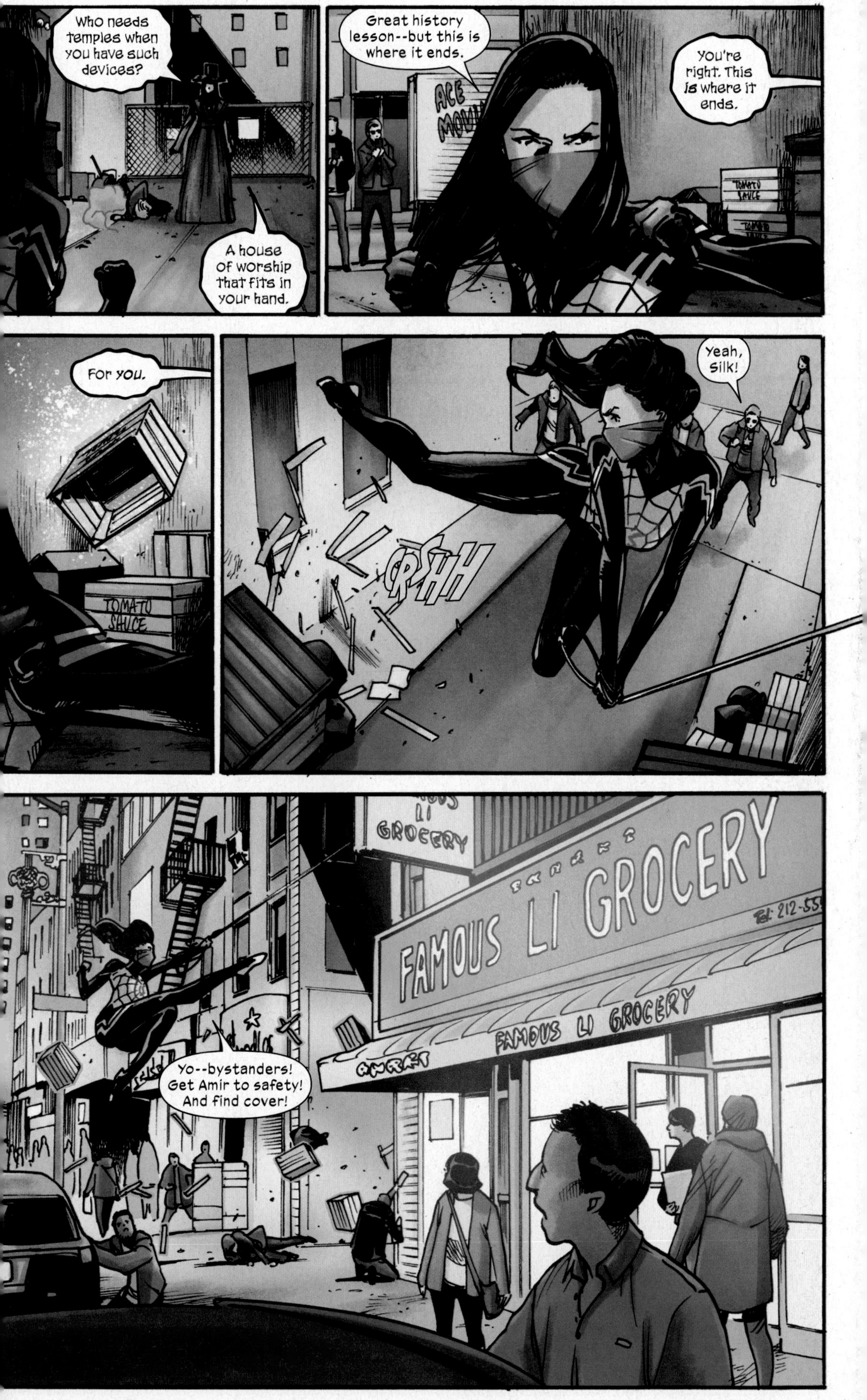

Who needs temples when you have such devices?
A house of worship that fits in your hand.
Great history lesson--but this is where it ends.
You're right. This is where it ends.
ACE
TOMATO SAUCE
For you.
TOMATO SAUCE
Yeah, Silk!
CRSHH
GROCERY
FAMOUS LI GROCERY
Tel: 212-55
FAMOUS LI GROCERY
Yo--bystanders! Get Amir to safety! And find cover!

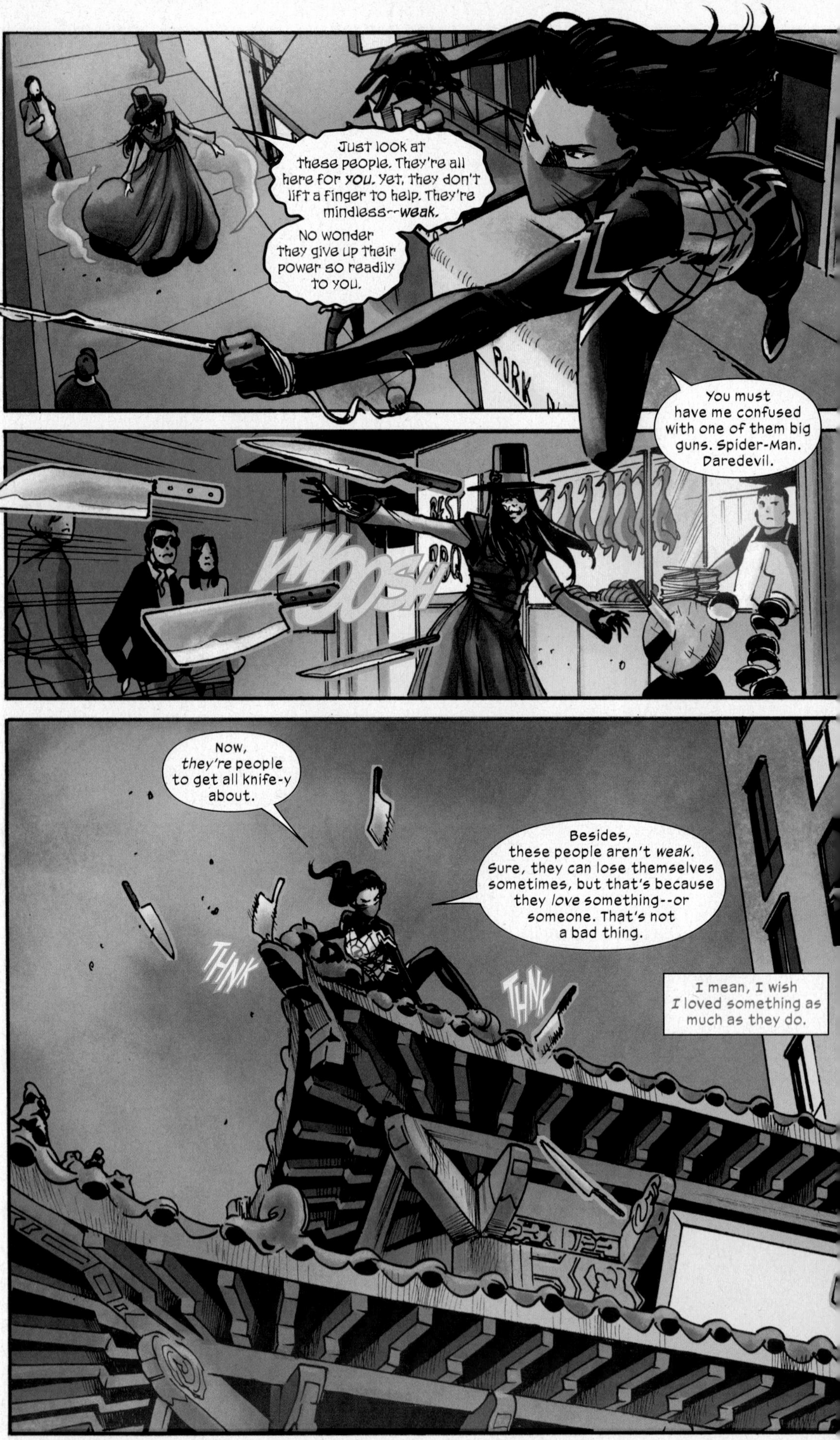
Just look at these people. They're all here for YOU. Yet, they don't lift a finger to help. They're mindless--weak.
No wonder they give up their power so readily to you.
PORK
You must have me confused with one of them big guns. Spider-Man. Daredevil.
VWOOSH
Now, they're people to get all knife-y about.
Besides, these people aren't weak. Sure, they can lose themselves sometimes, but that's because they love something--or someone. That's not a bad thing.
THNK
THNK
I mean, I wish I loved something as much as they do.

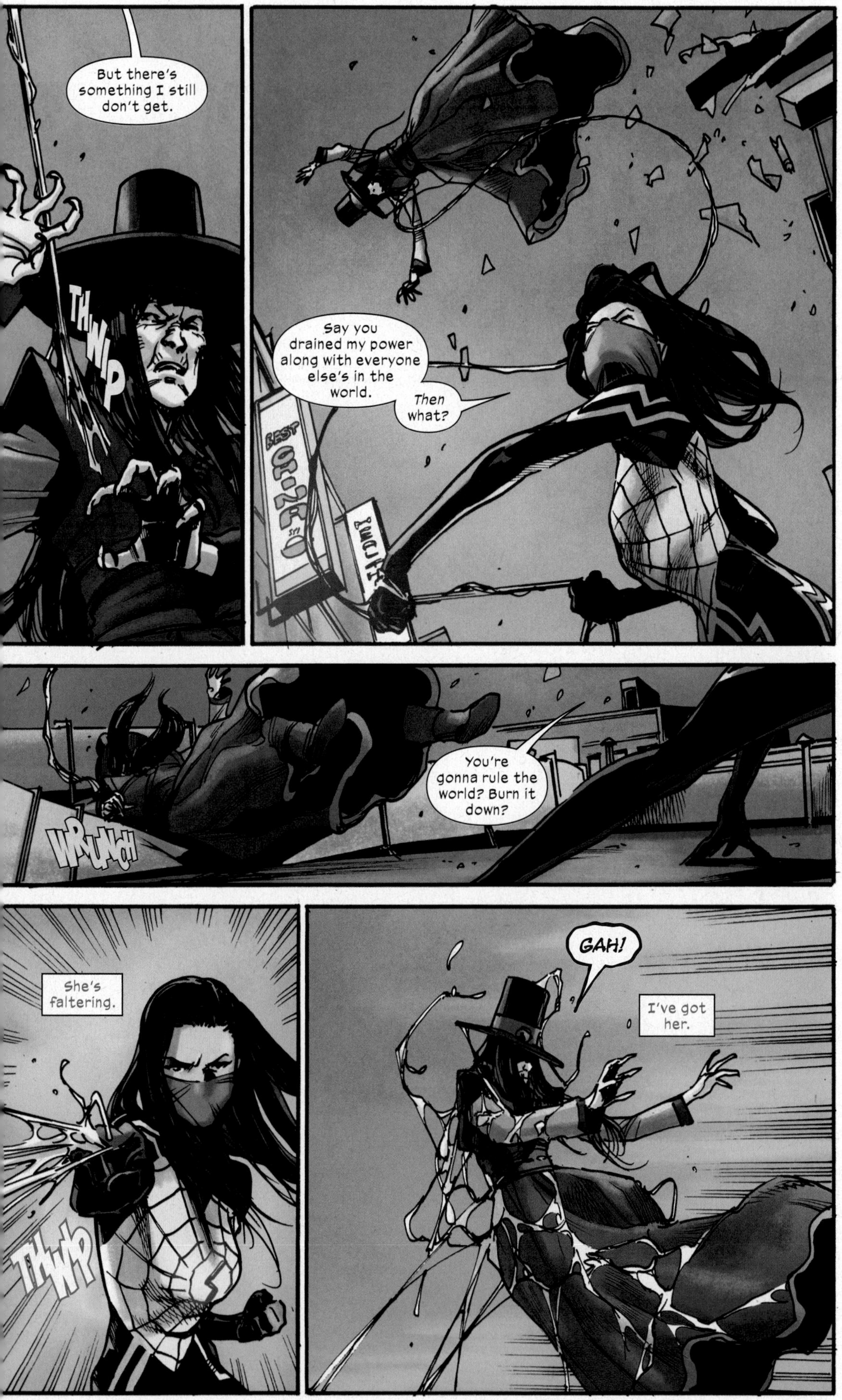
But there's something I still don't get.
THWIP
Say you drained my power along with everyone else's in the world.
Then what?
BEST
You're gonna rule the world? Burn it down?
WRUNCH
She's faltering.
THWIP
GAH!
I've got her.

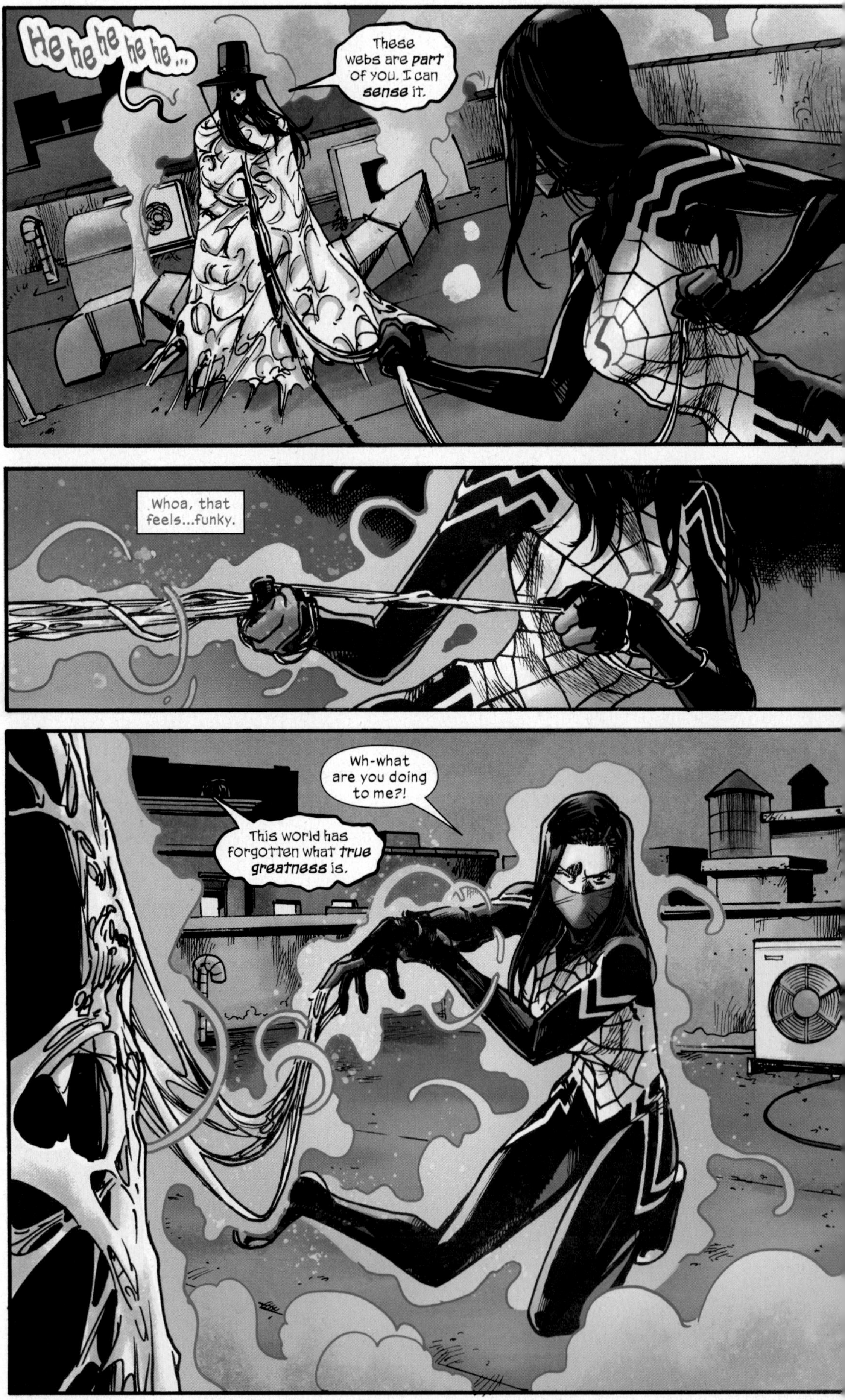
He he he he he...
These webs are part of you. I can sense it.
Whoa, that feels...funky.
Wh-what are you doing to me?!
This world has forgotten what true greatness is.

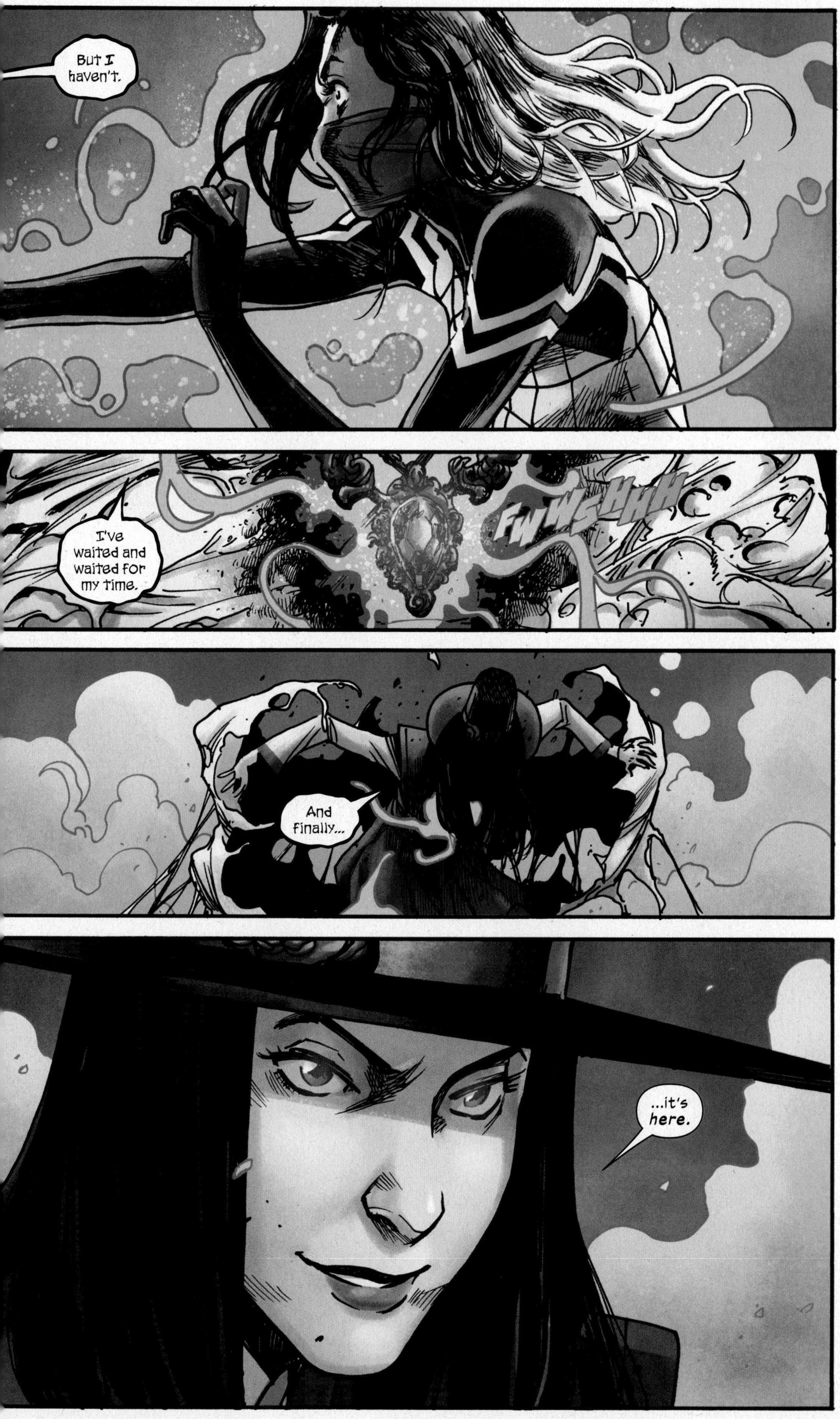
But I haven't.
I've waited and waited for my time.
FWWSHHH
And finally...
...it's here.

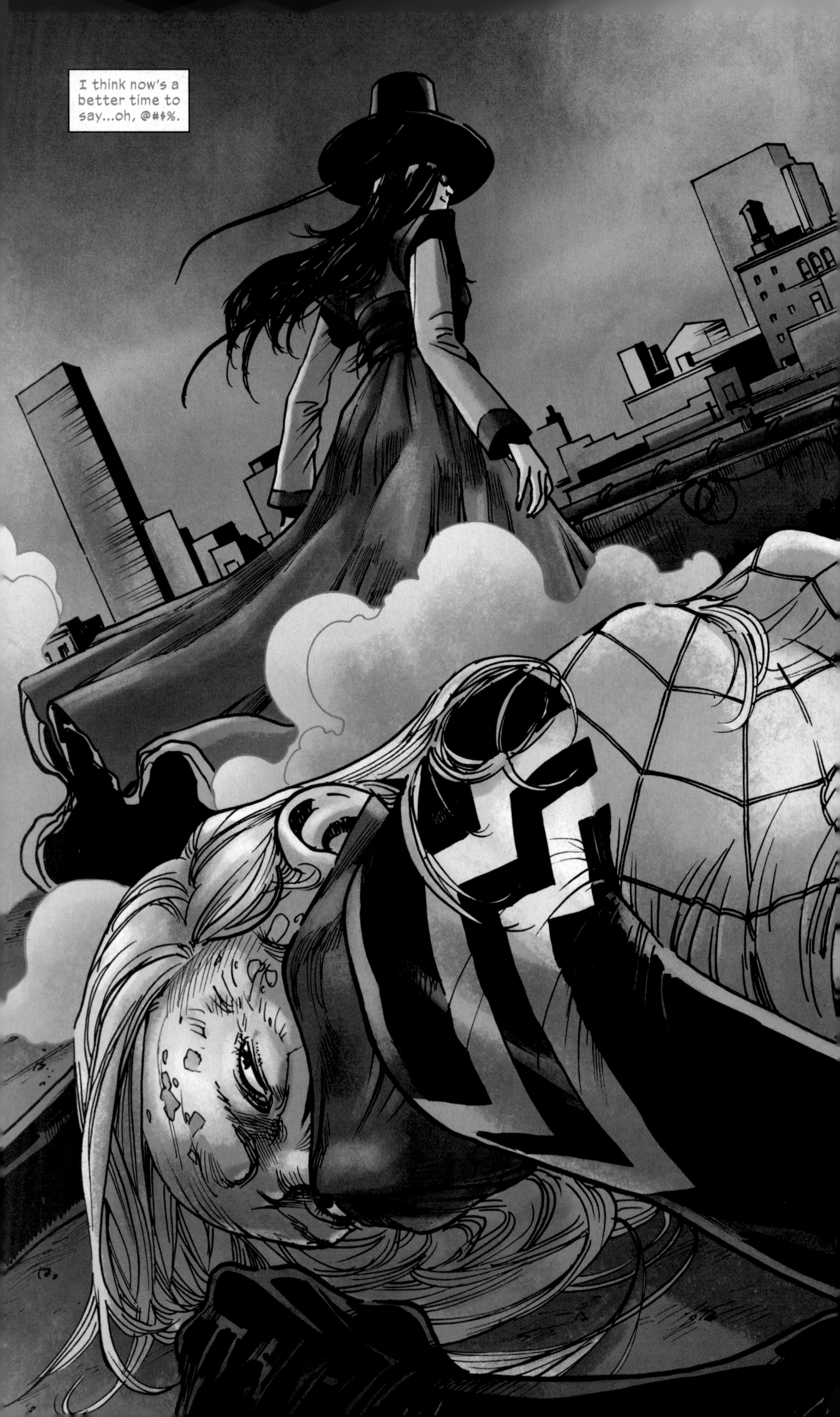
I think now's a better time to say...oh, @#$%.

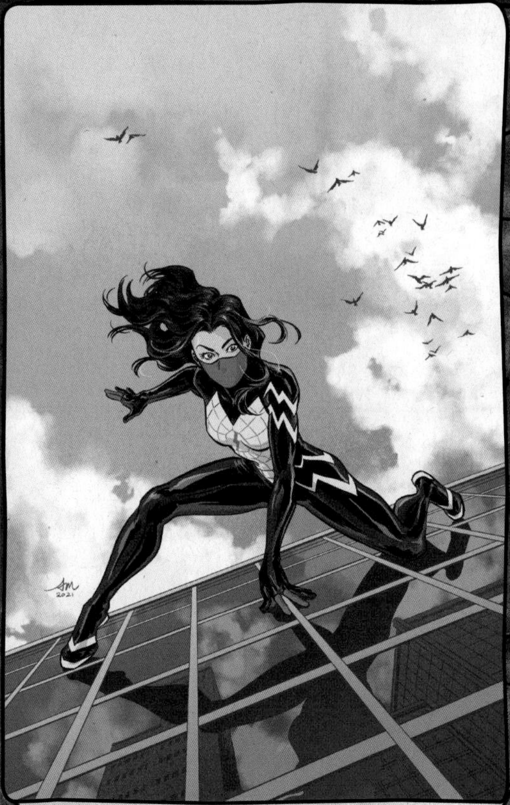

#1 VARIANT by Audrey Mok

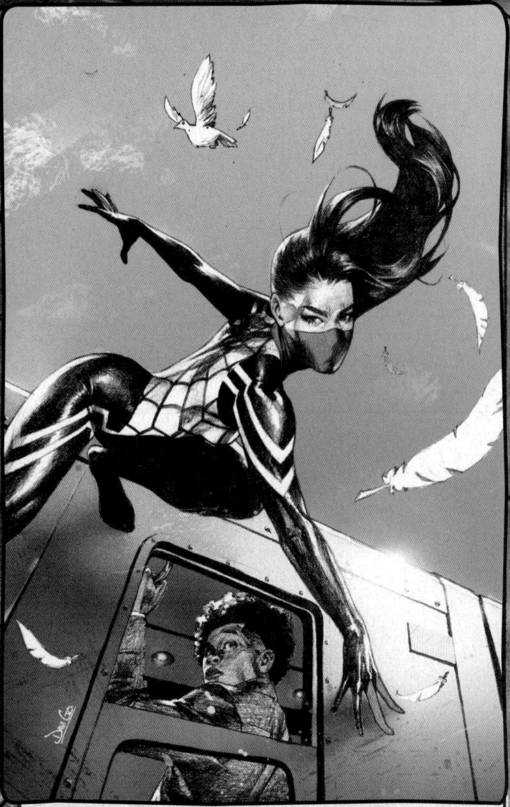

#1 VARIANT by Davi Go

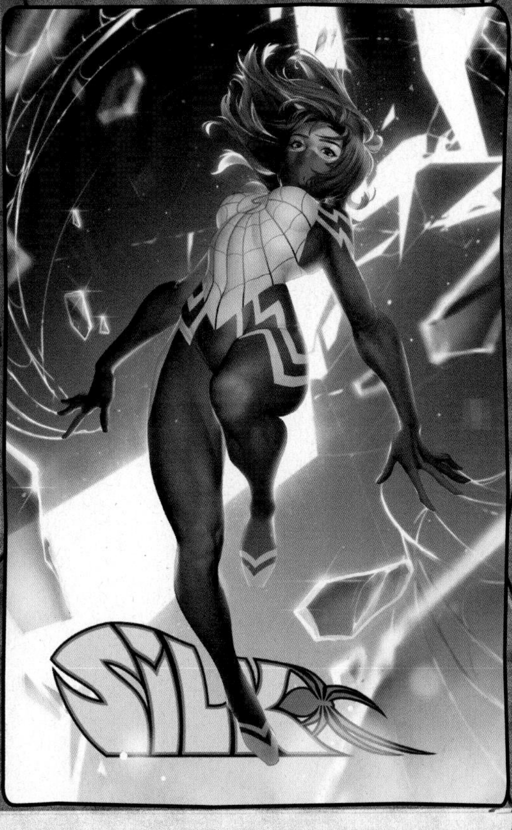

#1 VARIANT by RIcO

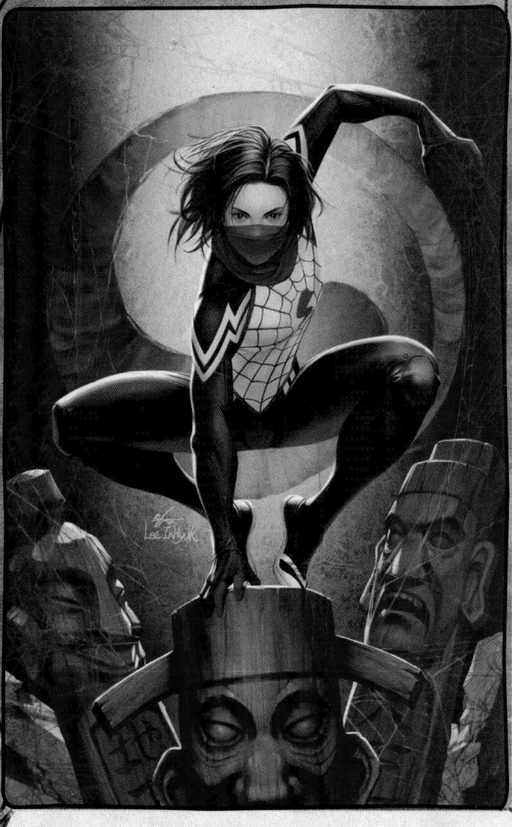

#1 2ND PRINTING VARIANT by InHyuk Lee

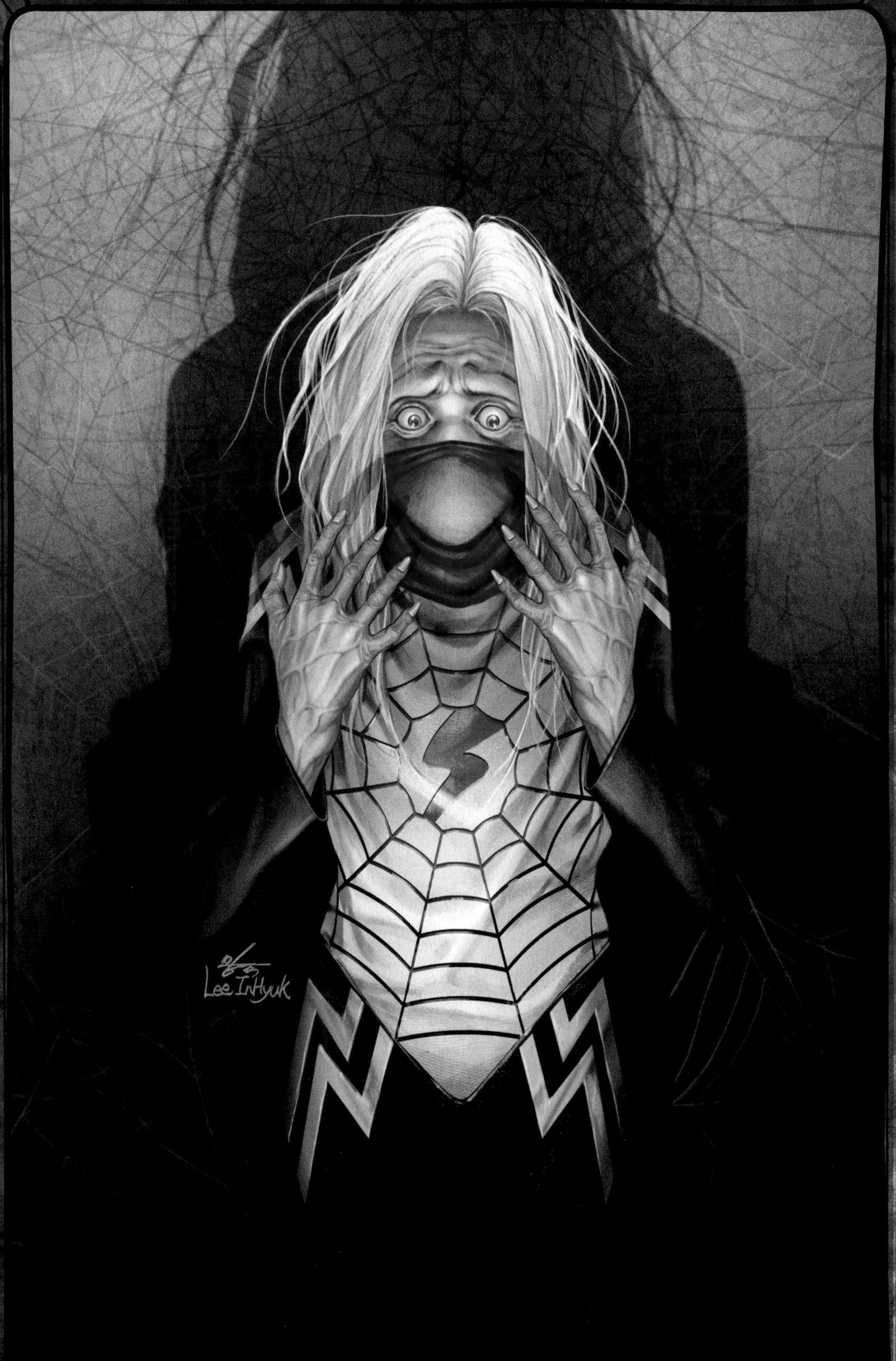
Lee InHyuk

SILK #4

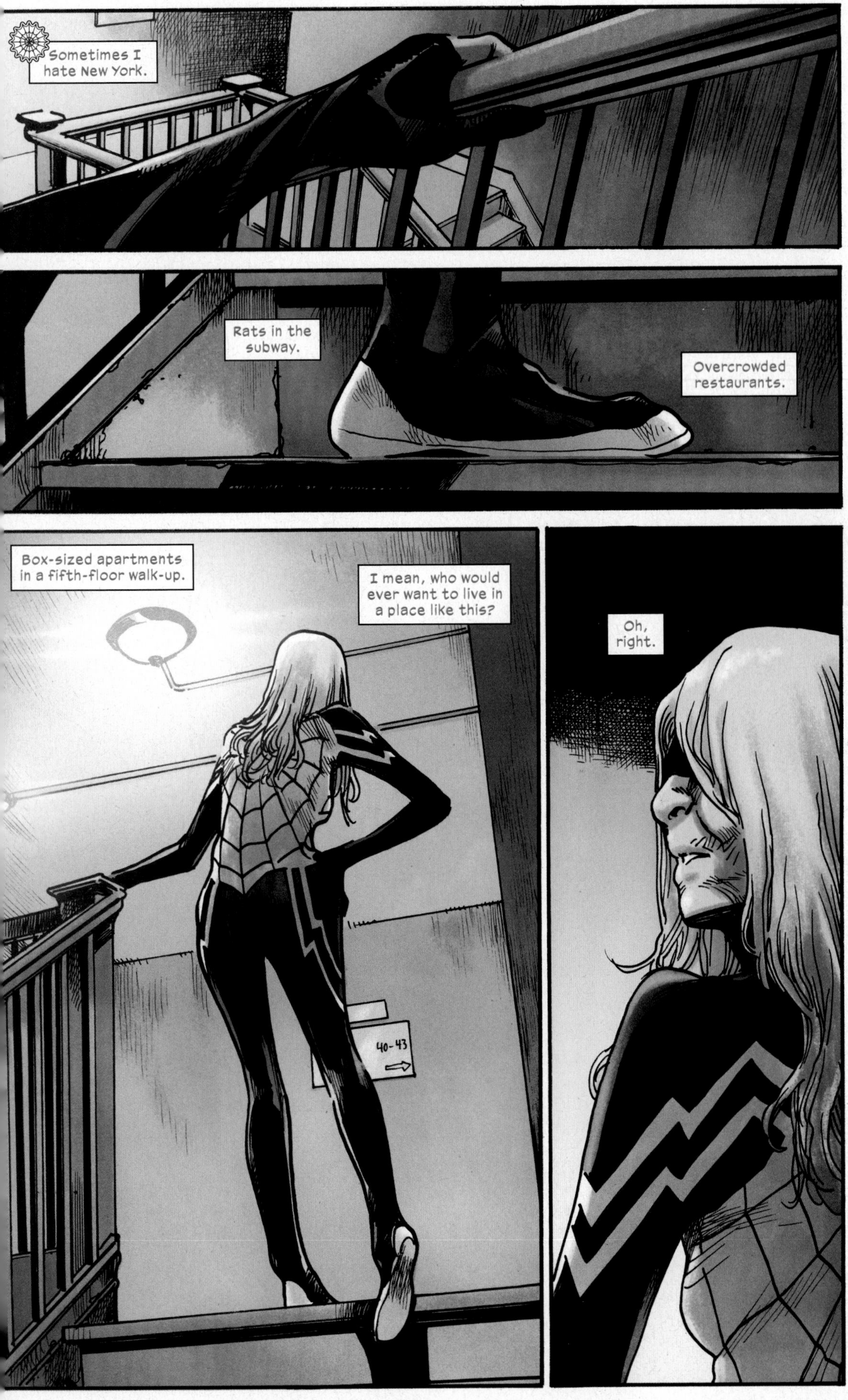
Sometimes I hate New York.
Rats in the subway.
Overcrowded restaurants.
Box-sized apartments in a fifth-floor walk-up.
I mean, who would ever want to live in a place like this?
40-43
Oh, right.

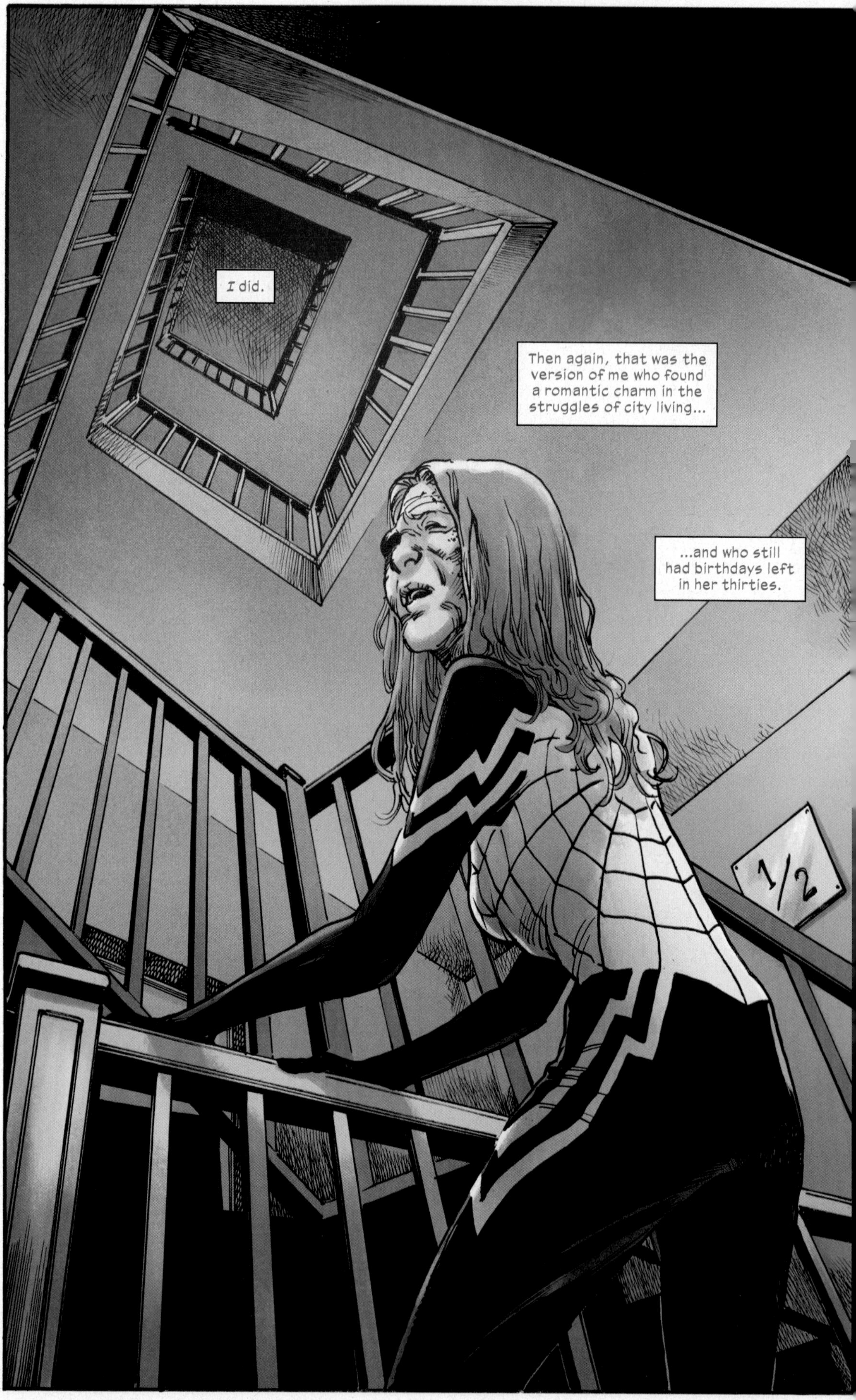
I did.
Then again, that was the version of me who found a romantic charm in the struggles of city living...
...and who still had birthdays left in her thirties.
1/2

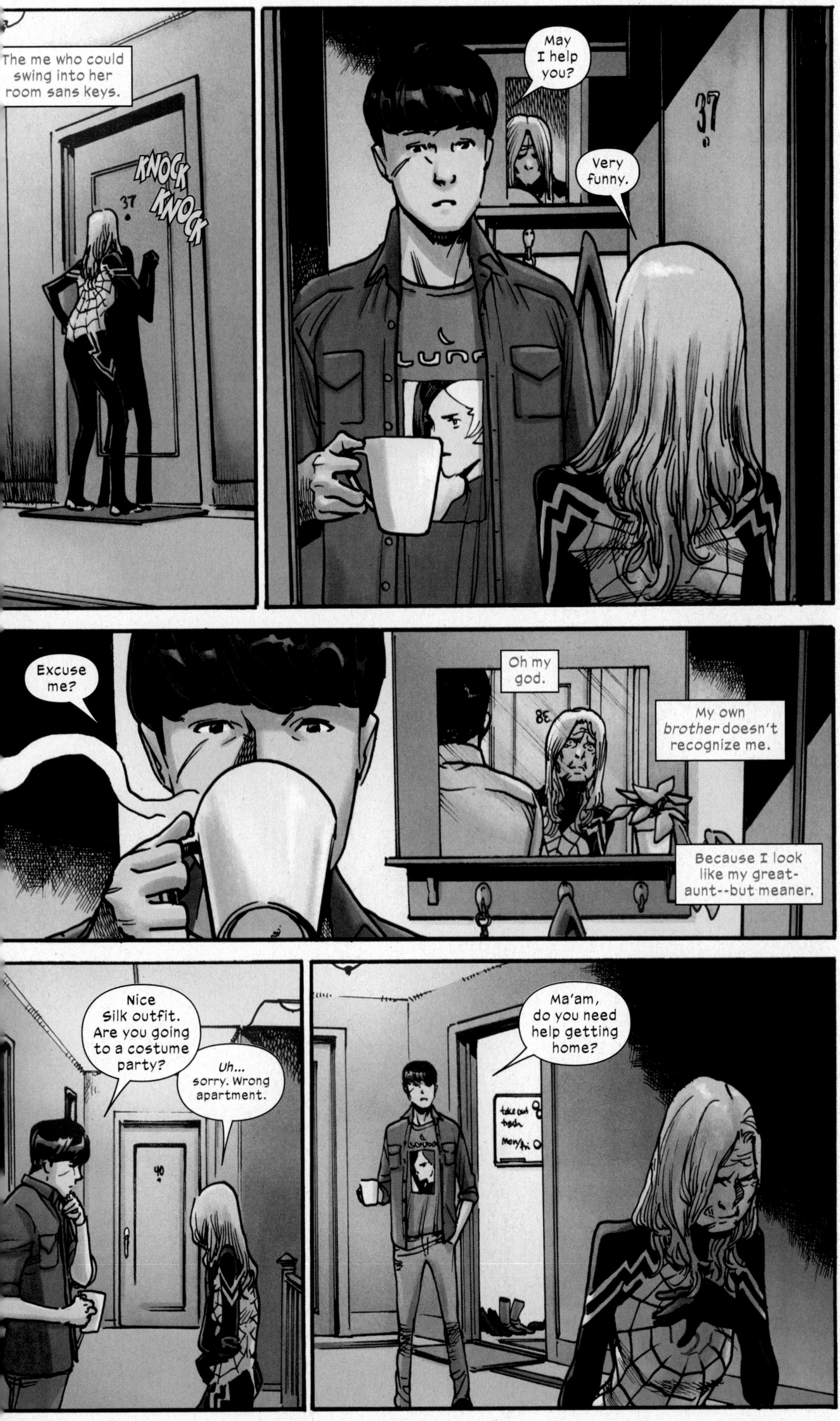

The me who could swing into her room sans keys.
KNOCK KNOCK
May I help you?
Very funny.
Excuse me?
Oh my god.
My own *brother* doesn't recognize me.
Because I look like my great-aunt--but meaner.
Nice Silk outfit. Are you going to a costume party?
Uh... sorry. Wrong apartment.
Ma'am, do you need help getting home?

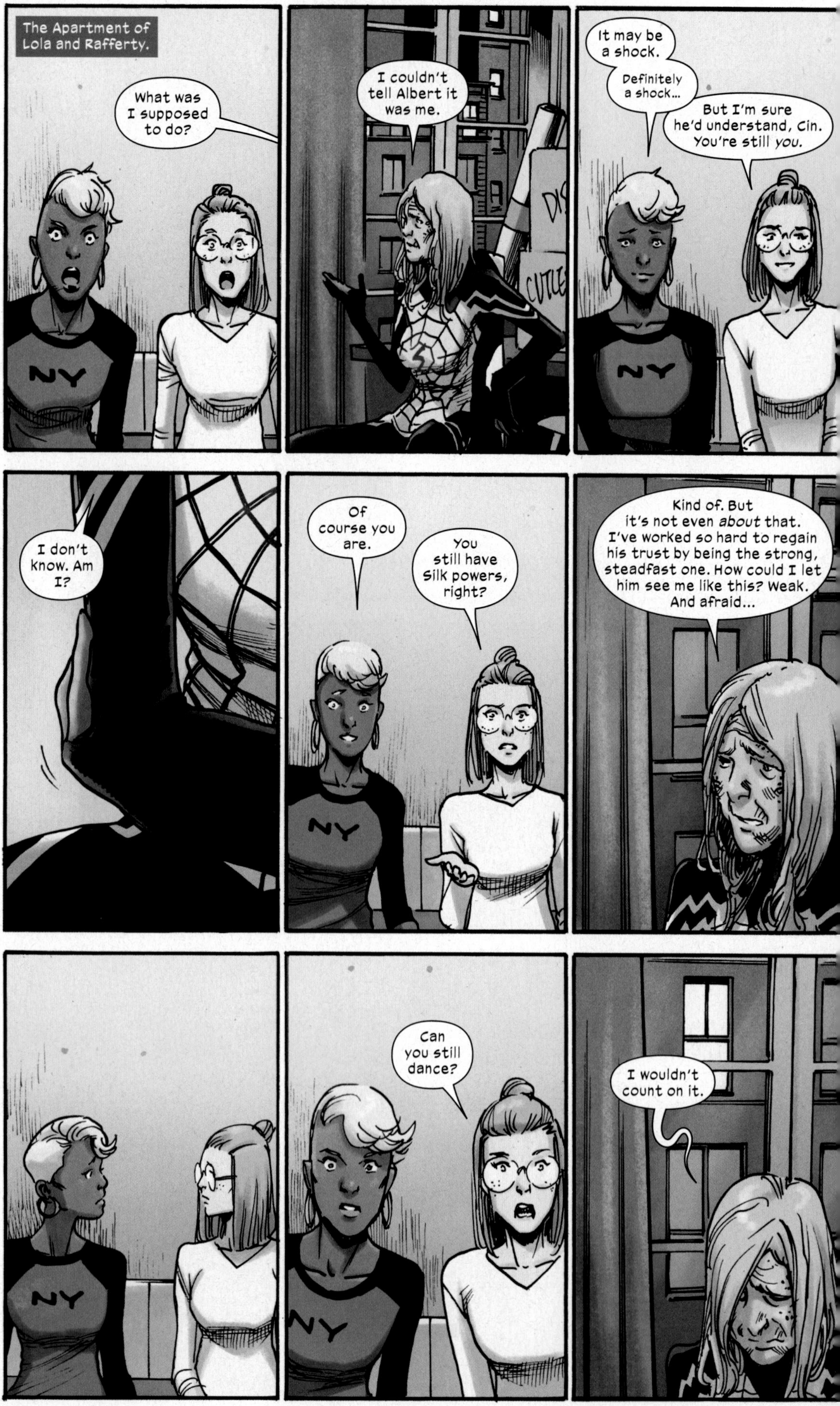

The Apartment of Lola and Rafferty.
What was I supposed to do?
I couldn't tell Albert it was me.
It may be a shock.
Definitely a shock...
But I'm sure he'd understand, Cin. You're still *you*.
I don't know. Am I?
Of course you are.
You still have Silk powers, right?
Kind of. But it's not even *about* that. I've worked so hard to regain his trust by being the strong, steadfast one. How could I let him see me like this? Weak. And afraid...
Can you still dance?
I wouldn't count on it.

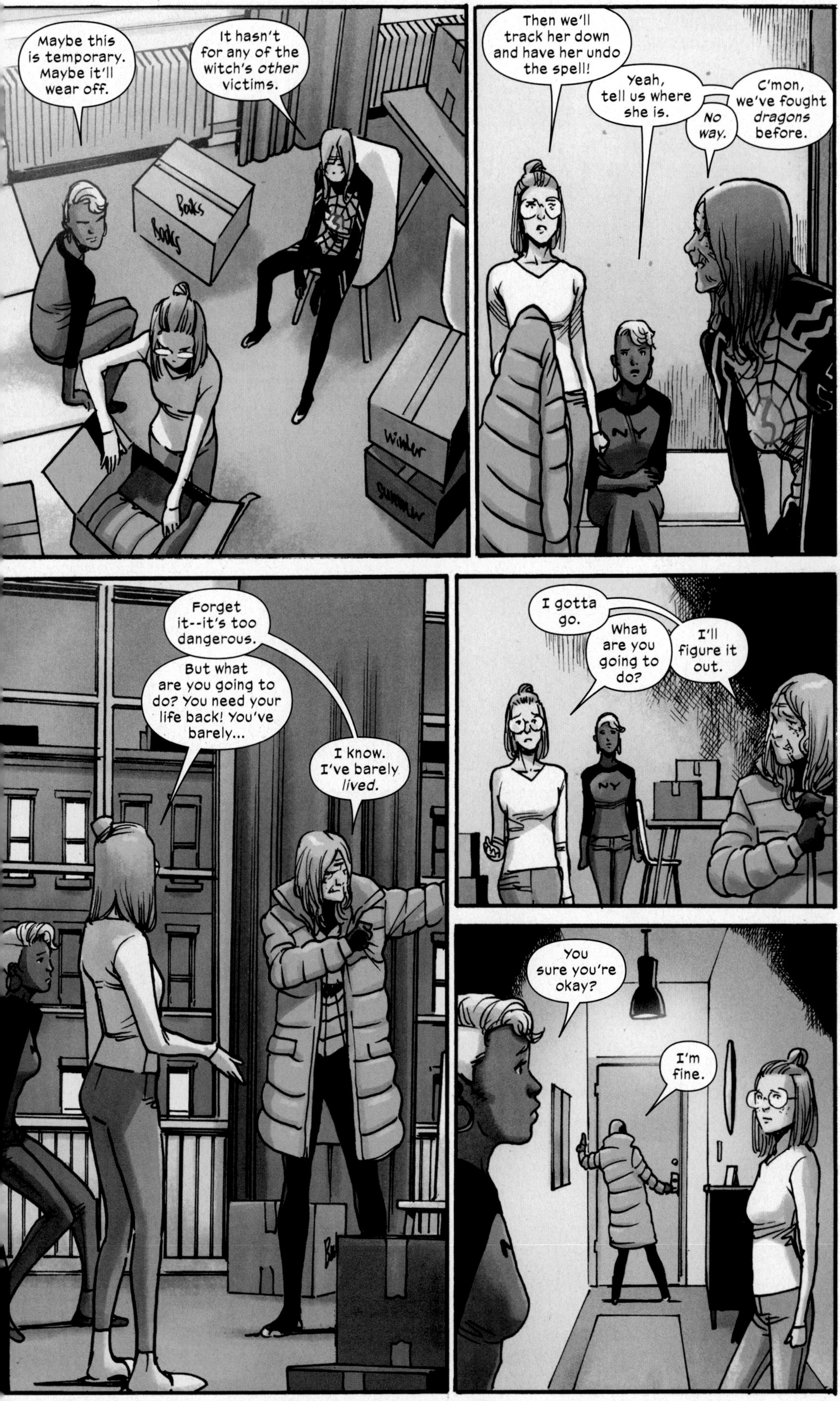
Maybe this is temporary. Maybe it'll wear off.
It hasn't for any of the witch's *other* victims.
Books
Books
Winter
Summer
Then we'll track her down and have her undo the spell!
Yeah, tell us where she is.
No way.
C'mon, we've fought *dragons* before.
NY
Forget it--it's too dangerous.
But what are you going to do? You need your life back! You've barely...
I know. I've barely *lived.*
I gotta go.
What are you going to do?
I'll figure it out.
NY
You sure you're okay?
I'm fine.

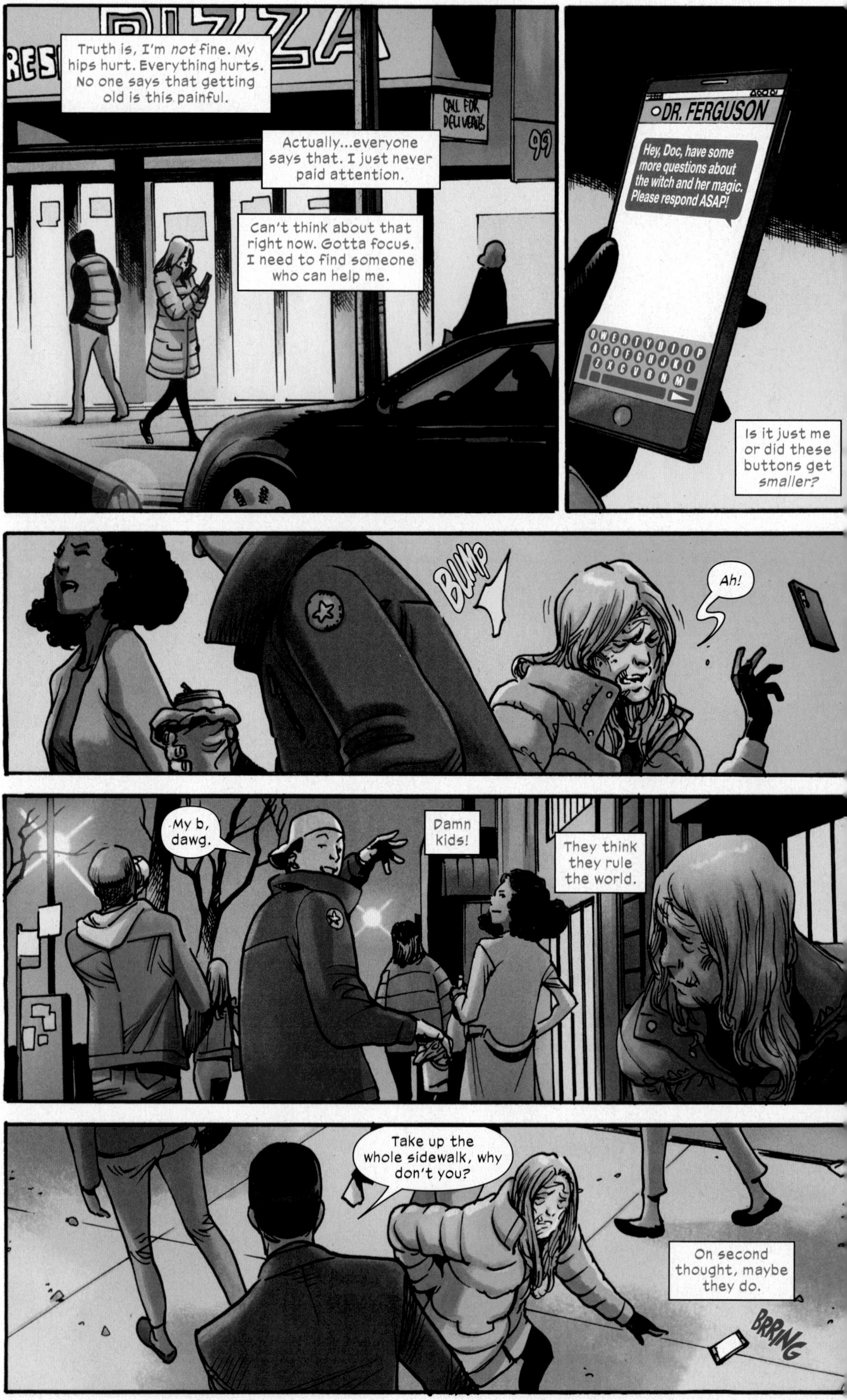
PIZZA
RES
Truth is, I'm *not* fine. My hips hurt. Everything hurts. No one says that getting old is this painful.
CALL FOR DELIVERIES
99
Actually...everyone says that. I just never paid attention.
Can't think about that right now. Gotta focus. I need to find someone who can help me.
DR. FERGUSON
Hey, Doc, have some more questions about the witch and her magic. Please respond ASAP!
Is it just me or did these buttons get *smaller?*
BUMP
Ah!
My b, dawg.
Damn kids!
They think they rule the world.
Take up the whole sidewalk, why don't you?
On second thought, maybe they do.
BRRING

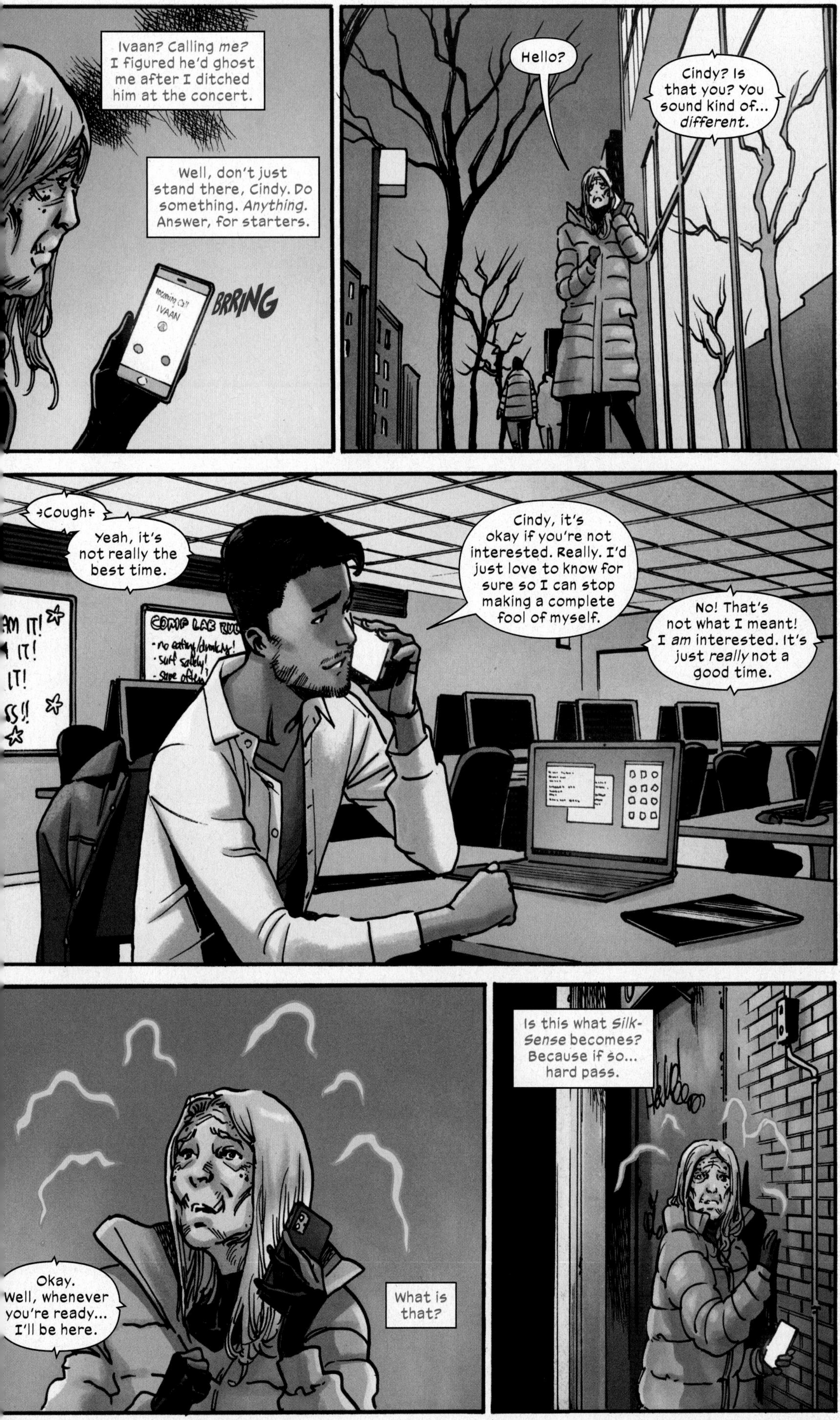
Ivaan? Calling *me?* I figured he'd ghost me after I ditched him at the concert.
Well, don't just stand there, Cindy. Do something. *Anything.* Answer, for starters.
Incoming Call IVAAN
BRRING
Hello?
Cindy? Is that you? You sound kind of... *different.*
Cough
Yeah, it's not really the best time.
Cindy, it's okay if you're not interested. Really. I'd just love to know for sure so I can stop making a complete fool of myself.
No! That's not what I meant! I *am* interested. It's just *really* not a good time.
Okay. Well, whenever you're ready... I'll be here.
What is that?
Is this what *Silk-Sense* becomes? Because if so... hard pass.

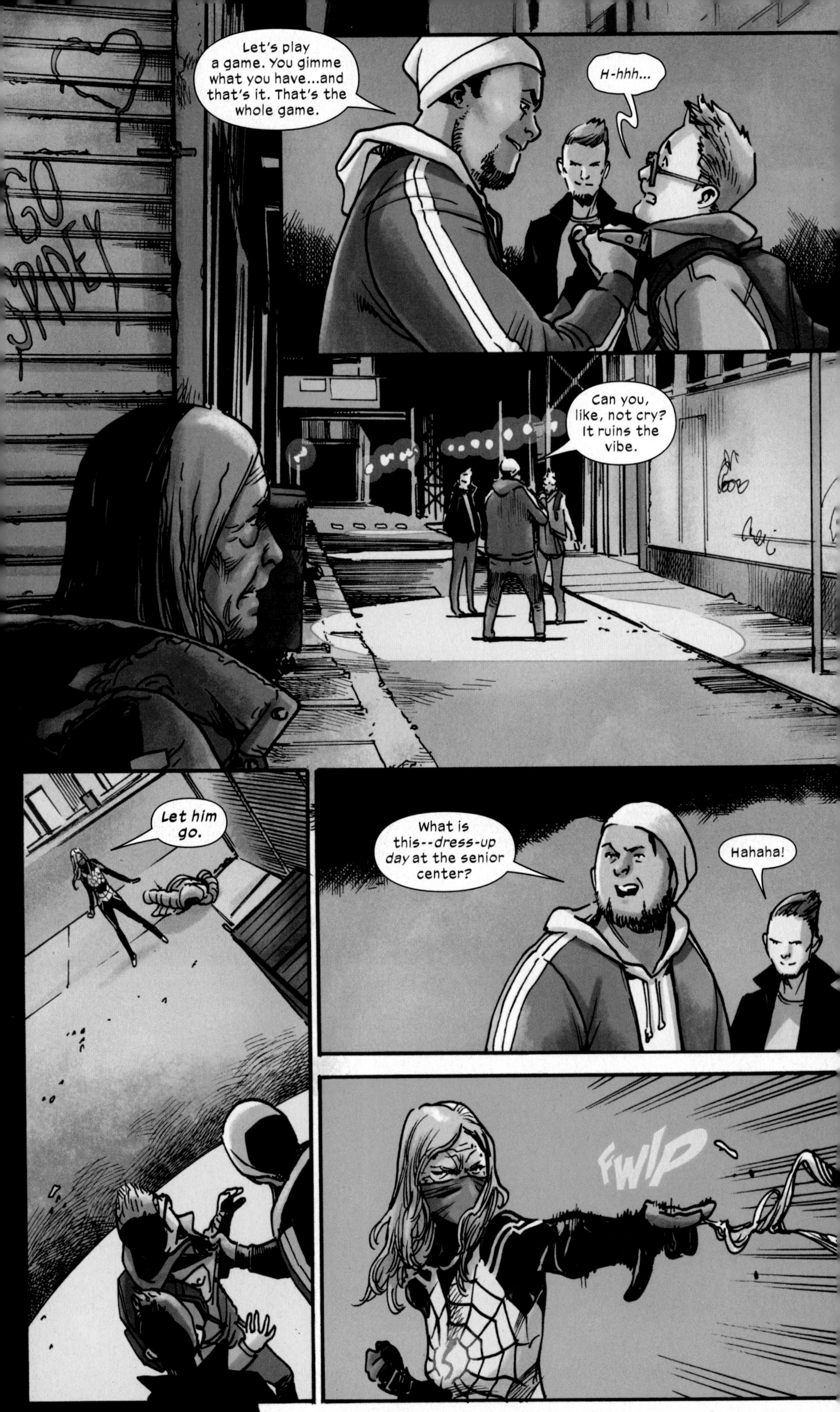

Let's play a game. You gimme what you have...and that's it. That's the whole game.
H-hhh...
GO SPIDEY
Can you, like, not cry? It ruins the vibe.
Let him go.
What is this--*dress-up day* at the senior center?
Hahaha!
FWIP

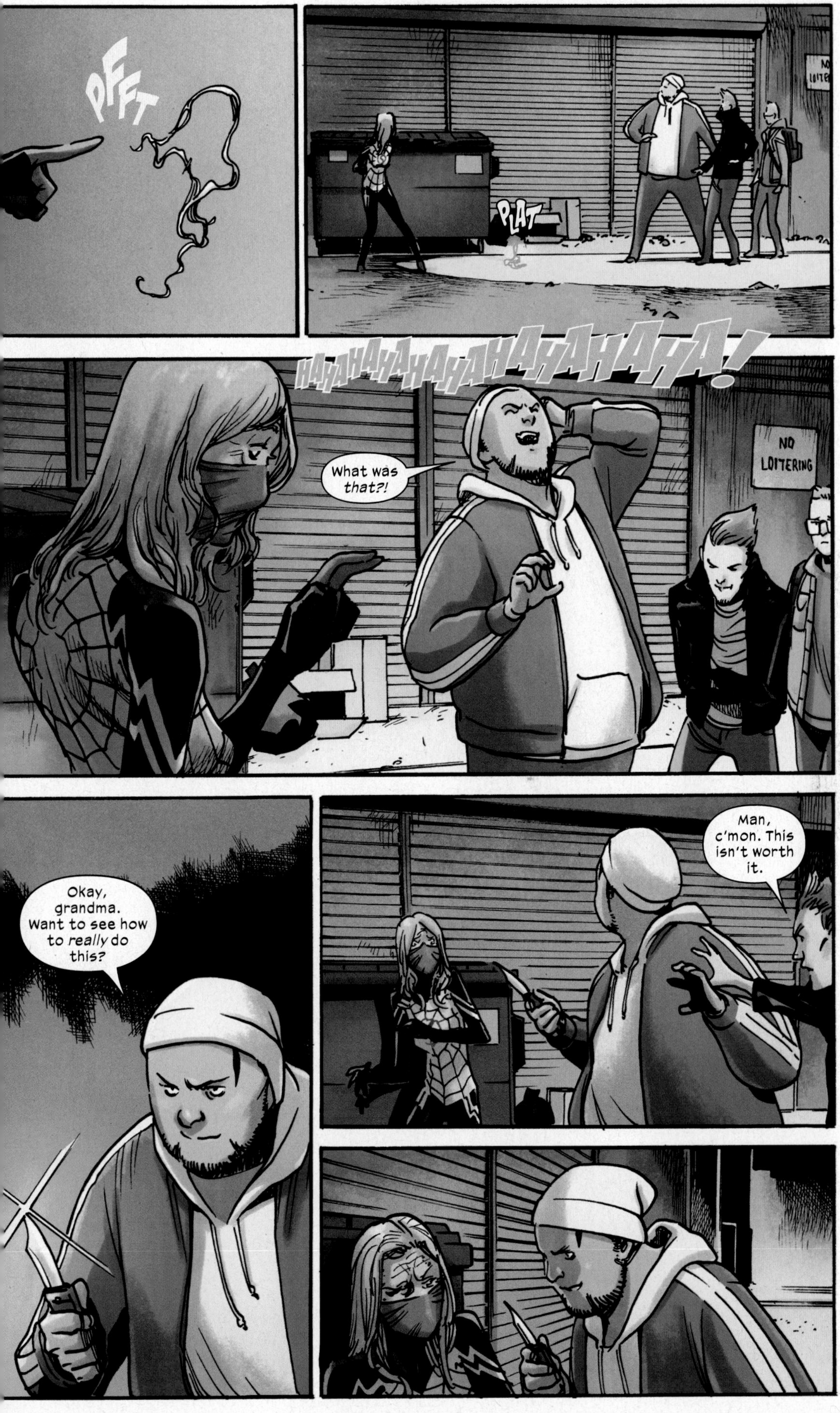
PFFT
NO LOITER
PLAT
HAHAHAHAHAHAHAHAHAHAHAHA!
What was *that?!*
NO LOITERING
Okay, grandma. Want to see how to *really* do this?
Man, c'mon. This isn't worth it.

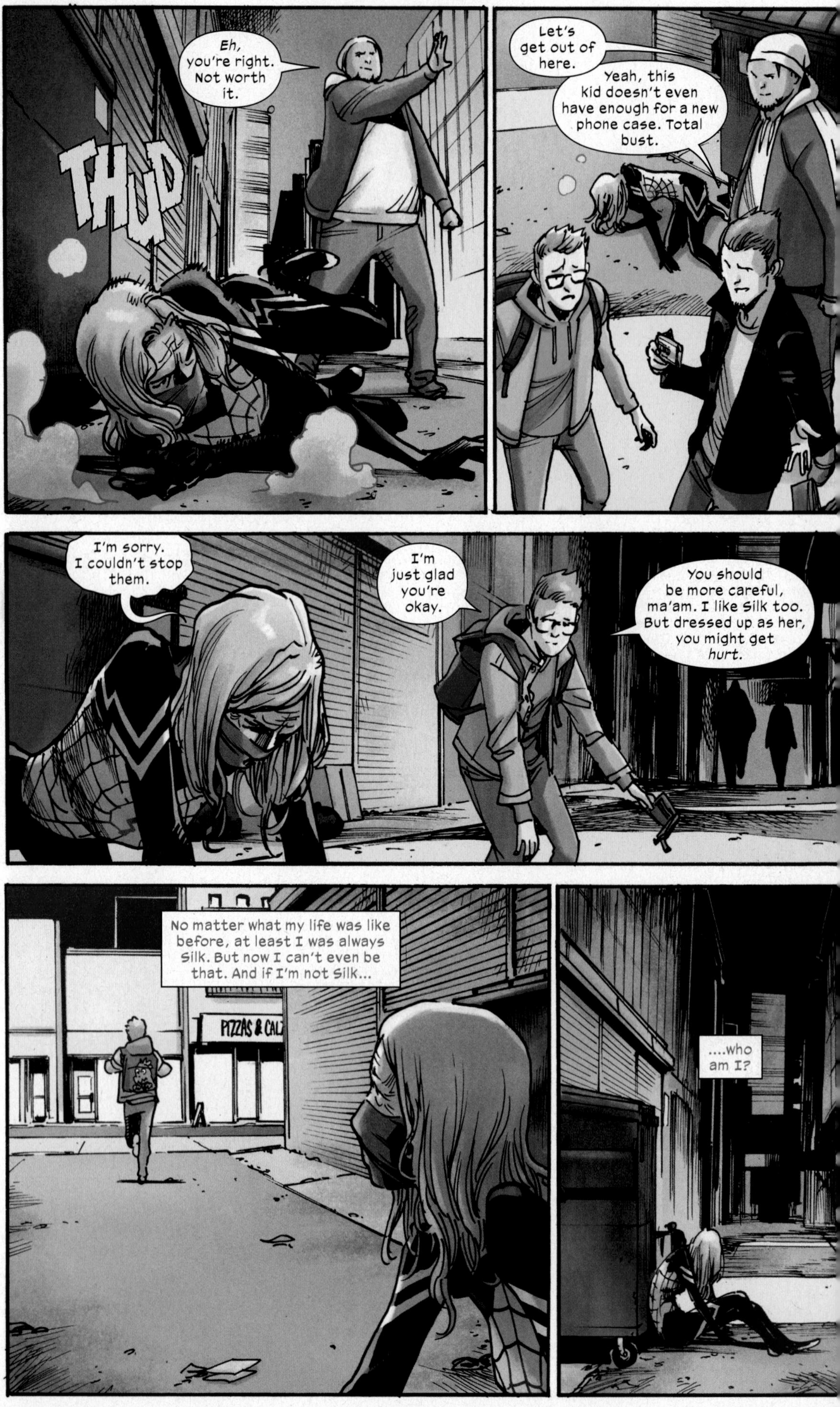
Eh, you're right. Not worth it.
THUD
Let's get out of here.
Yeah, this kid doesn't even have enough for a new phone case. Total bust.
I'm sorry. I couldn't stop them.
I'm just glad you're okay.
You should be more careful, ma'am. I like Silk too. But dressed up as her, you might get hurt.
No matter what my life was like before, at least I was always Silk. But now I can't even be that. And if I'm not Silk...
PIZZAS & CAL
....who am I?

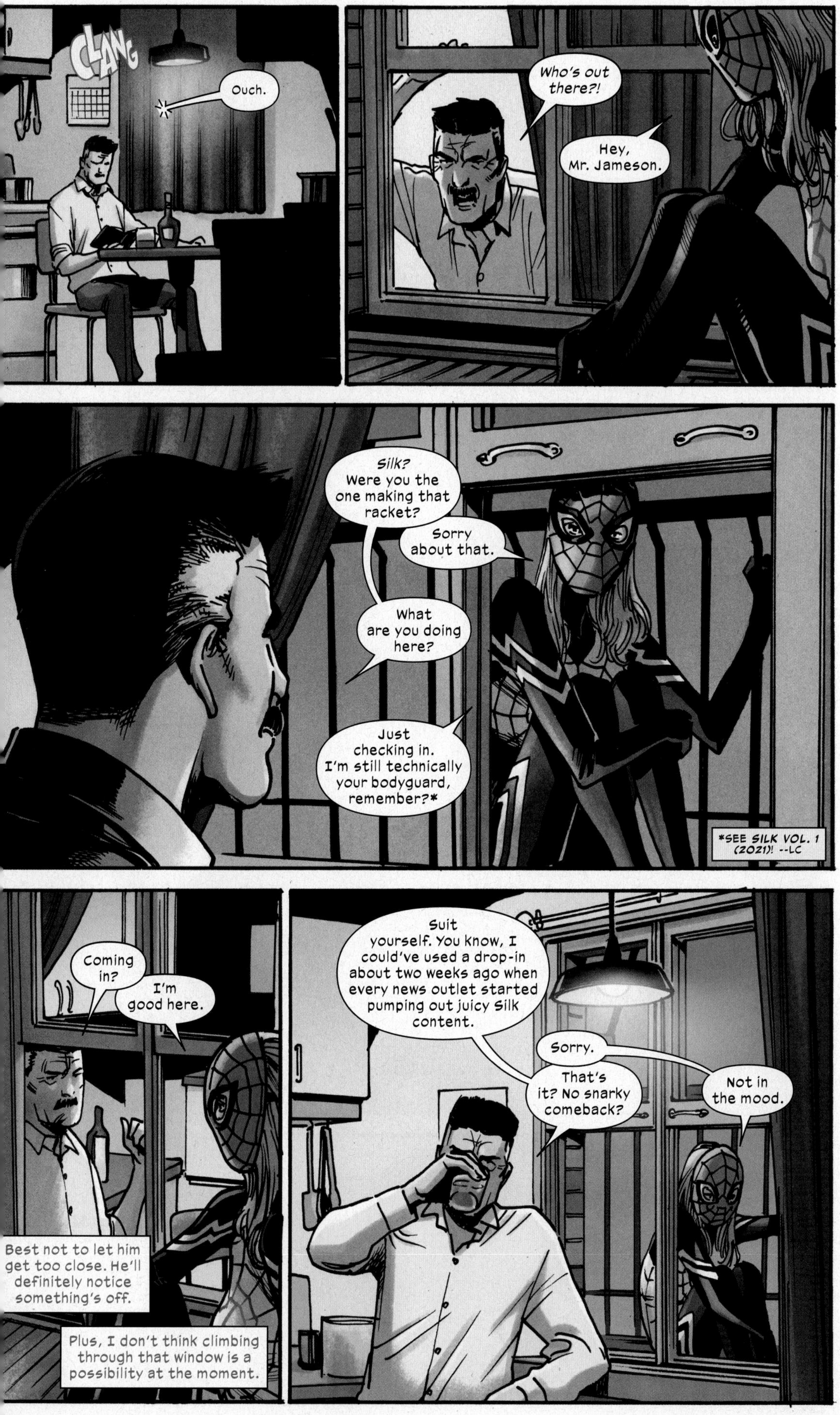
CLANG
Ouch.
Who's out there?!
Hey, Mr. Jameson.
Silk? Were you the one making that racket?
Sorry about that.
What are you doing here?
Just checking in. I'm still technically your bodyguard, remember?*
*SEE SILK VOL. 1 (2021)! --LC
Coming in?
I'm good here.
Best not to let him get too close. He'll definitely notice something's off.
Plus, I don't think climbing through that window is a possibility at the moment.
Suit yourself. You know, I could've used a drop-in about two weeks ago when every news outlet started pumping out juicy Silk content.
Sorry.
That's it? No snarky comeback?
Not in the mood.

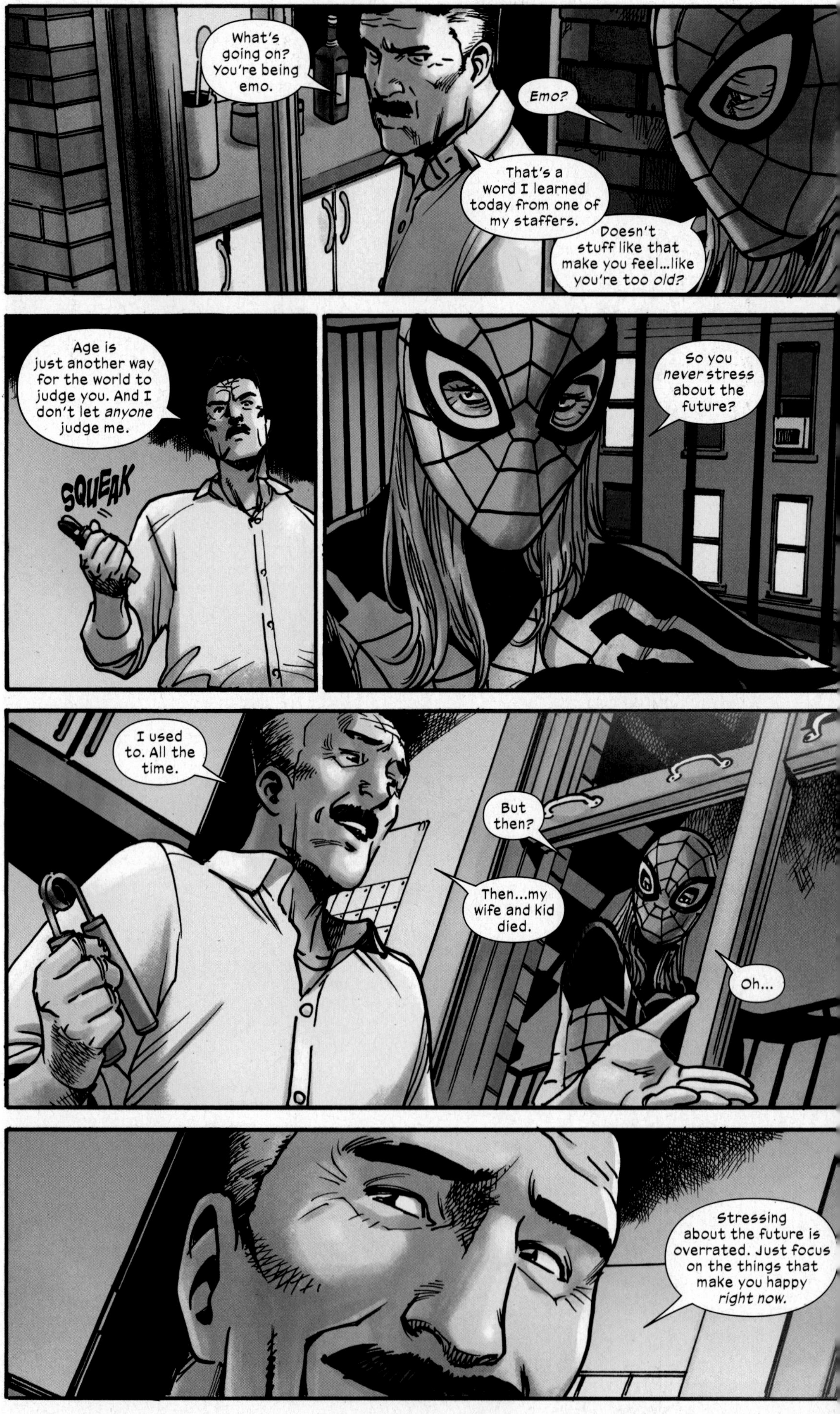

What's going on? You're being emo.
Emo?
That's a word I learned today from one of my staffers.
Doesn't stuff like that make you feel...like you're too *old?*
Age is just another way for the world to judge you. And I don't let *anyone* judge me.
SQUEAK
So you *never* stress about the future?
I used to. All the time.
But then?
Then...my wife and kid died.
Oh...
Stressing about the future is overrated. Just focus on the things that make you happy *right now.*

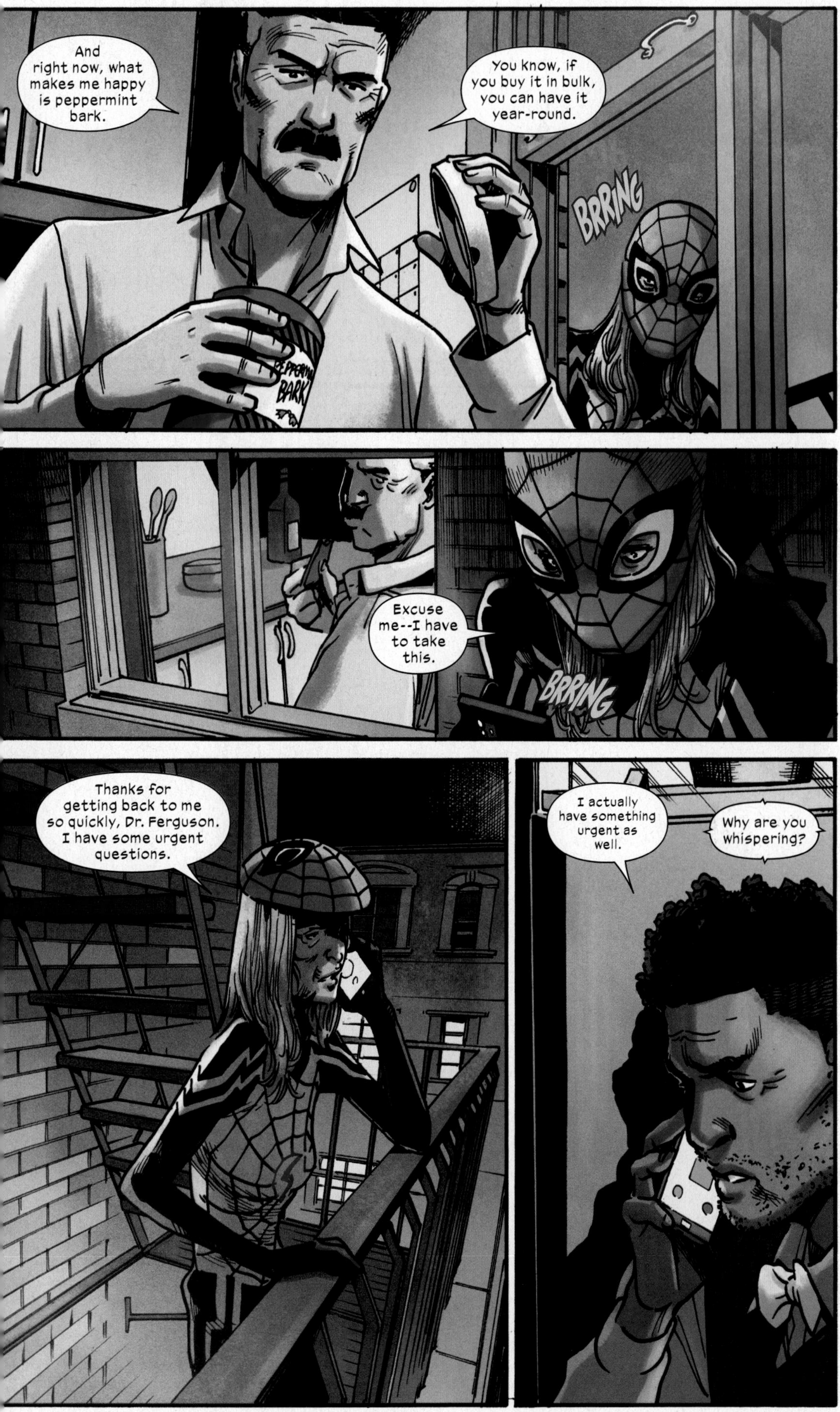
And right now, what makes me happy is peppermint bark.
You know, if you buy it in bulk, you can have it year-round.
BRRING
Excuse me--I have to take this.
BRRING
Thanks for getting back to me so quickly, Dr. Ferguson. I have some urgent questions.
I actually have something urgent as well.
Why are you whispering?

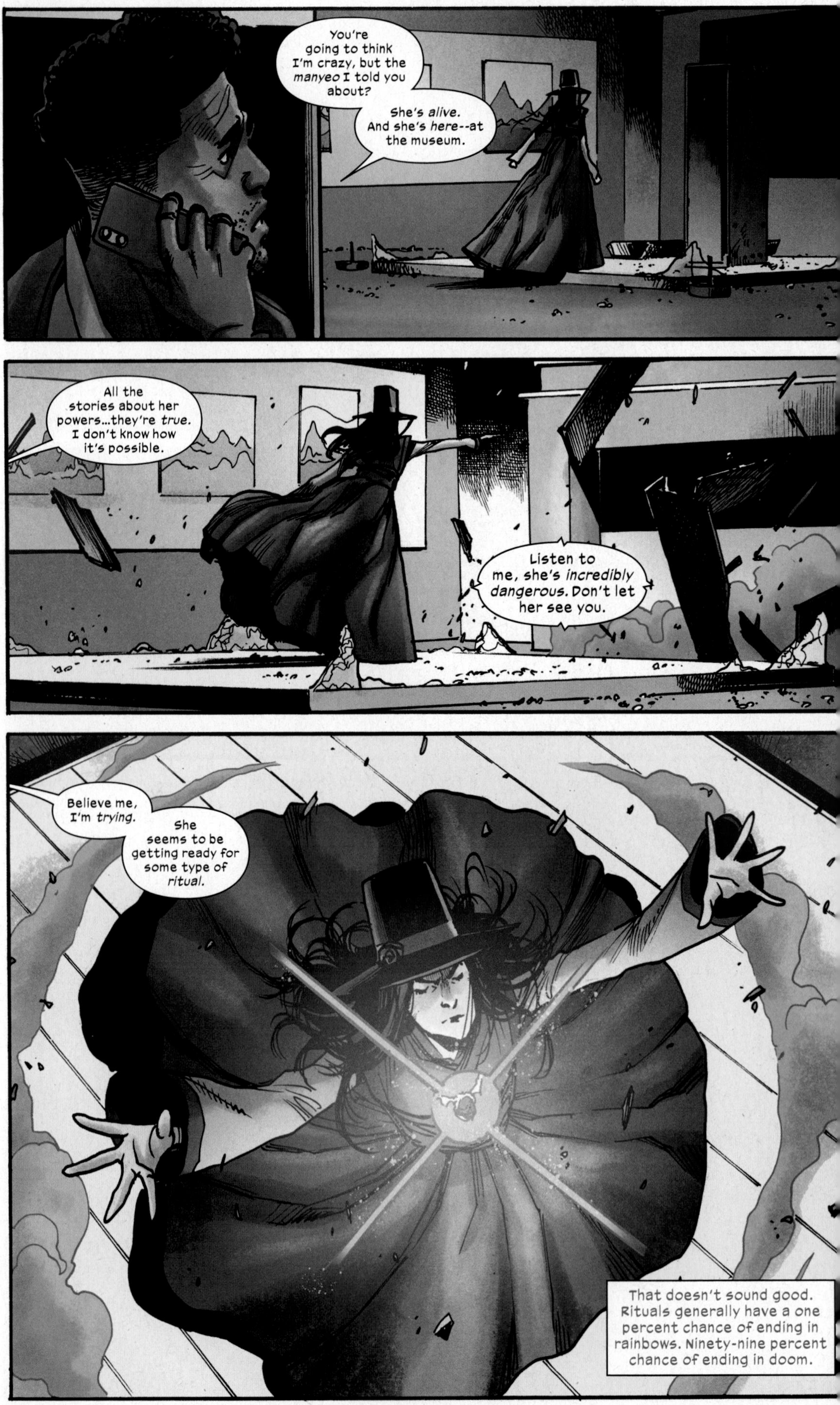

You're going to think I'm crazy, but the *manyeo* I told you about?
She's *alive.* And she's *here*--at the museum.
All the stories about her powers...they're *true.* I don't know how it's possible.
Listen to me, she's *incredibly dangerous.* Don't let her see you.
Believe me, I'm *trying.*
She seems to be getting ready for some type of *ritual.*
That doesn't sound good. Rituals generally have a one percent chance of ending in rainbows. Ninety-nine percent chance of ending in doom.

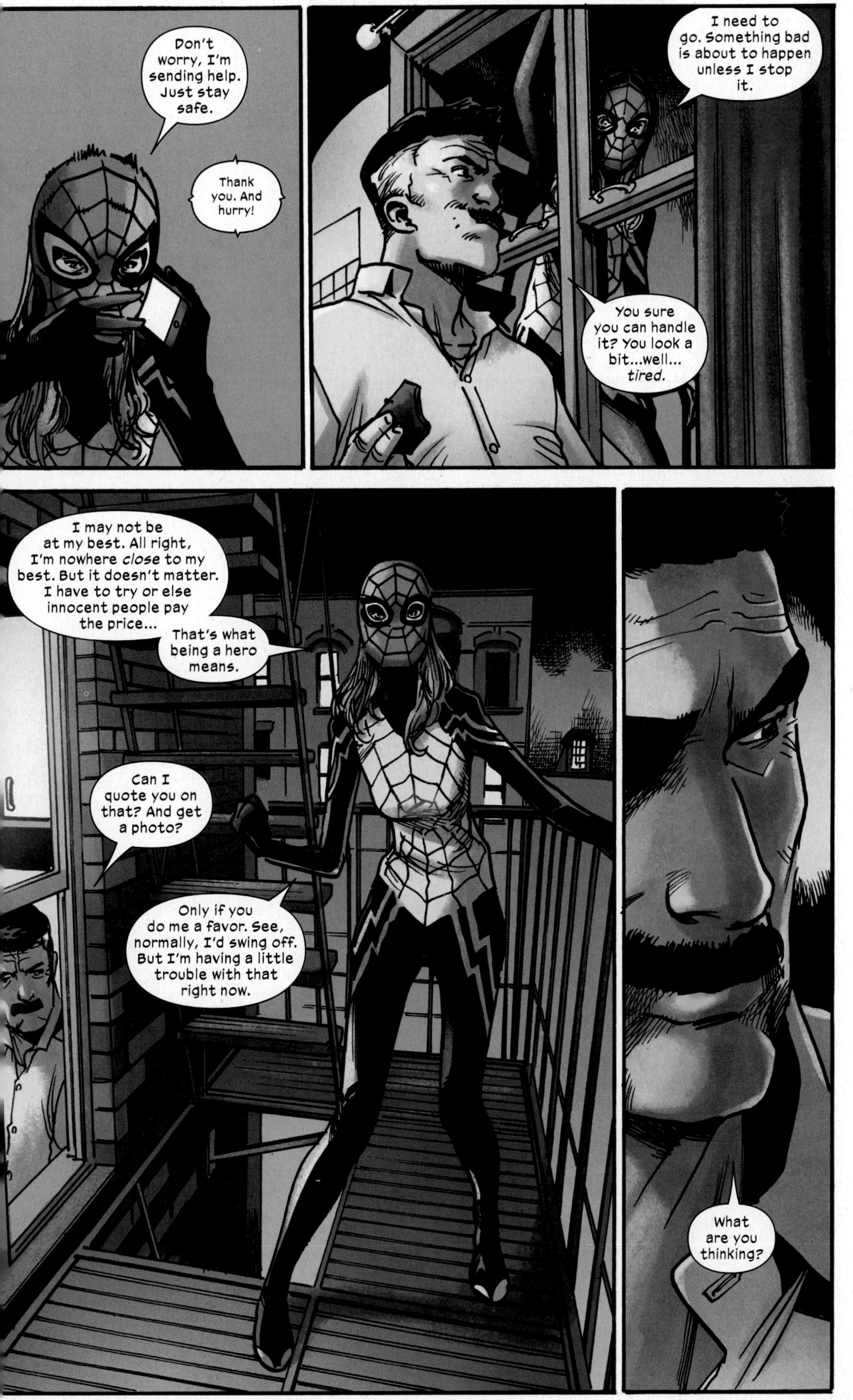
Don't worry, I'm sending help. Just stay safe.
Thank you. And hurry!
I need to go. Something bad is about to happen unless I stop it.
You sure you can handle it? You look a bit...well... *tired.*
I may not be at my best. All right, I'm nowhere *close* to my best. But it doesn't matter. I have to try or else innocent people pay the price...
That's what being a hero means.
Can I quote you on that? And get a photo?
Only if you do me a favor. See, normally, I'd swing off. But I'm having a little trouble with that right now.
What are you thinking?

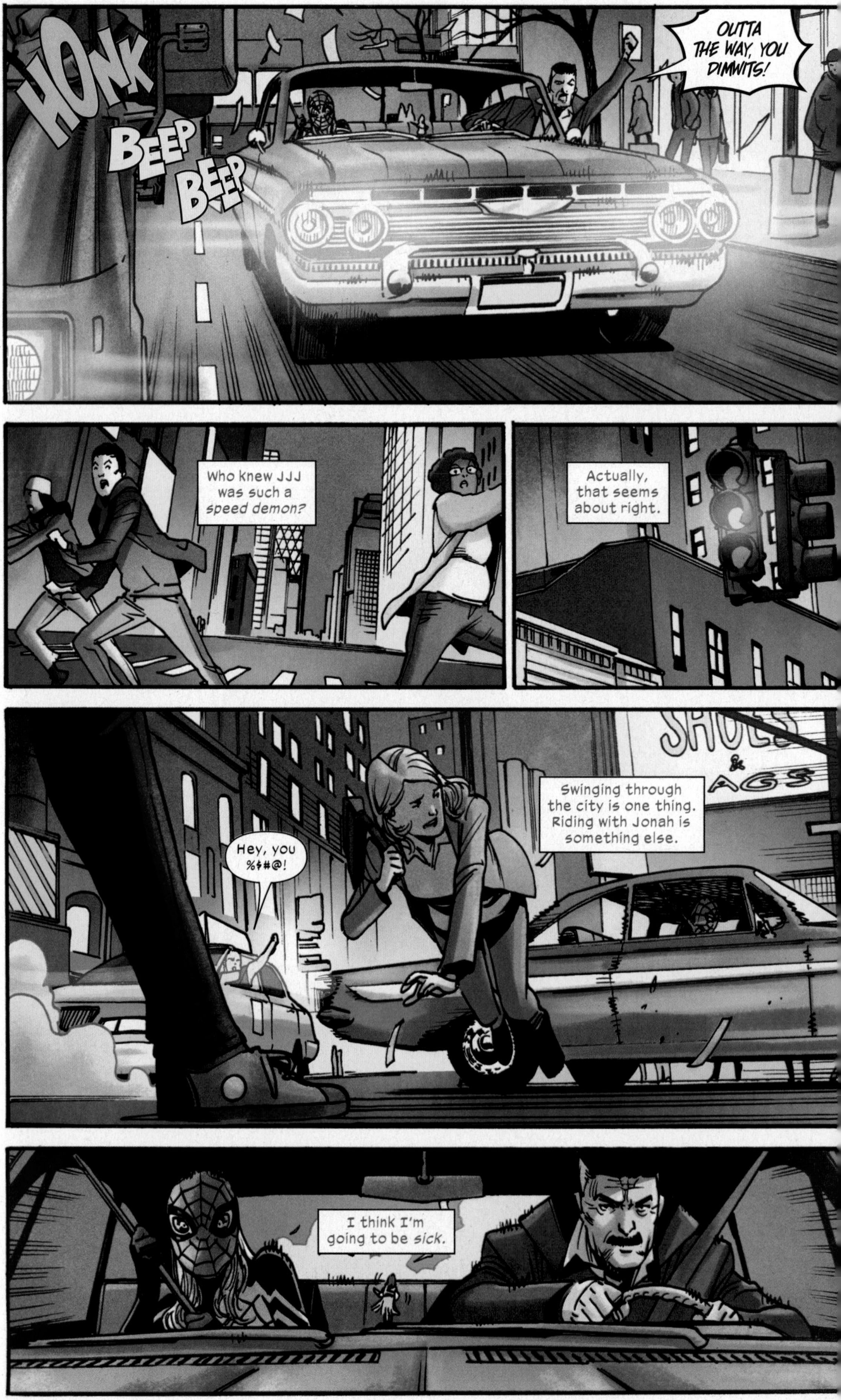
HONK
BEEP BEEP
BEEP
OUTTA THE WAY, YOU DIMWITS!
Who knew JJJ was such a speed demon?
Actually, that seems about right.
Swinging through the city is one thing. Riding with Jonah is something else.
Hey, you %$#@!
I think I'm going to be sick.

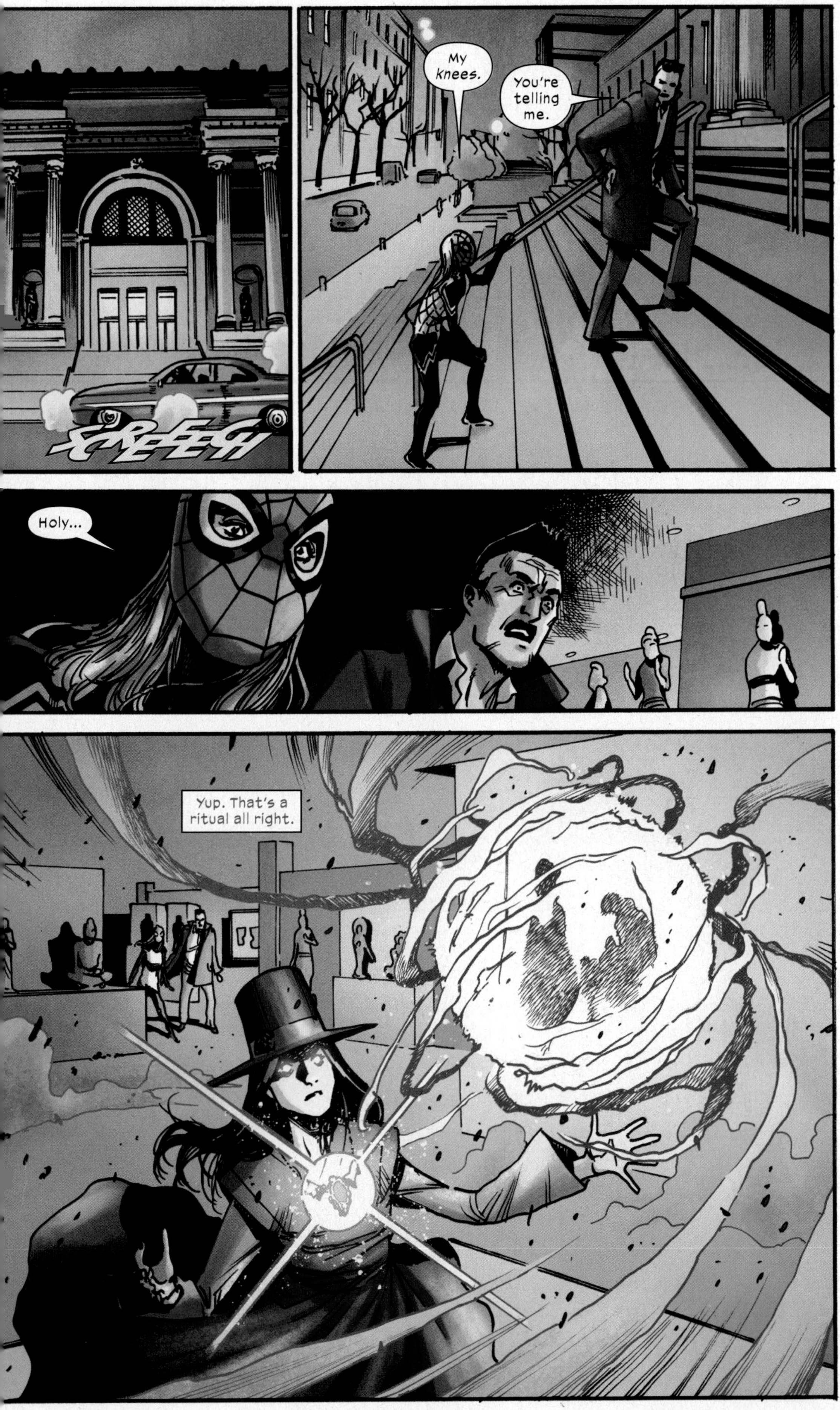
SCREEEECH
My knees.
You're telling me.
Holy...
Yup. That's a ritual all right.

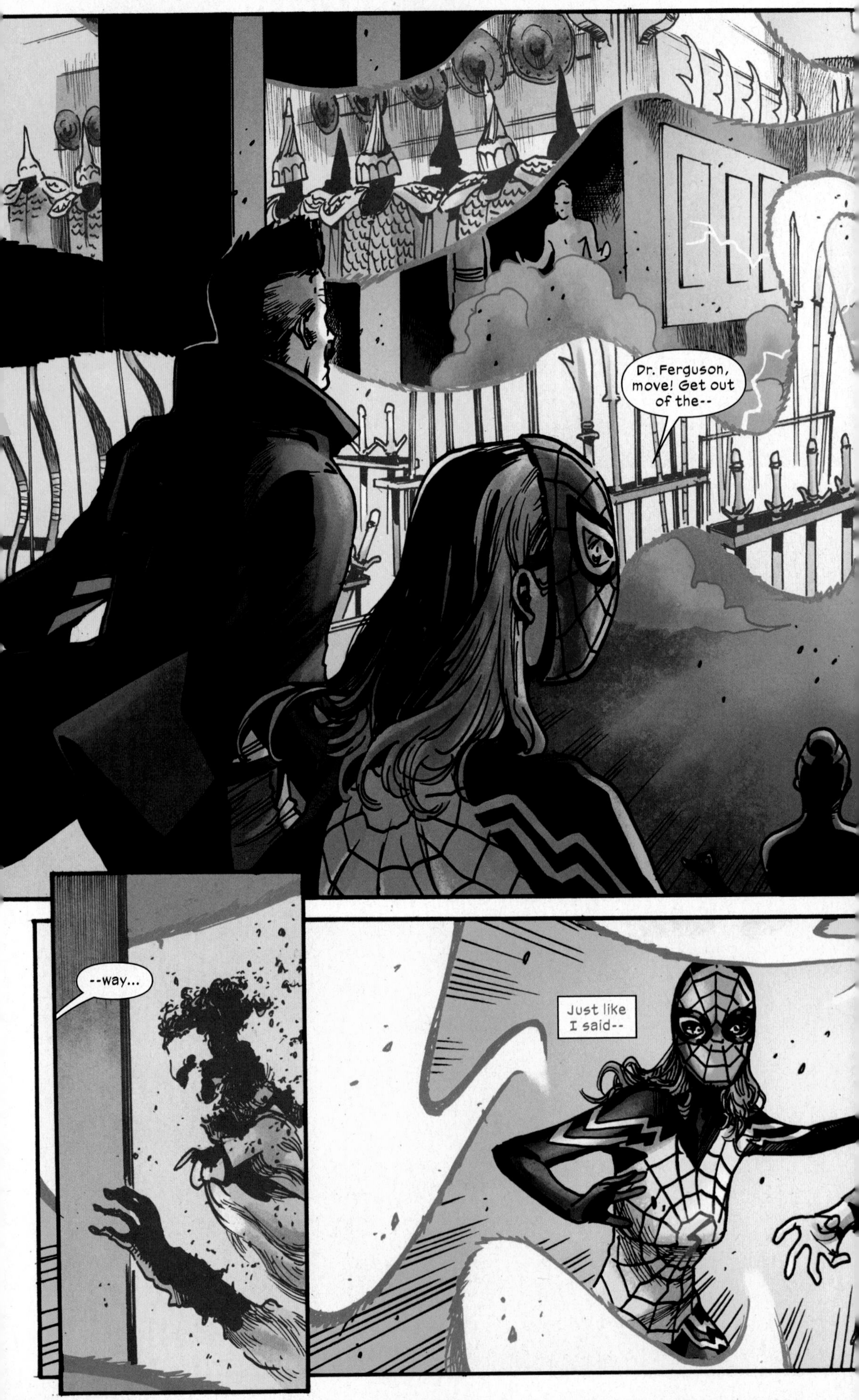
Dr. Ferguson, move! Get out of the--
--way...
Just like I said--

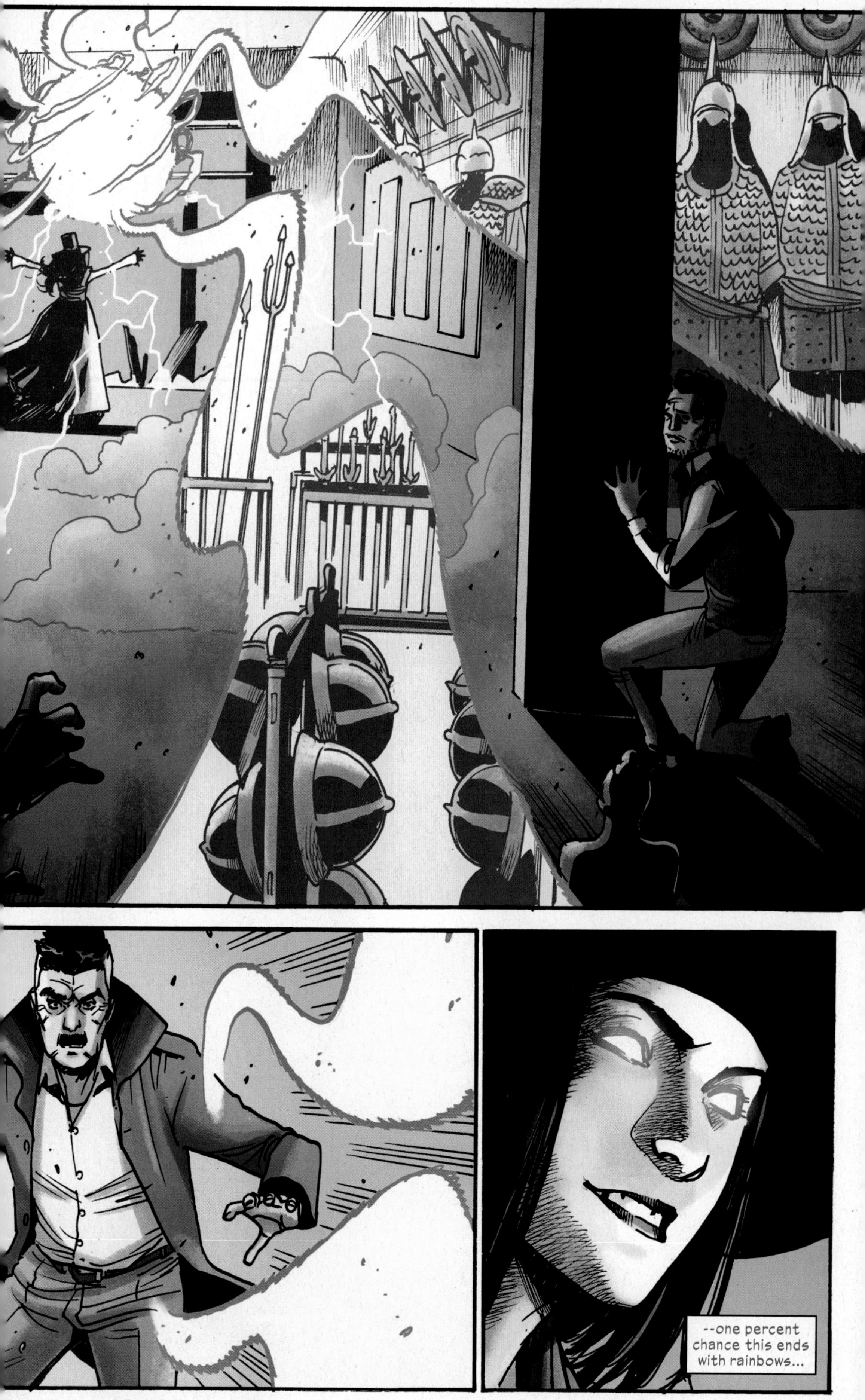
--one percent chance this ends with rainbows...

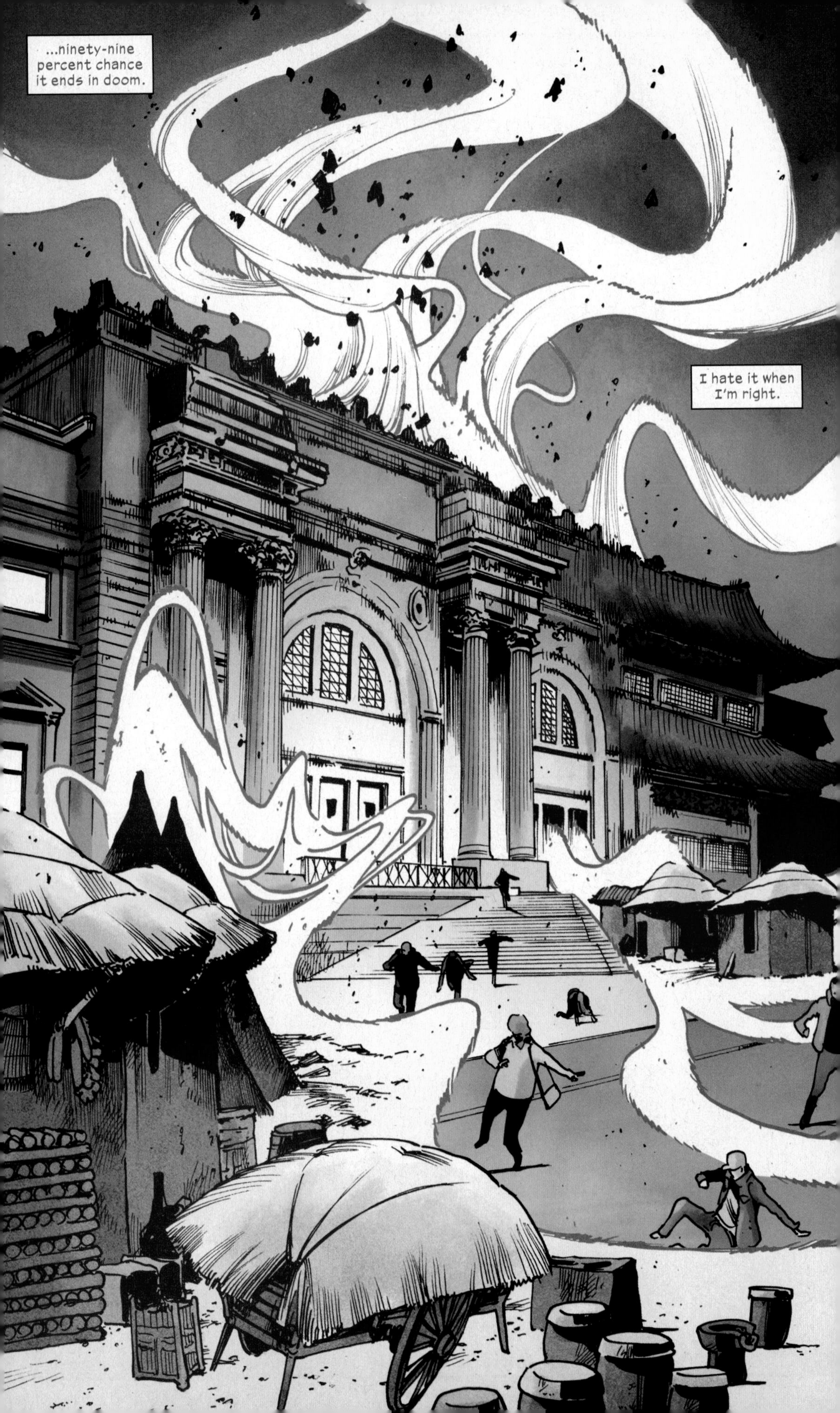
...ninety-nine percent chance it ends in doom.
I hate it when I'm right.

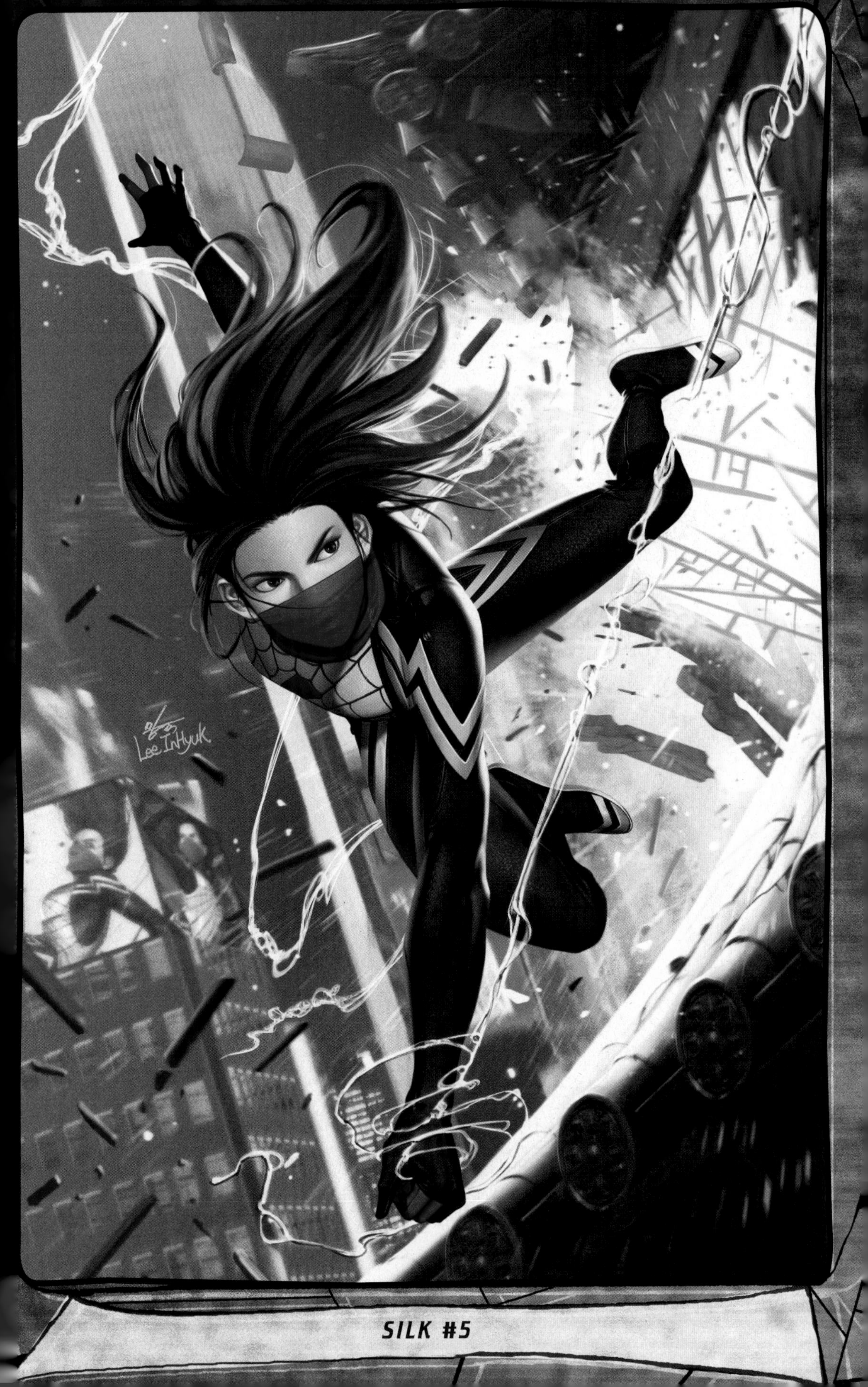
Lee InHyuk.

SILK #5

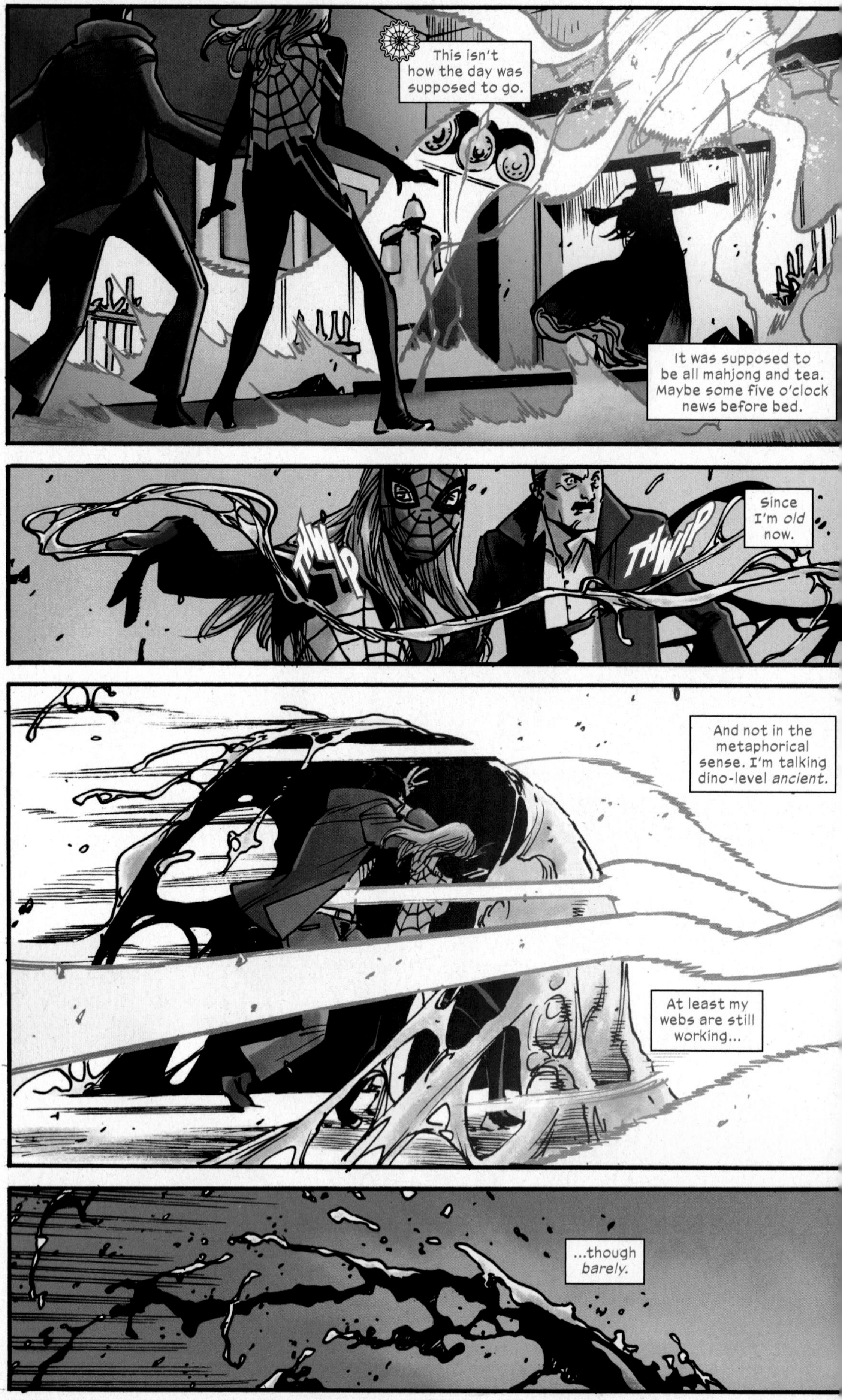
This isn't how the day was supposed to go.
It was supposed to be all mahjong and tea. Maybe some five o'clock news before bed.
THWIP
THWIP
Since I'm *old* now.
And not in the metaphorical sense. I'm talking dino-level *ancient*.
At least my webs are still working...
...though *barely*.

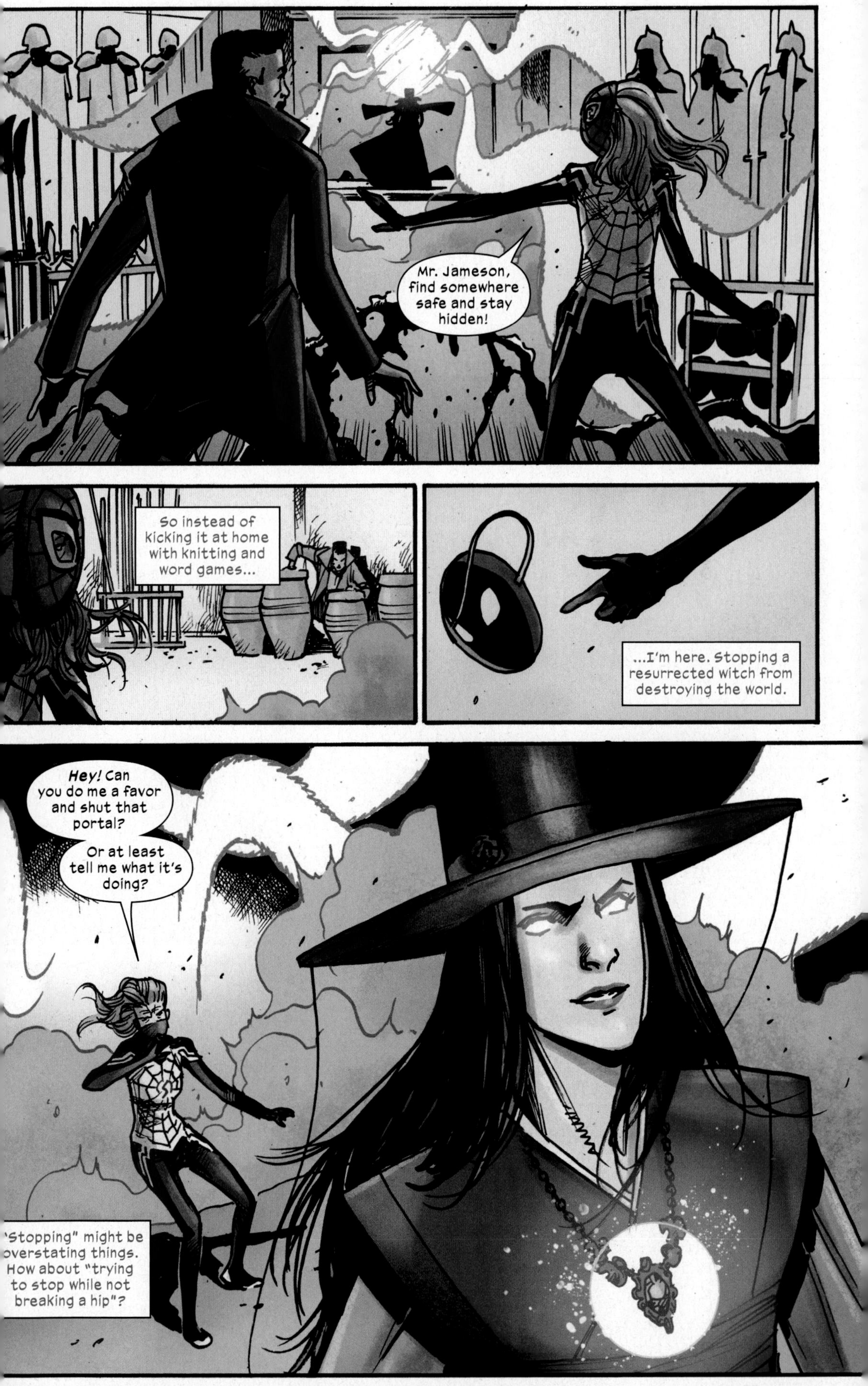

Mr. Jameson, find somewhere safe and stay hidden!
So instead of kicking it at home with knitting and word games...
...I'm here. Stopping a resurrected witch from destroying the world.
Hey! Can you do me a favor and shut that portal?
Or at least tell me what it's doing?
"Stopping" might be overstating things. How about "trying to stop while not breaking a hip"?

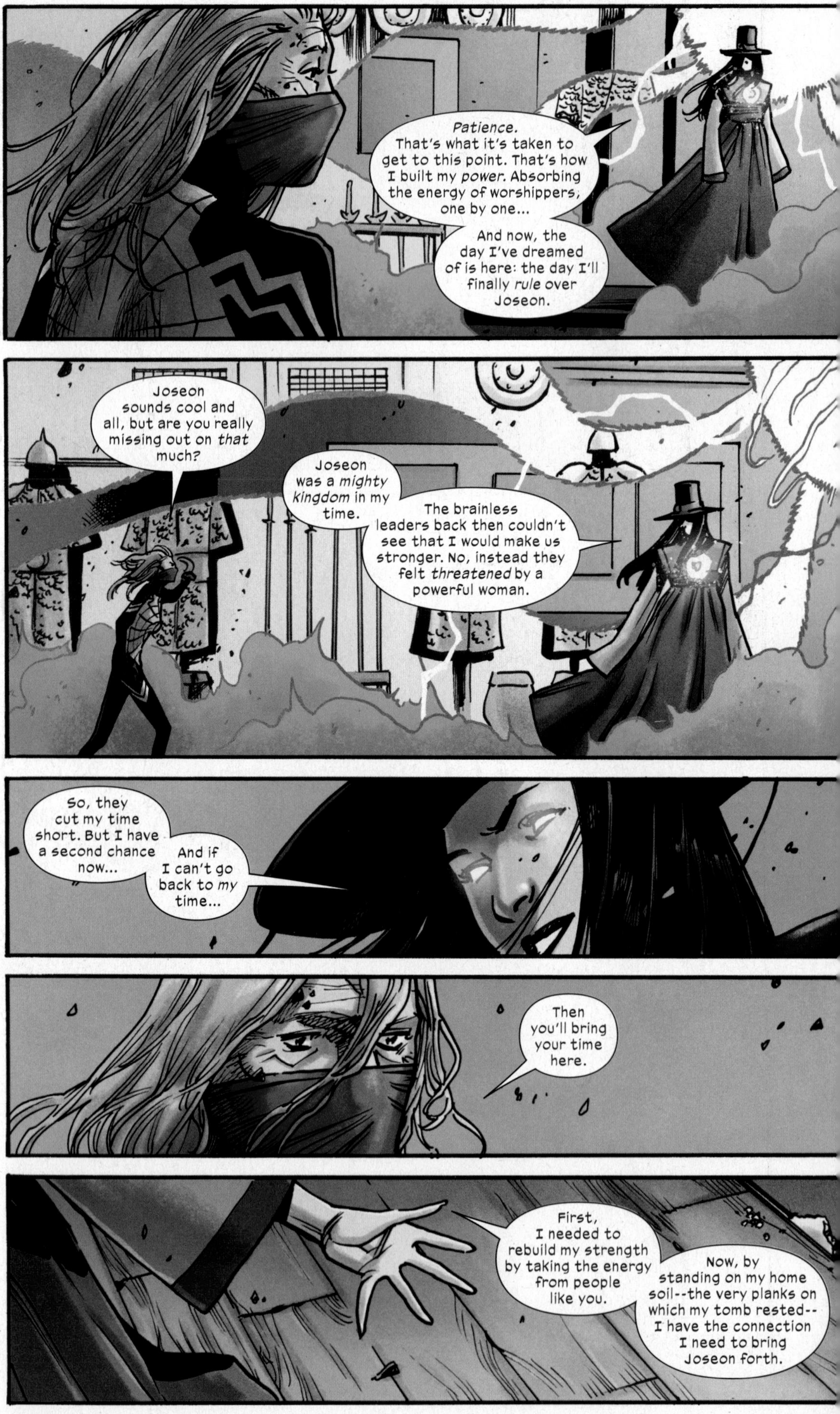
Patience. That's what it's taken to get to this point. That's how I built my power. Absorbing the energy of worshippers, one by one...
And now, the day I've dreamed of is here: the day I'll finally rule over Joseon.
Joseon sounds cool and all, but are you really missing out on that much?
Joseon was a mighty kingdom in my time.
The brainless leaders back then couldn't see that I would make us stronger. No, instead they felt threatened by a powerful woman.
So, they cut my time short. But I have a second chance now...
And if I can't go back to my time...
Then you'll bring your time here.
First, I needed to rebuild my strength by taking the energy from people like you.
Now, by standing on my home soil--the very planks on which my tomb rested--I have the connection I need to bring Joseon forth.

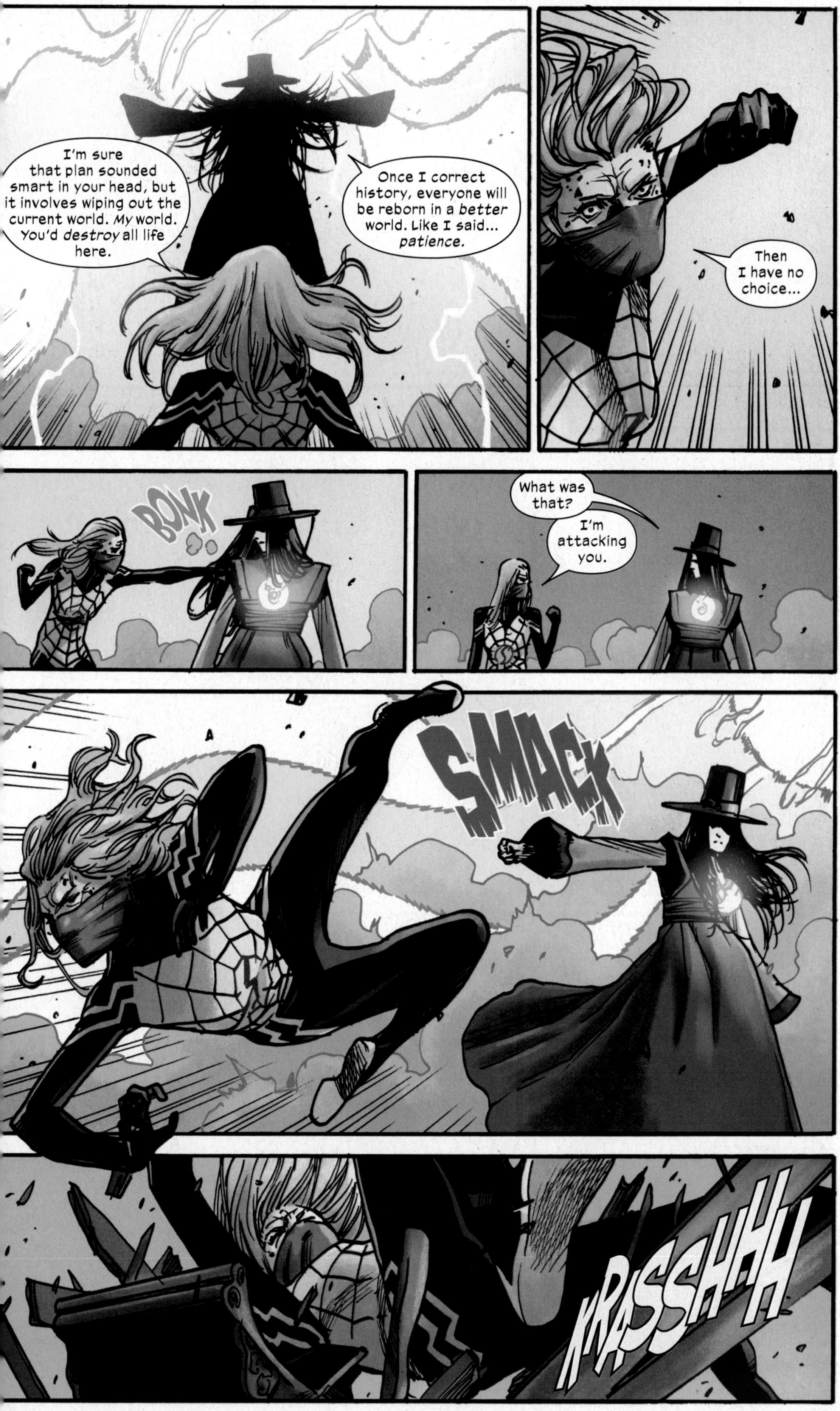
I'm sure that plan sounded smart in your head, but it involves wiping out the current world. *My* world. You'd *destroy* all life here.
Once I correct history, everyone will be reborn in a *better* world. Like I said... *patience.*
Then I have no choice...
BONK
What was that?
I'm attacking you.
SMACK
KRASSHHH

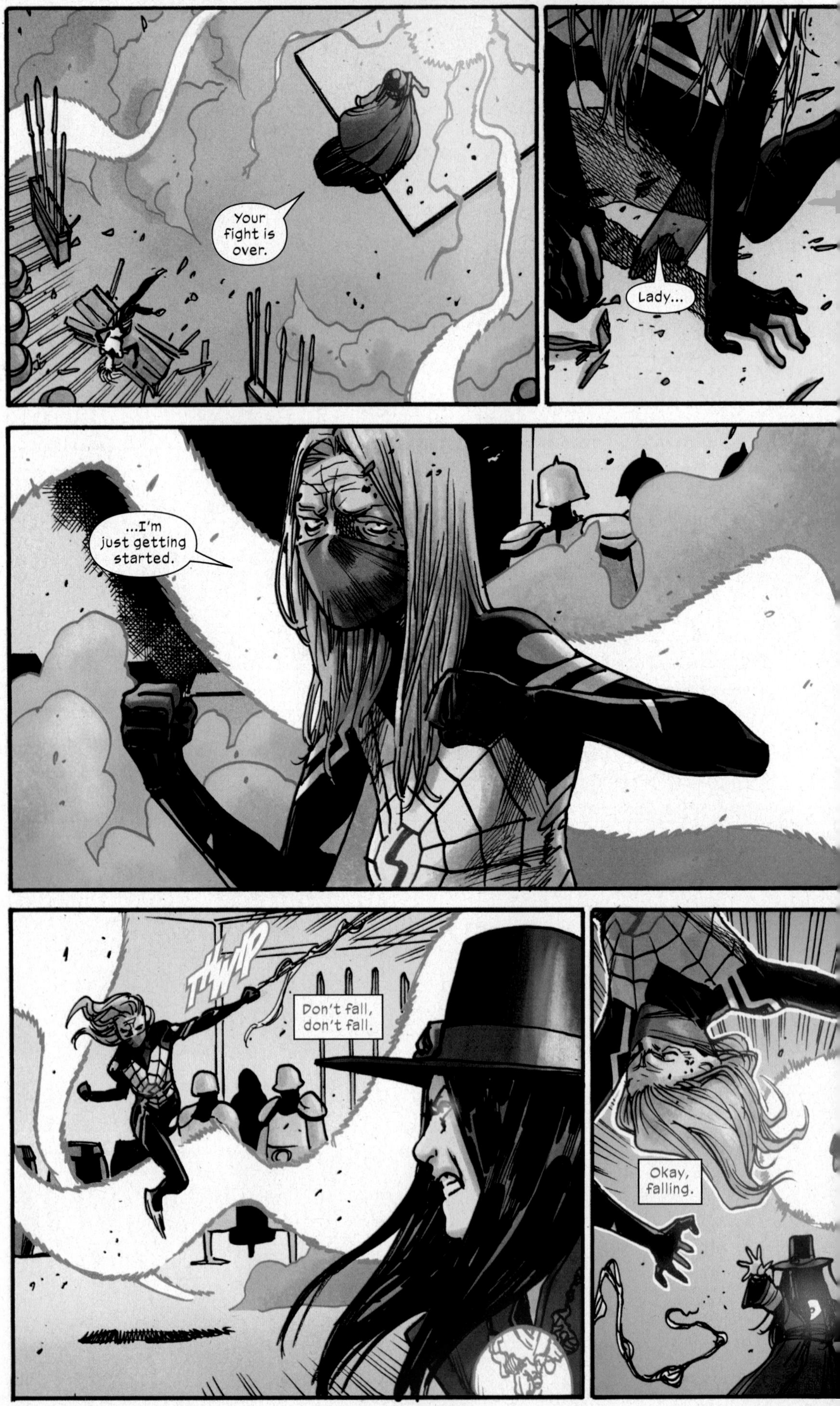
Your fight is over.
Lady...
...I'm just getting started.
THWIP
Don't fall, don't fall.
Okay, falling.

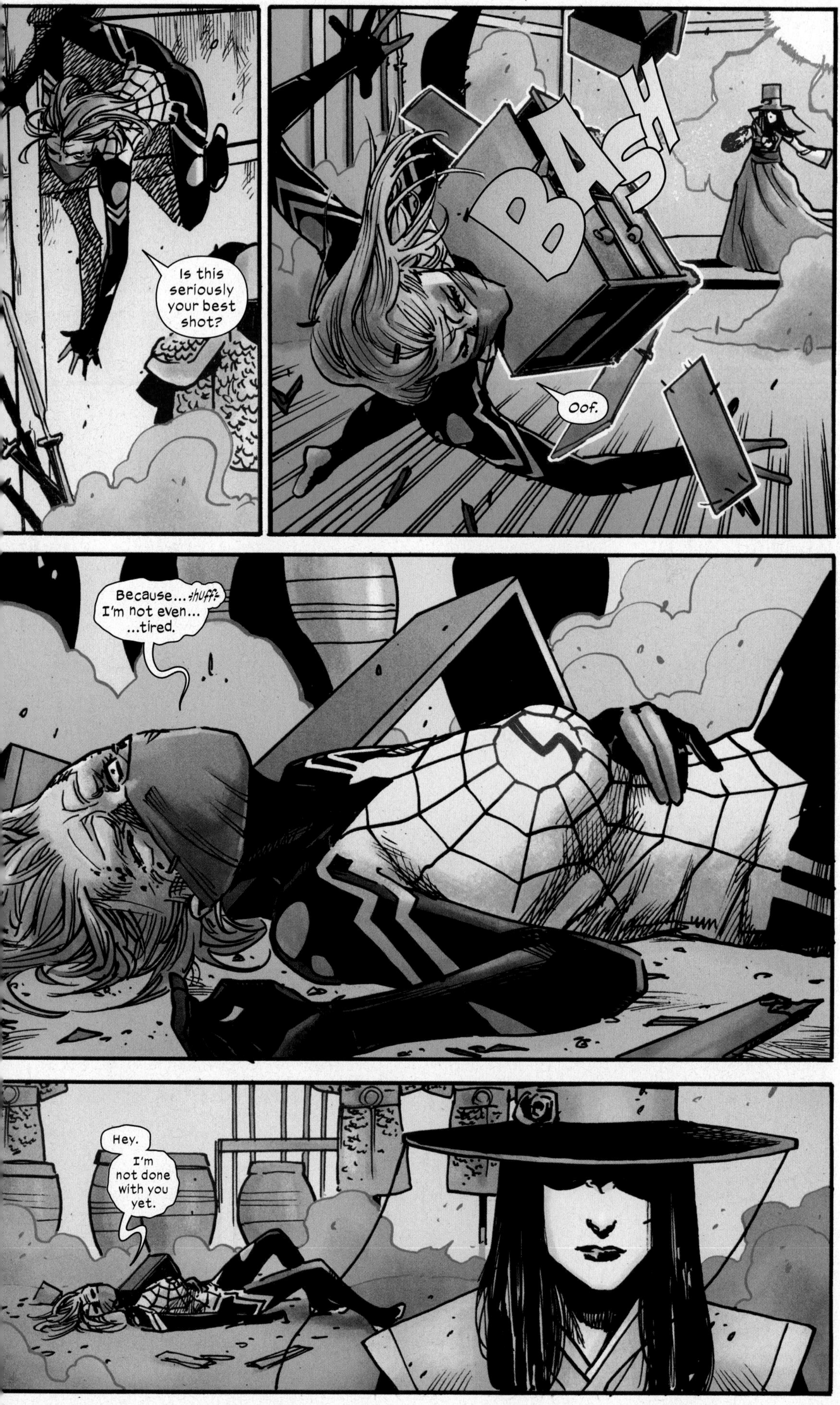
Is this seriously your best shot?
BASH
Oof.
Because... shuff I'm not even... ...tired.
Hey.
I'm not done with you yet.

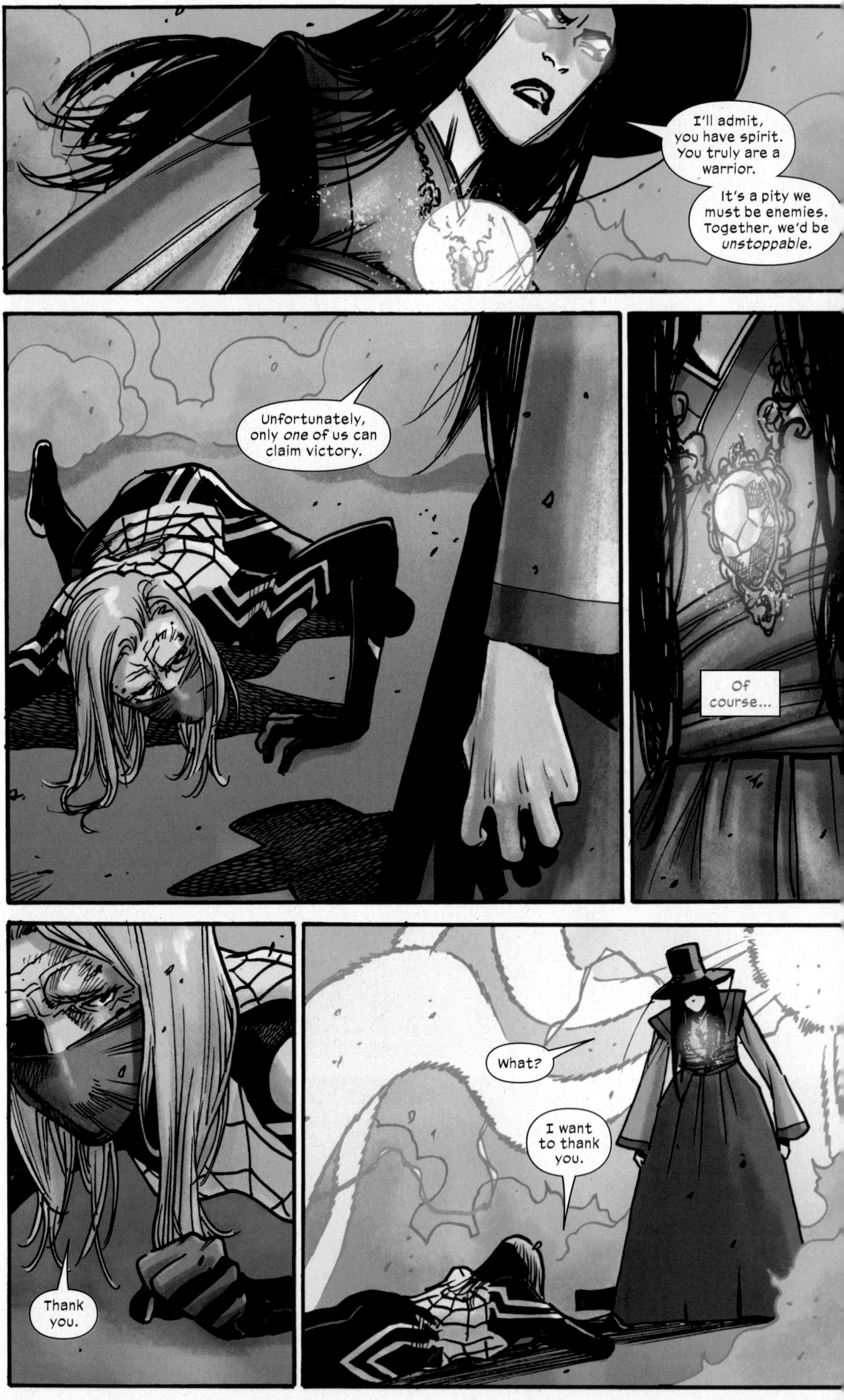
I'll admit, you have spirit. You truly are a warrior.
It's a pity we must be enemies. Together, we'd be *unstoppable*.
Unfortunately, only *one* of us can claim victory.
Of course...
Thank you.
What?
I want to thank you.

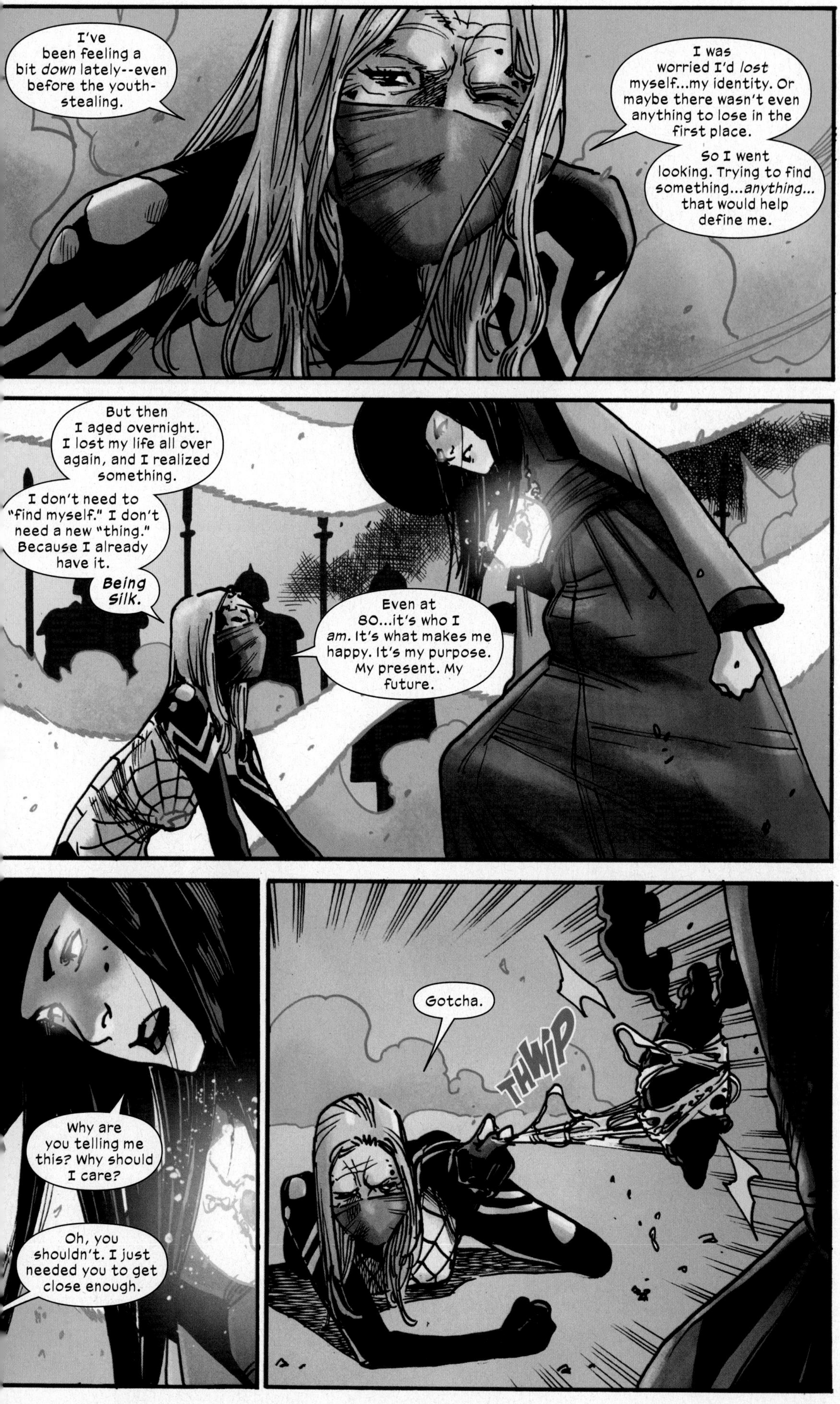
I've been feeling a bit *down* lately--even before the youth-stealing.
I was worried I'd *lost* myself...my identity. Or maybe there wasn't even anything to lose in the first place.
So I went looking. Trying to find something...*anything*... that would help define me.
But then I aged overnight. I lost my life all over again, and I realized something.
I don't need to "find myself." I don't need a new "thing." Because I already have it.
Being Silk.
Even at 80...it's who I *am*. It's what makes me happy. It's my purpose. My present. My future.
Why are you telling me this? Why should I care?
Oh, you shouldn't. I just needed you to get close enough.
Gotcha.
THWIP

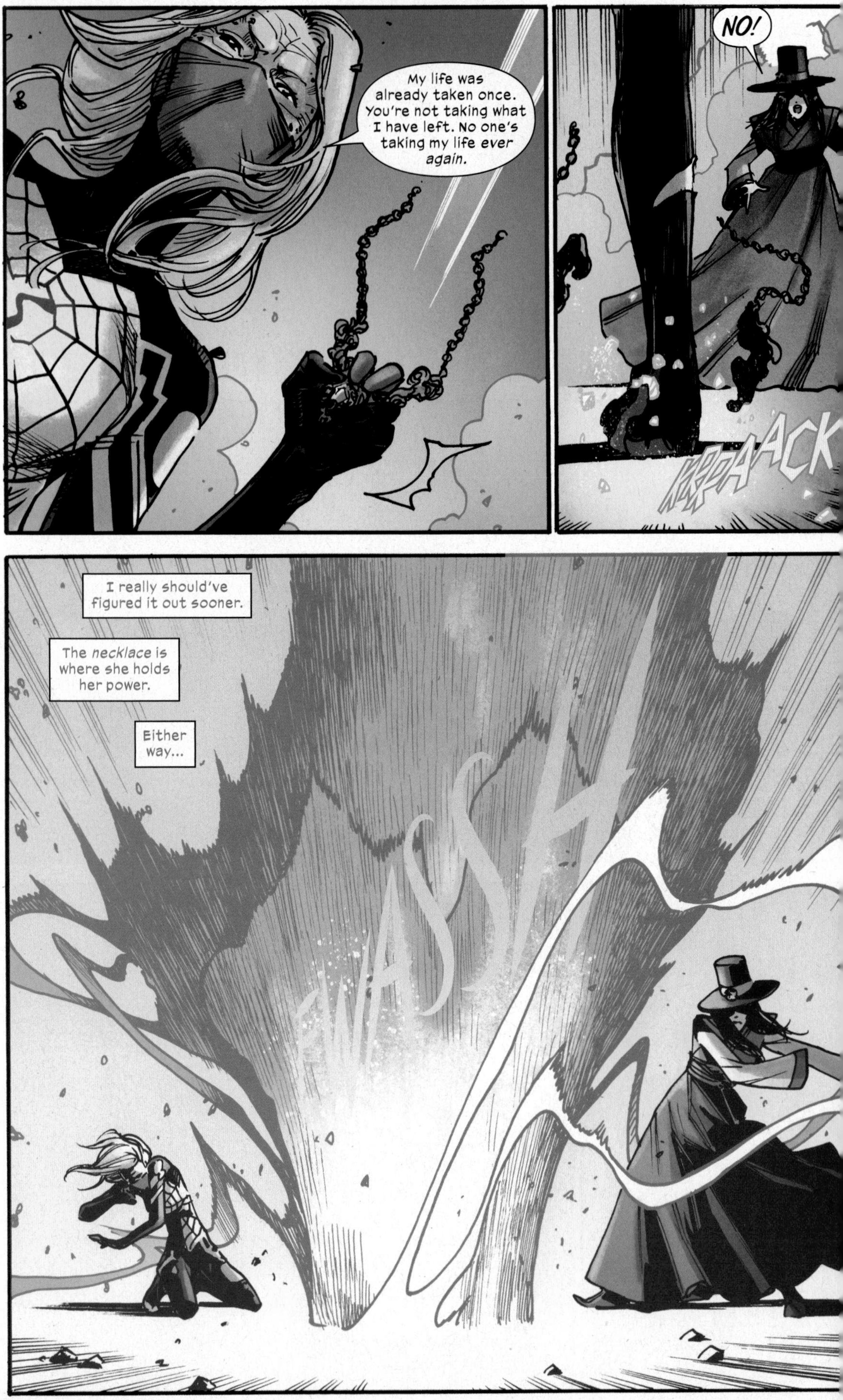
My life was already taken once. You're not taking what I have left. No one's taking my life *ever* again.
NO!
KRRAACK
I really should've figured it out sooner.
The *necklace* is where she holds her power.
Either way...
FWASSH

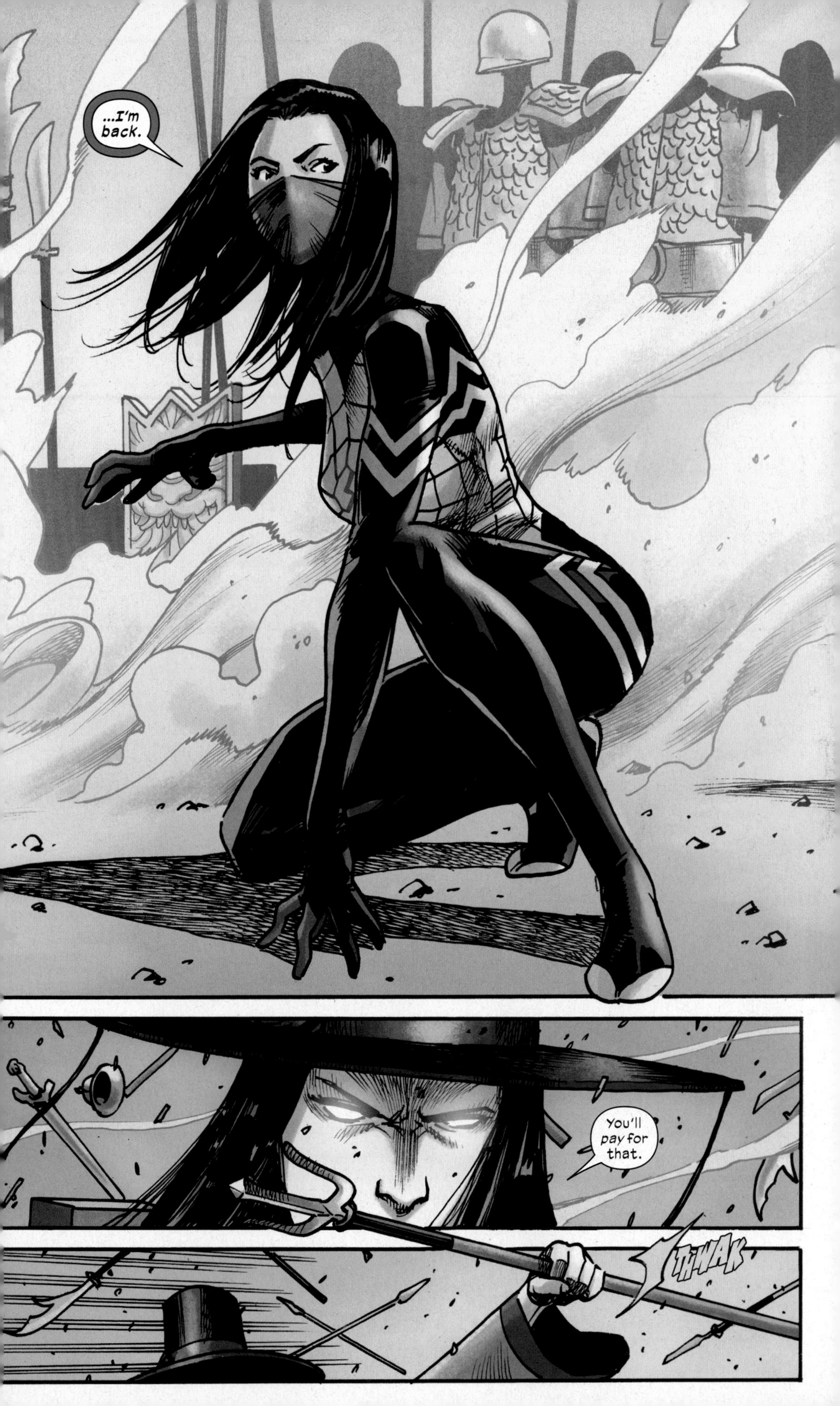
...I'm back.
You'll pay for that.
THWAK

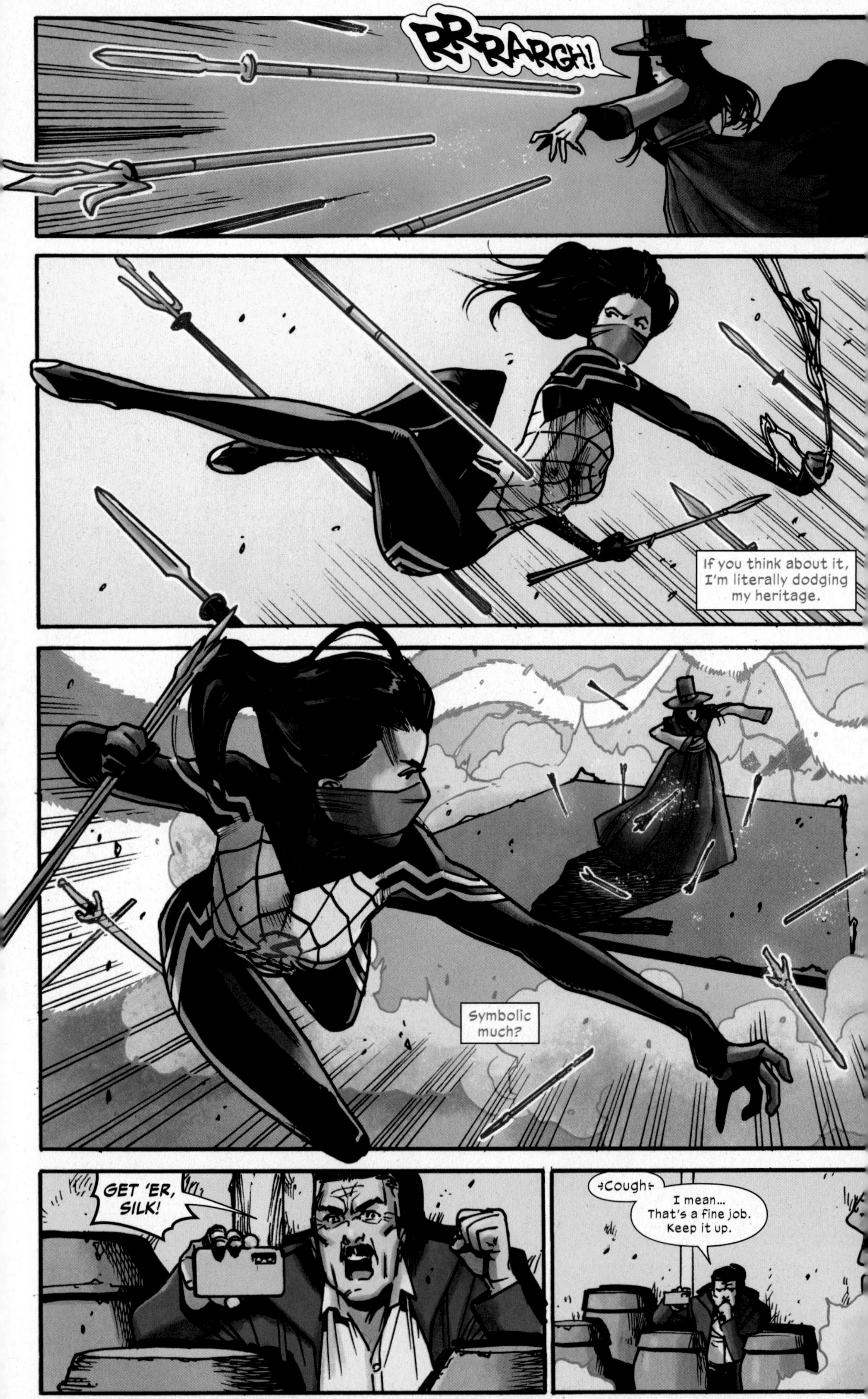
RRRARGH!
If you think about it, I'm literally dodging my heritage.
Symbolic much?
GET 'ER, SILK!
Cough
I mean... That's a fine job. Keep it up.

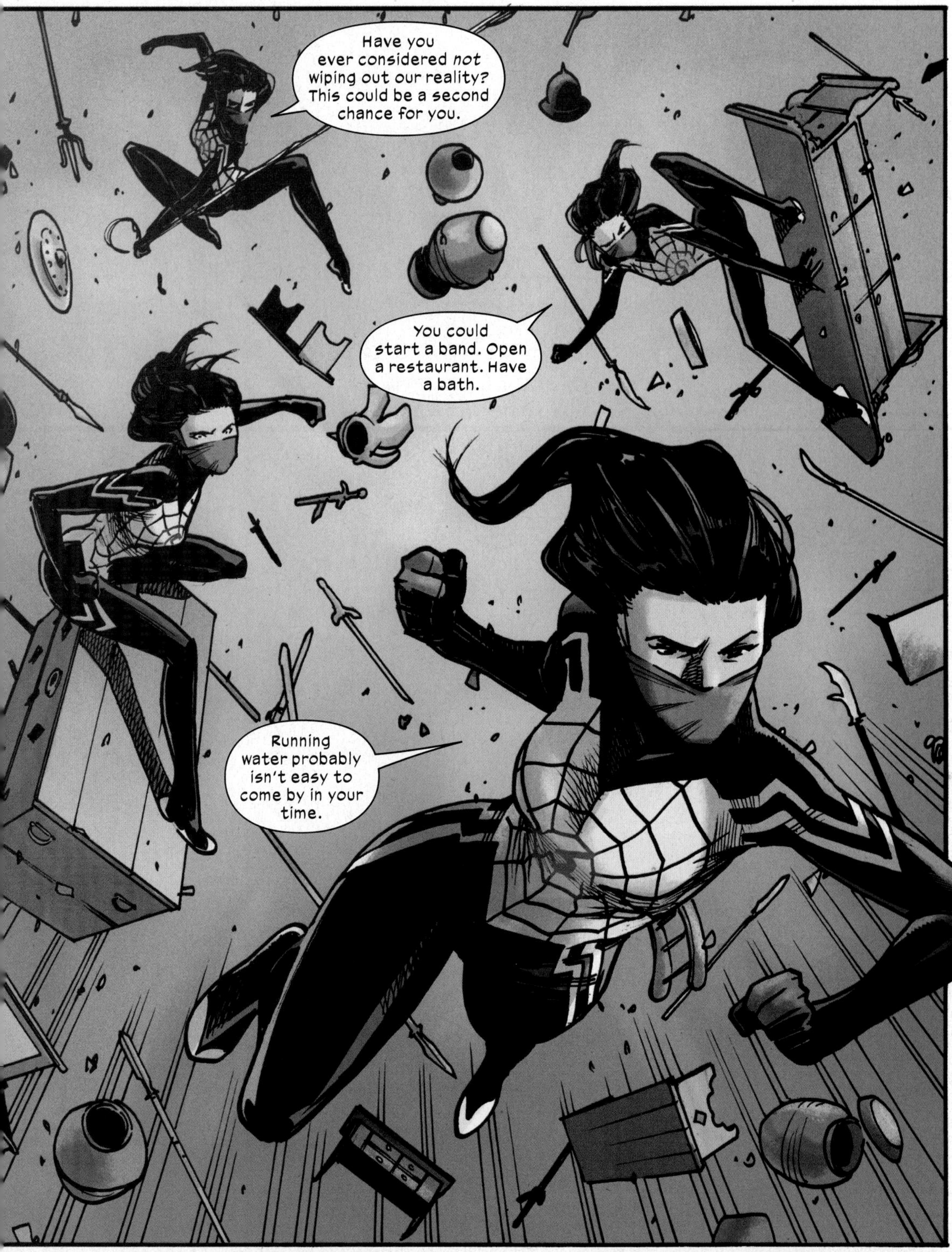
Have you ever considered *not* wiping out our reality? This could be a second chance for you.
You could start a band. Open a restaurant. Have a bath.
Running water probably isn't easy to come by in your time.

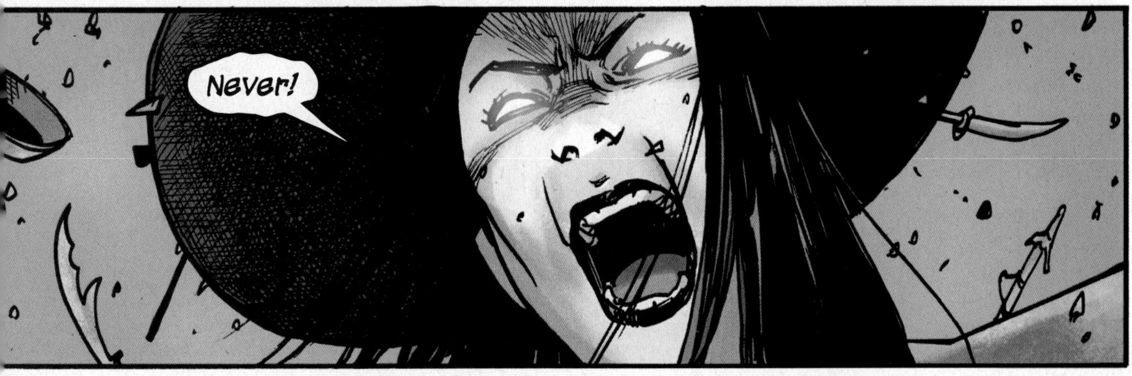
Never!

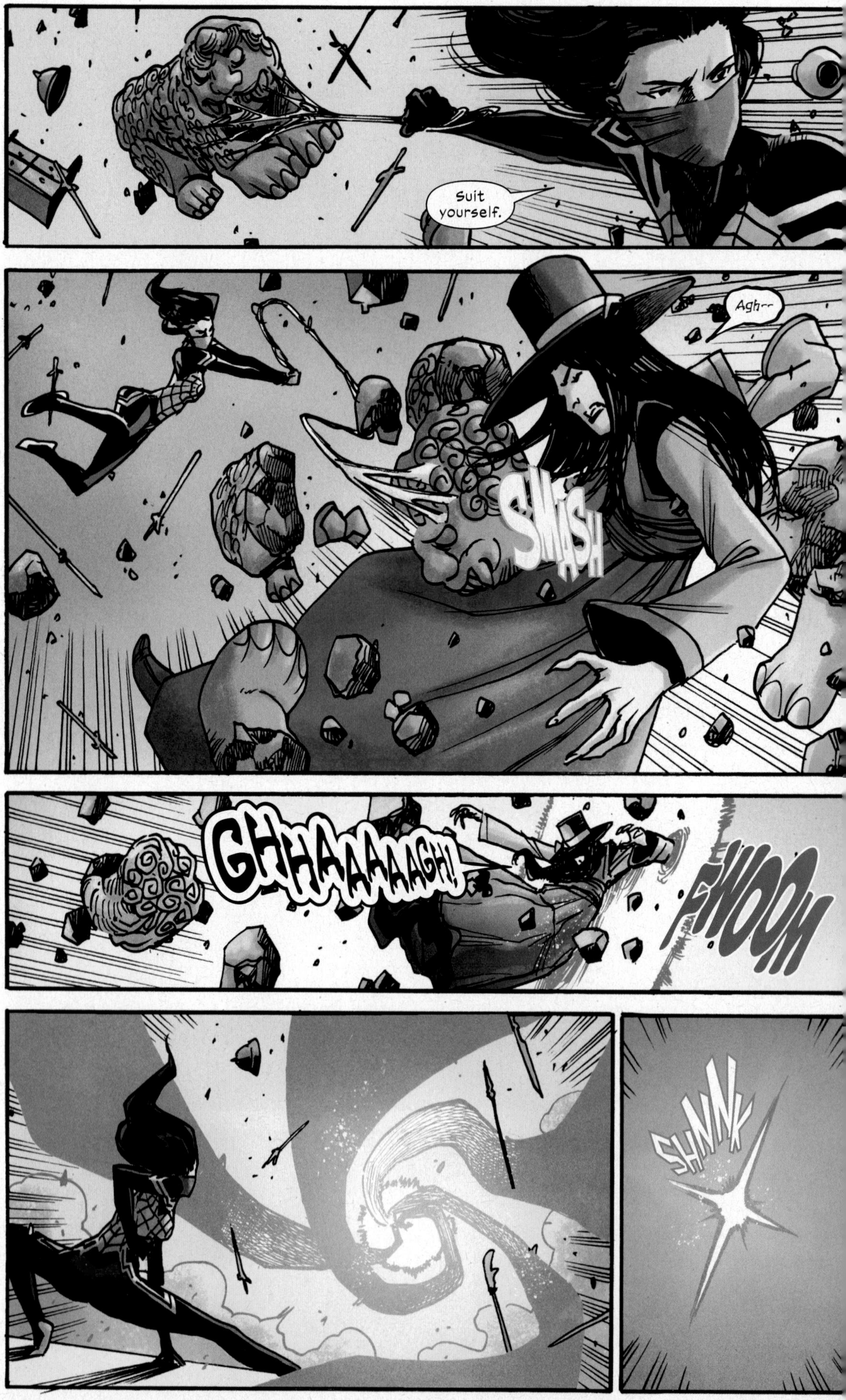
Suit yourself.
Agh--
SMASH
GHHAAAAAAGH!
FWOOM
SHNNK

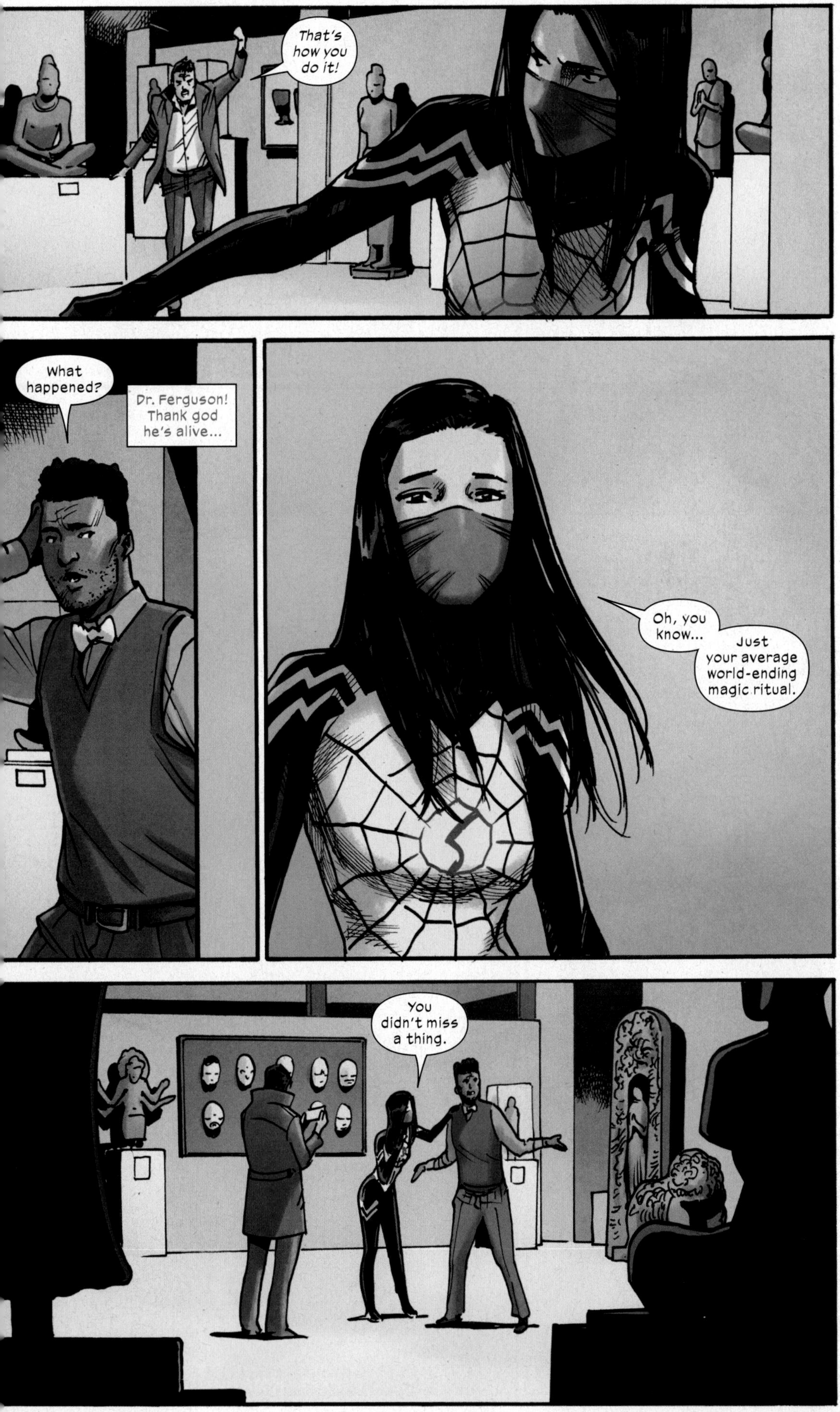
That's how you do it!
What happened?
Dr. Ferguson! Thank god he's alive...
Oh, you know... Just your average world-ending magic ritual.
You didn't miss a thing.

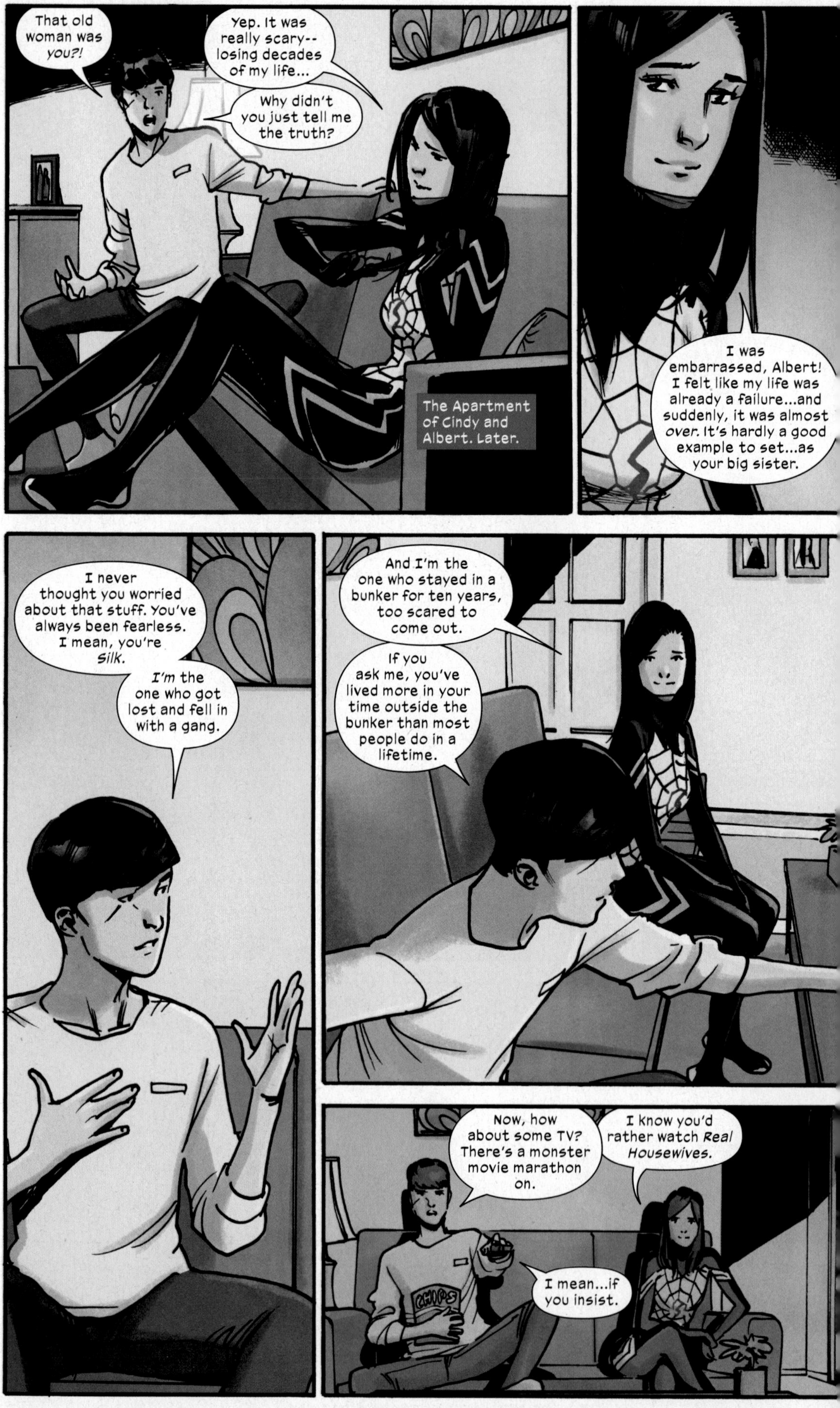
That old woman was *you?!*
Yep. It was really scary-- losing decades of my life...
Why didn't you just tell me the truth?
The Apartment of Cindy and Albert. Later.
I was embarrassed, Albert! I felt like my life was already a failure...and suddenly, it was almost *over.* It's hardly a good example to set...as your big sister.
I never thought you worried about that stuff. You've always been fearless. I mean, you're *Silk.*
I'm the one who got lost and fell in with a gang.
And I'm the one who stayed in a bunker for ten years, too scared to come out.
If you ask me, you've lived more in your time outside the bunker than most people do in a lifetime.
Now, how about some TV? There's a monster movie marathon on.
I know you'd rather watch *Real Housewives.*
I mean...if you insist.
CHIPS

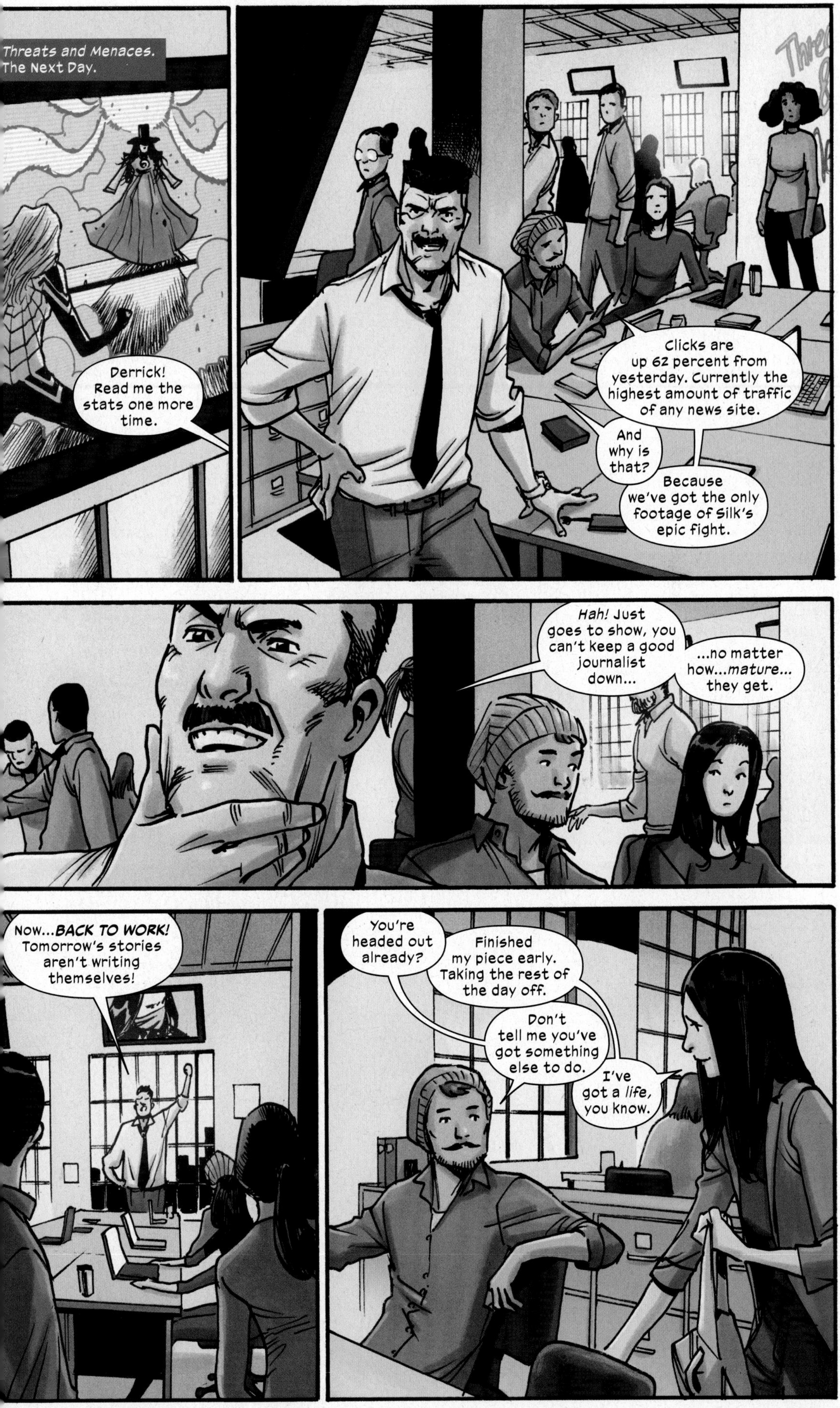
Threats and Menaces. The Next Day.
Derrick! Read me the stats one more time.
Clicks are up 62 percent from yesterday. Currently the highest amount of traffic of any news site.
And why is that?
Because we've got the only footage of Silk's epic fight.
Hah! Just goes to show, you can't keep a good journalist down...
...no matter how...*mature*... they get.
Now...***BACK TO WORK!*** Tomorrow's stories aren't writing themselves!
You're headed out already?
Finished my piece early. Taking the rest of the day off.
Don't tell me you've got something else to do.
I've got a *life,* you know.

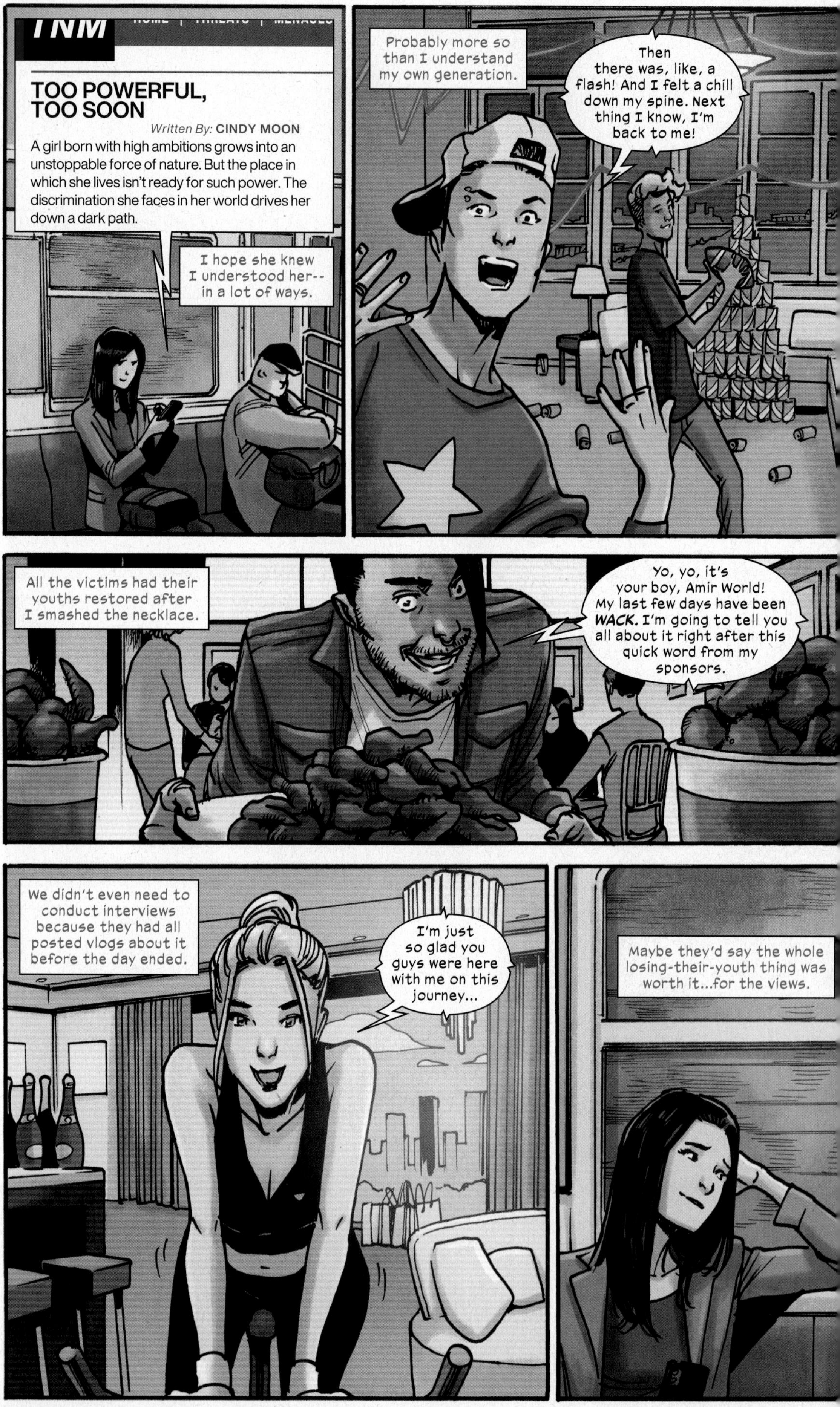
TNM
HOME | THREATS | MENACES
TOO POWERFUL, TOO SOON
Written By: CINDY MOON
A girl born with high ambitions grows into an unstoppable force of nature. But the place in which she lives isn't ready for such power. The discrimination she faces in her world drives her down a dark path.
I hope she knew I understood her--in a lot of ways.
Probably more so than I understand my own generation.
Then there was, like, a flash! And I felt a chill down my spine. Next thing I know, I'm back to me!
All the victims had their youths restored after I smashed the necklace.
Yo, yo, it's your boy, Amir World! My last few days have been WACK. I'm going to tell you all about it right after this quick word from my sponsors.
We didn't even need to conduct interviews because they had all posted vlogs about it before the day ended.
I'm just so glad you guys were here with me on this journey...
Maybe they'd say the whole losing-their-youth thing was worth it...for the views.

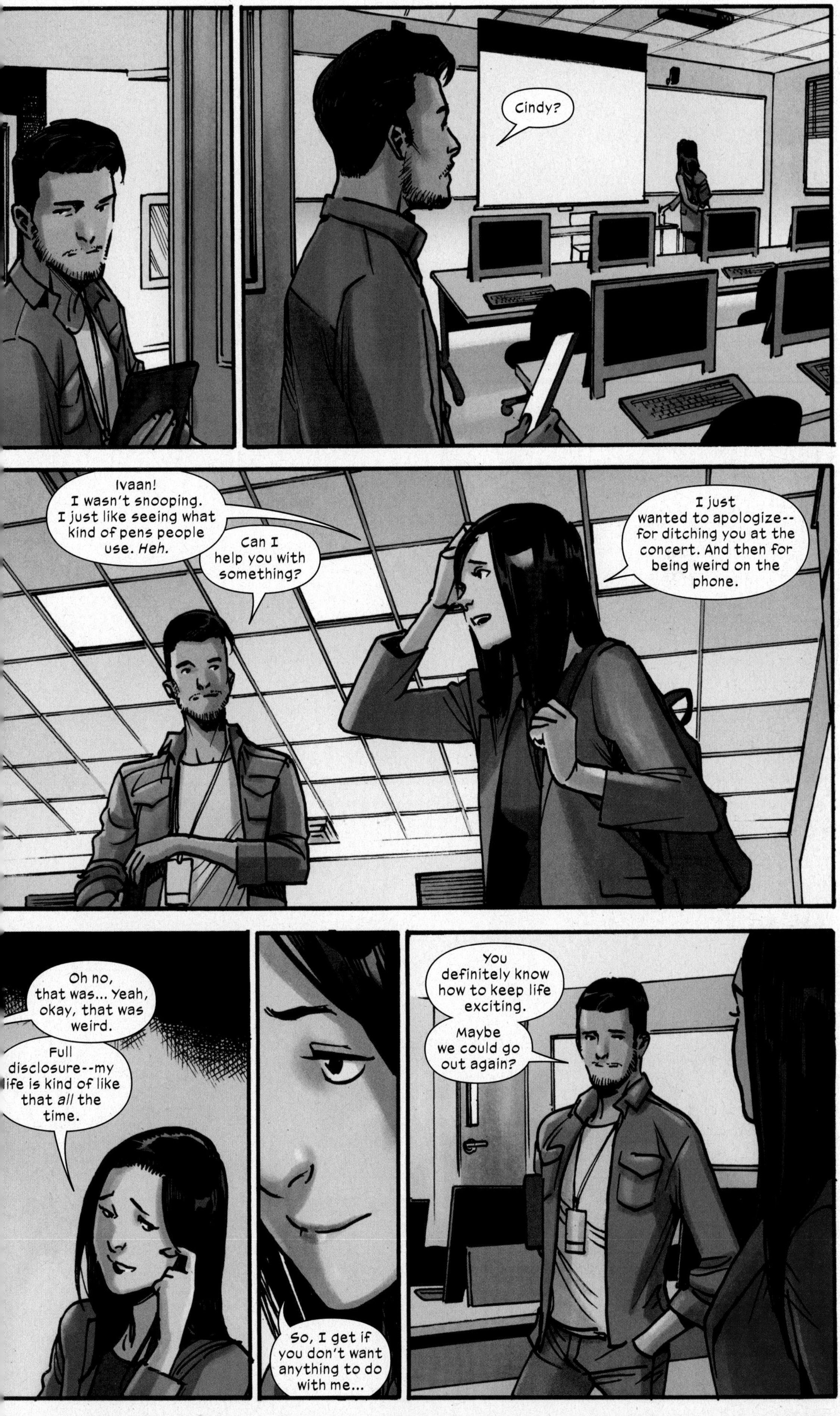
Cindy?
Ivaan! I wasn't snooping. I just like seeing what kind of pens people use. *Heh.*
Can I help you with something?
I just wanted to apologize--for ditching you at the concert. And then for being weird on the phone.
Oh no, that was... Yeah, okay, that was weird.
Full disclosure--my life is kind of like that *all* the time.
So, I get if you don't want anything to do with me...
You definitely know how to keep life exciting.
Maybe we could go out again?

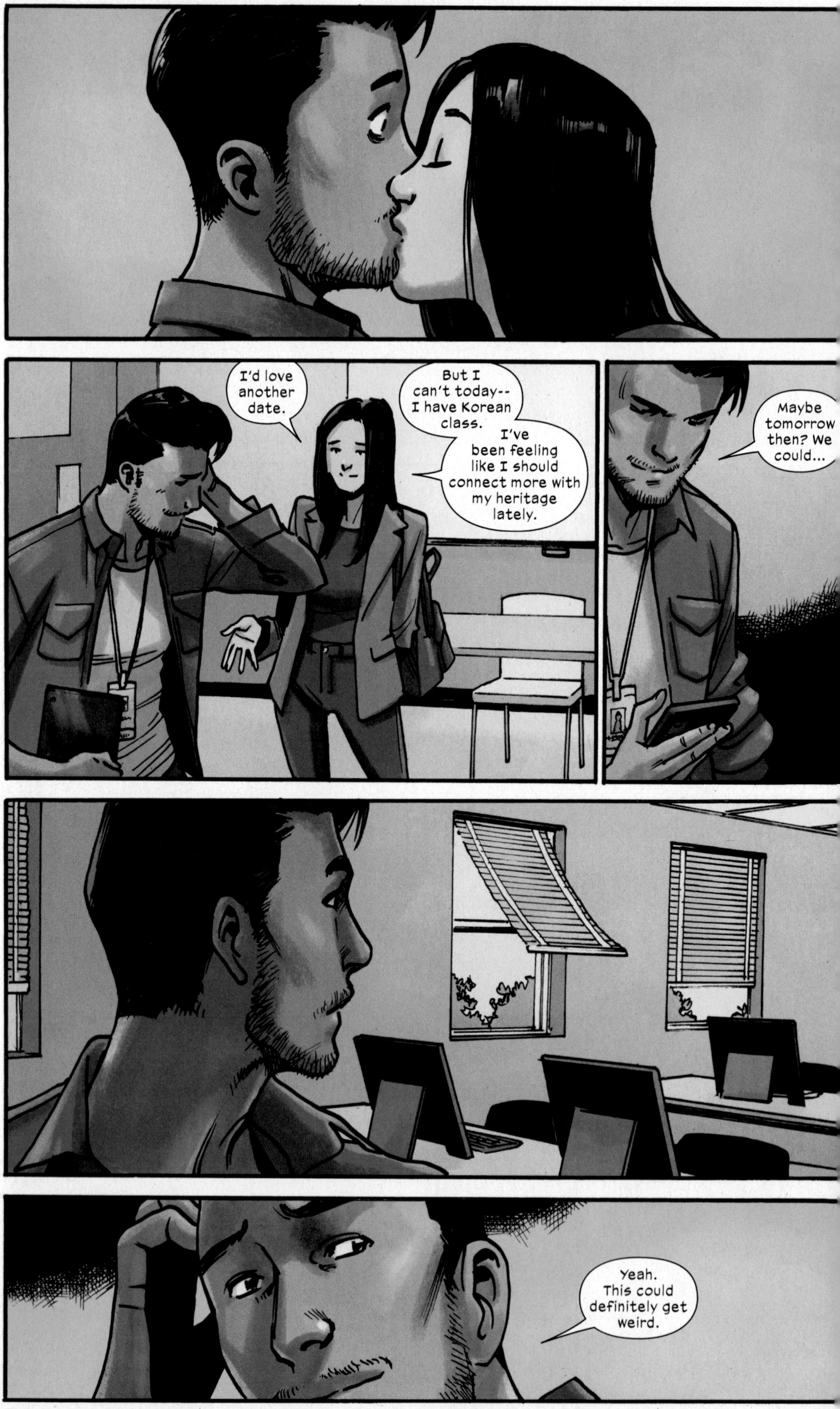
I'd love another date.
But I can't today-- I have Korean class.
I've been feeling like I should connect more with my heritage lately.
Maybe tomorrow then? We could...
Yeah. This could definitely get weird.

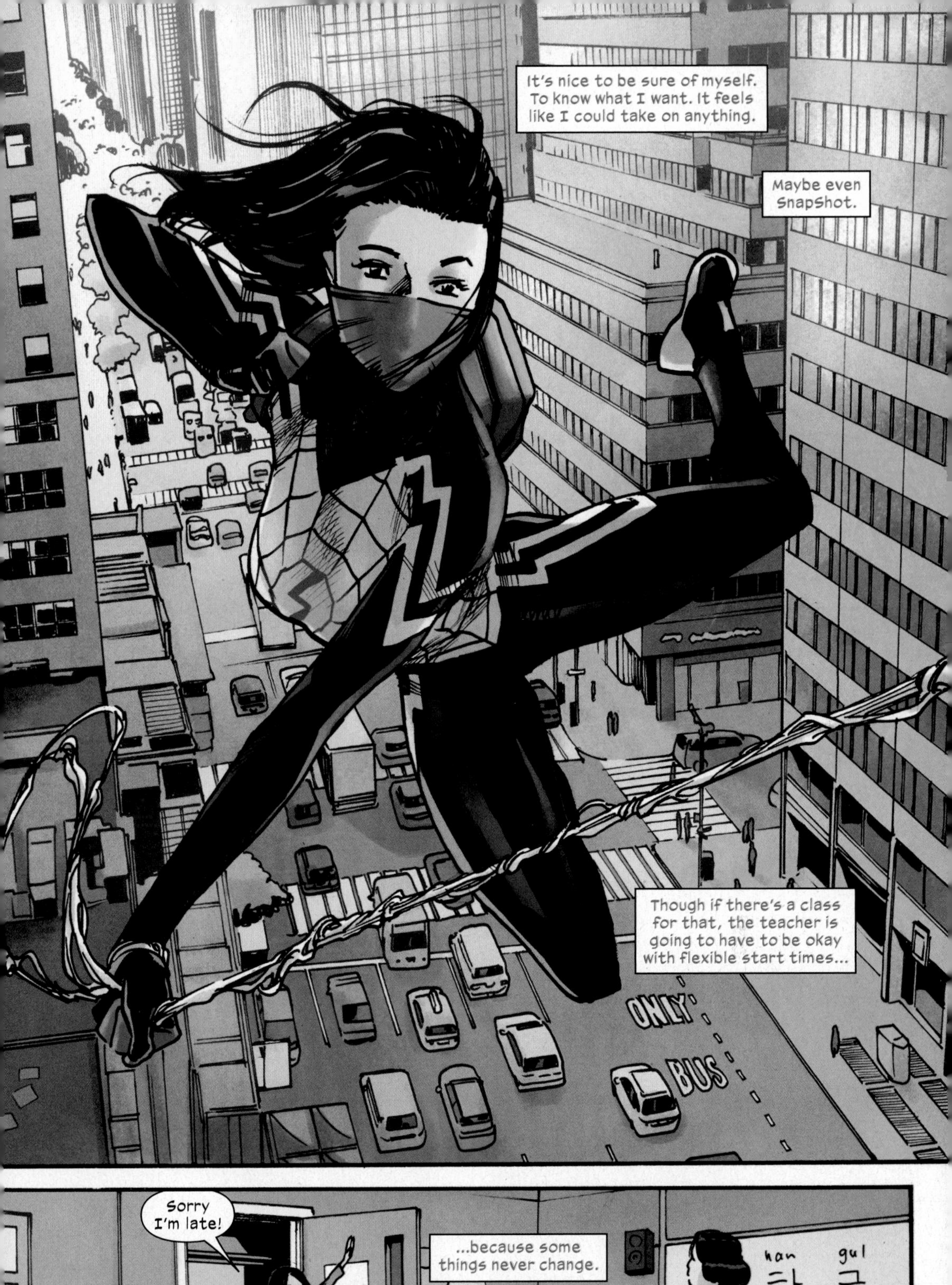
It's nice to be sure of myself. To know what I want. It feels like I could take on anything.
Maybe even SnapShot.
Though if there's a class for that, the teacher is going to have to be okay with flexible start times...
ONLY
BUS

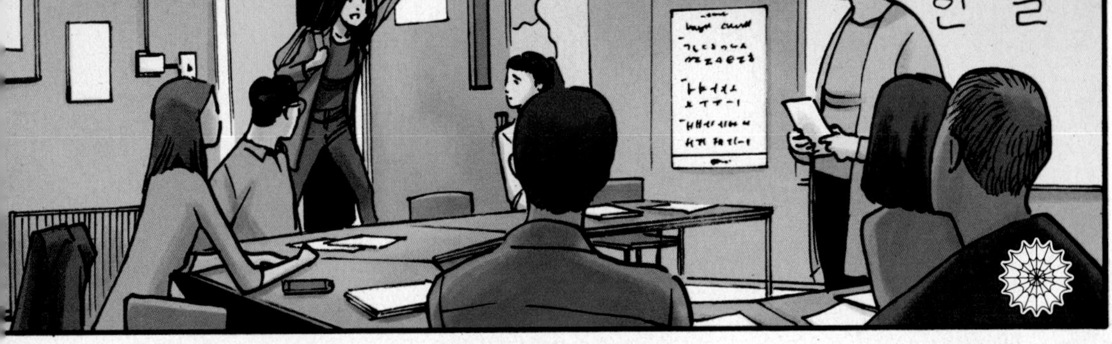
Sorry I'm late!
...because some things never change.
han
gul
한 글

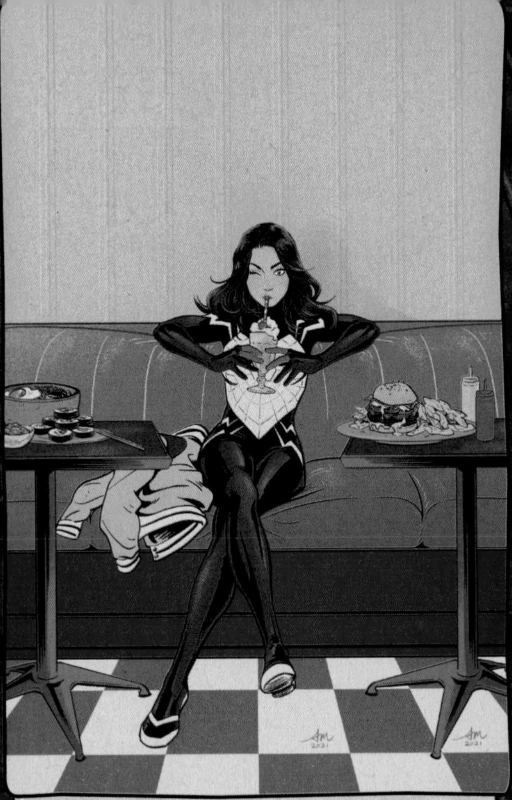

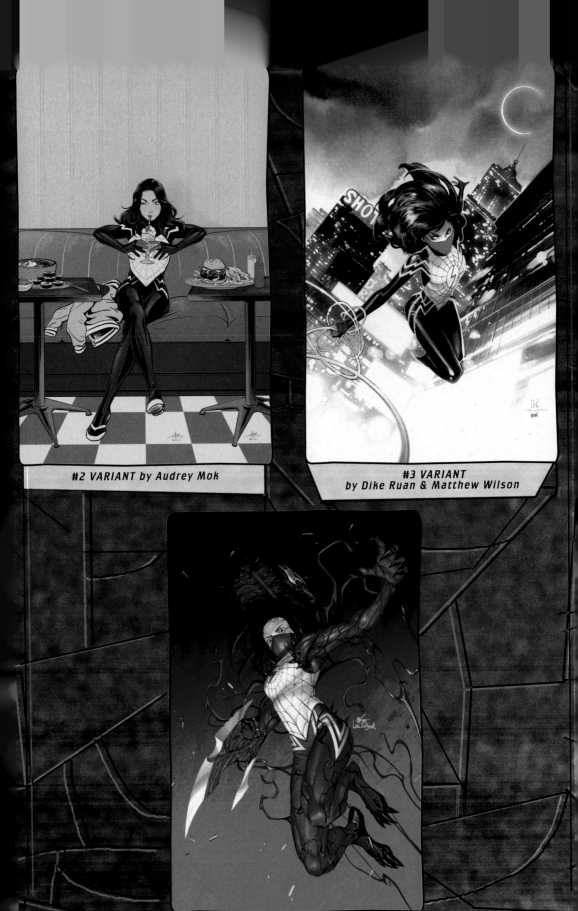

#2 VARIANT by Audrey Mok

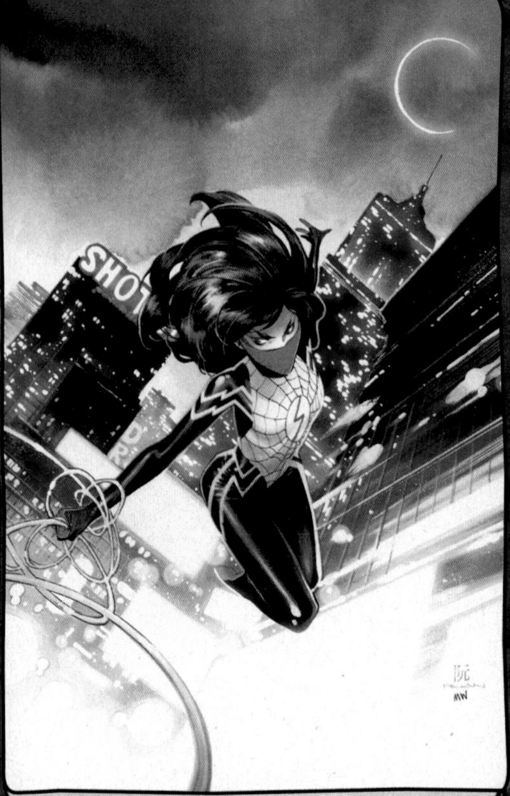
SHOT

#3 VARIANT
by Dike Ruan & Matthew Wilson

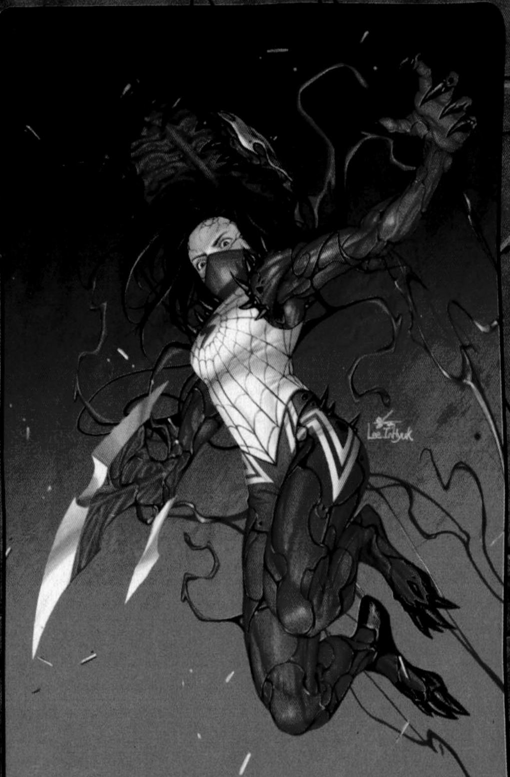

#3 CARNAGE FOREVER VARIANT by InHyuk Lee

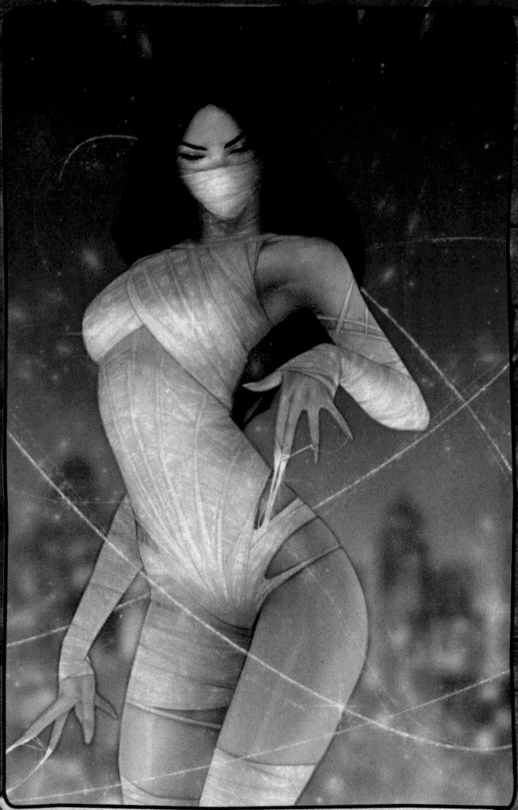

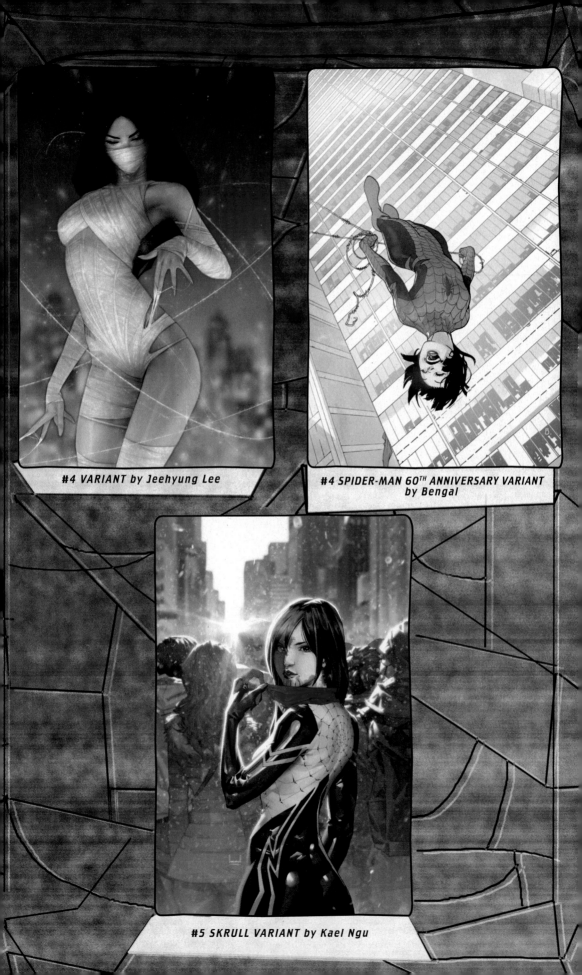

***#4 VARIANT** by Jeehyung Lee*

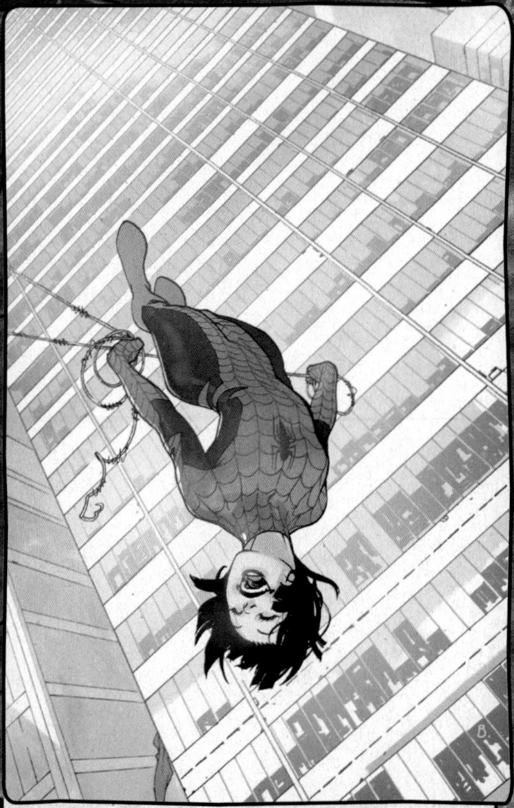

***#4 SPIDER-MAN 60TH ANNIVERSARY VARIANT** by Bengal*

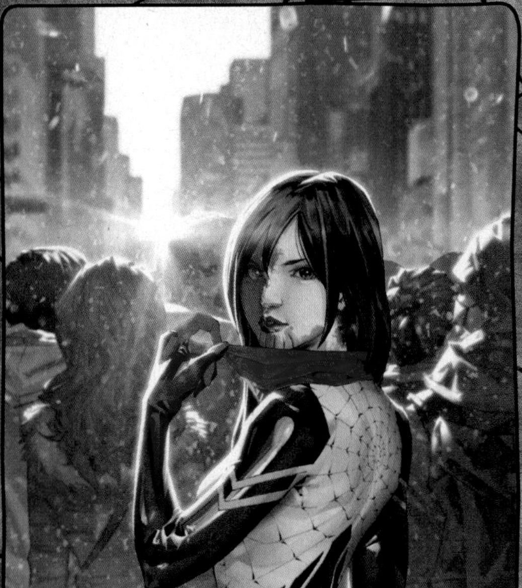

***#5 SKRULL VARIANT** by Kael Ngu*

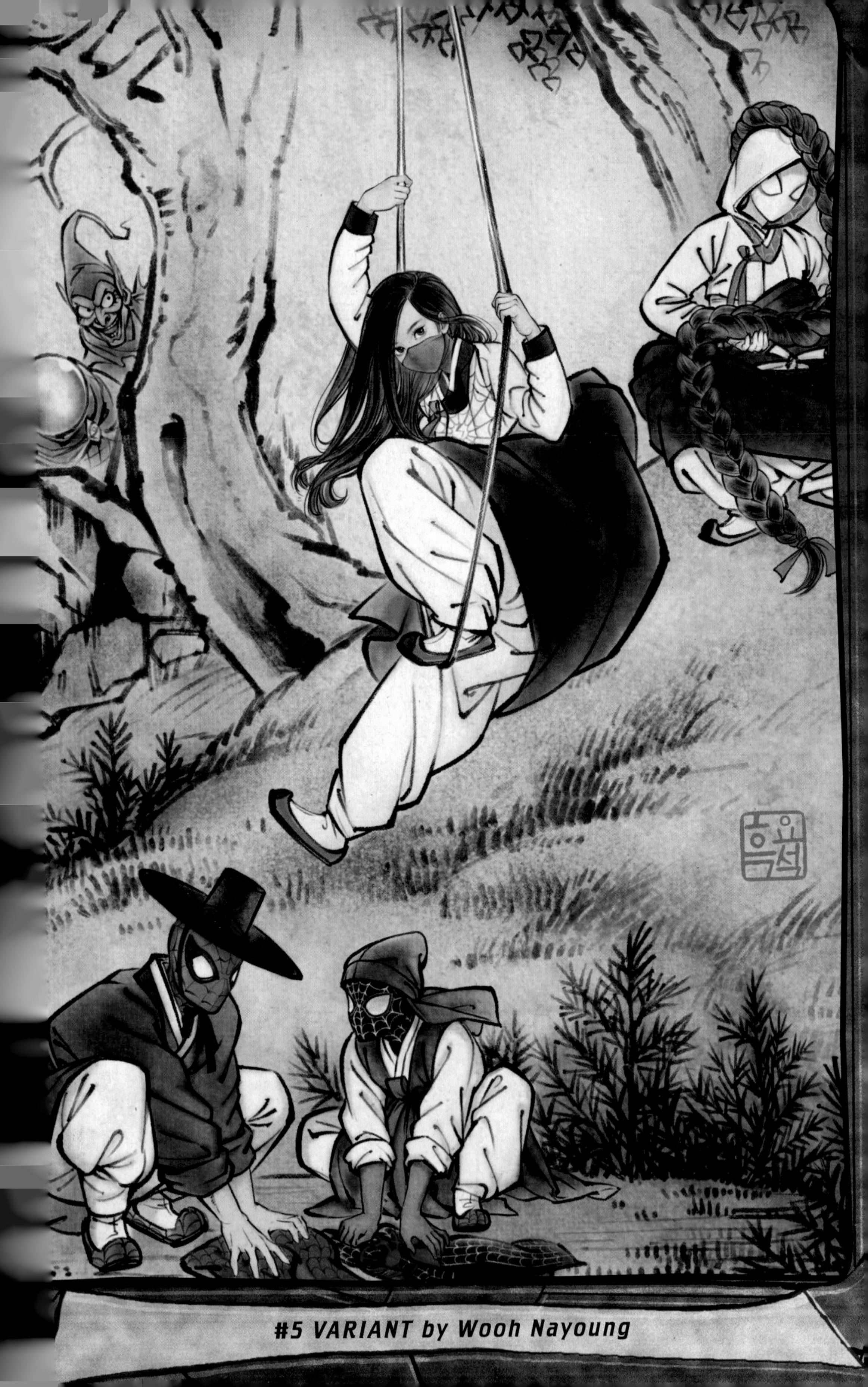

#5 VARIANT by Wooh Nayoung